Corporate Manslaughter and Regulatory Reform

Crime Prevention and Security Management

Series Editor: **Martin Gill**

Titles include:

Paul Almond
CORPORATE MANSLAUGHTER AND REGULATORY REFORM

Joshua Bamfield
SHOPPING AND CRIME

Mark Button
DOING SECURITY
Critical Reflections and an Agenda for Change

Paul Ekblom
CRIME PREVENTION, SECURITY AND COMMUNITY SAFETY USING THE 5Is FRAMEWORK

Janice Goldstraw-White
WHITE COLLAR CRIME
Accounts of Offending Behaviour

Bob Hoogenboom
THE GOVERNANCE OF POLICING AND SECURITY
Ironies, Myths and Paradoxes

Kate Moss
BALANCING LIBERTY AND SECURITY
Human Rights, Human Wrongs

Kate Moss
SECURITY AND LIBERTY
Restriction by Stealth

Tim Prenzler
POLICING AND SECURITY IN PRACTICE
Challenges and Achievements

Adam White
THE POLITICS OF PRIVATE SECURITY
Regulation, Reform and Re-Legitimation

Crime Prevention and Security Management
Series Standing Order ISBN 978–0–230–01355–1 hardback
978–0–230–01356–8 paperback
(*outside North America only*)

You can receive future titles in this series as they are published by placing a standing order. Please contact your bookseller or, in case of difficulty, write to us at the address below with your name and address, the title of the series and the ISBN quoted above.

Customer Services Department, Macmillan Distribution Ltd, Houndmills, Basingstoke, Hampshire RG21 6XS, England

---

Corporate Manslaughter and Regulatory Reform

Paul Almond
Senior Lecturer in Law, School of Law, University of Reading, UK

palgrave
macmillan

First published 2013 by
PALGRAVE MACMILLAN

Palgrave Macmillan in the UK is an imprint of Macmillan Publishers Limited, registered in England, company number 785998, of Houndmills, Basingstoke, Hampshire RG21 6XS.

Palgrave Macmillan in the US is a division of St Martin's Press LLC, 175 Fifth Avenue, New York, NY 10010.

Palgrave Macmillan is the global academic imprint of the above companies and has companies and representatives throughout the world.

Palgrave® and Macmillan® are registered trademarks in the United States, the United Kingdom, Europe and other countries.

ISBN 978–0–230–27452–5

This book is printed on paper suitable for recycling and made from fully managed and sustained forest sources. Logging, pulping and manufacturing processes are expected to conform to the environmental regulations of the country of origin.

A catalogue record for this book is available from the British Library.

Library of Congress Cataloging-in-Publication Data
Almond, Paul, 1979–
Corporate manslaughter and regulatory reform / Paul Almond.
p. cm.
Includes bibliographical references and index.
ISBN 978–0–230–27452–5
1. Manslaughter—Great Britain. 2. Criminal liability of juristic persons—Great Britain. 3. Employers' liability—Great Britain. 4. Industrial safety—Law and legislation—Great Britain—Criminal provisions. 5. Law reform—Great Britain. I. Title.
KD7965.A96 2013
344.4104'65—dc23 2012036832

10 9 8 7 6 5 4 3 2 1
22 21 20 19 18 17 16 15 14 13

For my parents
and
Ellen Doreen Bates (1922–2011)

Contents

List of Cases

United Kingdom:

Attorney-General's Reference (No. 2 of 1999) [2000] 3 All ER 183.
Austin Rover v HM Inspector of Factories [1989] 3 WLR 520.
Benham v United Kingdom (1996) 22 EHRR 293.
DPP v Kent and Sussex Contractors [1944] KB 146.
H. L. Bolton (Engineering) Co. Ltd. v TJ Graham & Sons Ltd. [1957] 1 QB 159.
Marshall v Gotham [1954] AC 360.
Meridian Global Funds Management Asia Ltd. v Securities Commission [1995] 2 AC 500 (PC).
Moore v Bresler [1944] 2 All ER 515.
Mousell v London and North Western Railway [1917] 2 KB 836.
Priestley v Fowler [1837] 150 EngRep 1030.
R v Adomako [1995] 1 AC 171.
R v Birmingham and Gloucester Railway Co. (1842) 3 QB 223.
R v British Steel [1995] 1 WLR 1356.
R v Cory Bros. [1927] 1 KB 810.
R v Cotswold Geotechnical (Holdings) Ltd. [2011] EWCA Crim 1337; [2011] All ER (D) 100 (May).
R v Dennis Clothier and Sons Ltd. (2002), Unreported, Bristol Crown Court 23 March 2002.
R v English Brothers Ltd. (2001), Unreported, Northampton Crown Court 30 July 2001.
R v F. Howe and Son (Engineers) Ltd. [1999] 2 CrAppR 37.
R v Great North of England Railway Co. (1846) 9 QB 315.
R v Great Western Trains Co. Ltd. (1999), Unreported, Central Criminal Court, 13 August 1999 (case ref. C7800570).
R v ICR Haulage [1944] KB 551.
R v Jackson Transport (Ossett) Ltd. (1996) Unreported, *Health and Safety at Work*, 11/1996 p. 4.
R v Lawrence [1982] AC 510.
R v Misra and Srivastava [2005] 1 CrAppR 328.
R v Northern Strip Mining Construction Co. (1965) Unreported.

R v OLL Ltd. (1994) Unreported, *The Independent*, 9 December 1994.
R v P&O European Ferries (Dover) Ltd. [1991] 93 CrAppR 72.
R v Seymour [1983] 2 AC 493.
R v Teglgaard Hardwood (UK) Ltd. (2003), Unreported, Hull Crown Court, 24 February 2004.
R v Wacker [2003] 4 All ER 295.
Tesco v Brent London Borough Council [1993] 2 All ER 718.
Tesco Supermarkets Ltd. v Nattrass [1972] AC 153.
Tipling v Pexall (1688) 80 ER 1085 (2 Bulstrode 233).

Australia:

R v Denbo Pty Ltd. (1994) 6 VIR 157.

Canada:

Canadian Dredge and Dock Co. v The Queen [1985] 1 SCR 662.

Netherlands:

Hospital Case, Rechtbank Leeuwarden, 23 December 1987 (NJ 1988, 981).
Ijzerdraad Case, Hoge Raad, 23 February 1954 (NJ 1954, 378).
Kabejauw Case, Hoge Raad, 1 July 1981 (NJ 1982, 80).

United States of America:

New York Central & Hudson Railroad Co. v United States 212 US 481 (1909).
People v Rochester Railway and Light Co. 195 NY 102 (1909).
State v Lehig Valley Railroad 103 A 685 (1917).
United States v Bank of New England 484 US 943 (1987).
United States v Basic Construction Co. 711 F2d 570 (4th c. 1983).
United States v Van Schaick 134 F 592 (1904).

List of Statutory Materials

United Kingdom:

Agriculture (Safety, Health and Welfare Provisions) Act 1956
Clean Air Act 1959
Corporate Manslaughter and Corporate Homicide Act 2007
Cotton Mills and Factories Act 1819
Education Act 1918
Factories Act 1844
Factories Act 1961
Factory Act 1833
Factory Act 1891
Factory Act 1901
Factory Acts (Extension) Act 1864
Factory and Workshop Act 1878
Factory and Workshop Act 1895
Gangmasters (Licensing) Act 2004
Health and Morals of Apprentices Act 1802
Health and Safety at Work Act 1974
Health and Safety (Offences) Act 2008
Mines and Quarries Act 1954
Nuclear Installations Act 1959
Nuclear Installations Act 1965
Offices, Shops and Railway Premises Act 1963
Poor Law Amendment Act 1844
Reform Act 1832
Reporting of Injuries, Diseases and Dangerous Occurrences Regulations (1995) S.I. No. 3163
Road Traffic Act 1988
Road Vehicles (Construction & Use) Regulations 1986
Statute of Artificers 1563
Statute of Labourers 1351
Workman's Compensation Act 1897

Australia:

Crimes (Industrial Manslaughter) Act 2003 (ACT)
Criminal Code Act 1995

Belgium:

Belgian Penal Code

Canada:

Bill C-45: An Act to Amend the Criminal Code (Criminal Liability of Organizations) (2003)
Criminal Code (RSC 1985, c. C-46)

China:

The Labour Law of the People's Republic of China

Denmark:

Danish Criminal Code

European Union:

1989 Framework Directive (89/391/EEC)
1999 Convention of the Council of Europe on Corruption

Finland:

Penal Code of Finland

France:

French Penal Code

Netherlands:

Netherlands Criminal Code

New Zealand:

Crimes Act 1961
Interpretation Act 1999

Portugal:

Portuguese Penal Code

Sweden:

Swedish Penal Code
1977 Work Environment Act

United States of America:

Occupational Safety and Health Act 1970

Preface

It was while conducting interviews with HSE inspectors in 2003 that the idea for the research question at the heart of this book first began to formulate. I was a PhD student, undertaking fieldwork for my study of health and safety inspectors' attitudes in relation to work-related fatality cases, and I was speaking with a very experienced inspector about his 30-year career and the changes he had witnessed during that time. He identified what he saw as a paradox underpinning this area of regulation:

> When I joined HSE 27 years ago it wasn't a very important job to be honest, but it just seems to have grown and grown in importance... I remember investigating fatalities when nobody was interested in what was going on, it was just one of those things, people go to work and get killed, but it's a big event now. I wonder why, when actually we're safer, the importance of the subject seems to keep rising? In the time I've been an inspector, employee fatalities have fallen from about six or seven hundred a year down to about two hundred a year. You'd expect people to have said 'right, we can pack in now', but they don't, the importance keeps growing. It's a conundrum. I know you're not being interviewed, but what are your thoughts?
>
> (2003: I7)

The inspector's frankness, and the reversal of the interviewer–interviewee dynamic, had thrown me, and I was not well-prepared enough to give him any more than a very general answer. But afterwards I was struck by this seeming contradiction and the way that it seemed to map across onto the whole topic of health and safety regulation. Why was there a movement towards criminalisation, and a greater sense of public concern over death and disaster, at a time when the quantitative scale of the problem of work-related death and injury was ostensibly in decline? Why were criminalisation and a 'toughening' of the law being pursued at the same time as rates of inspection, enforcement, and prosecution were falling? And how had this issue managed to retain such a high level of perceived significance at a time when health and safety regulation faced a climate of sustained public and political hostility, mistrust, and opposition arguably far greater than at any other time during the last 100 years?

Having started out with a doctoral study that tried to understand the corporate manslaughter reforms in practice, I subsequently focused on trying to make sense of that process in more sociological terms. One potential explanation for this phenomenon can be found via reference to the work of scholars within a 'risk society' paradigm, who identify a climate of widespread public insecurity over risk as leading to the formation of policies that reflect a new 'risk management' role for government, such as those involving the punitive, expressive use of the law to reassure the public about the dangers inherent in modern society. But this line of argument alone did not seem able to explain the reality of public attitudes in this area that I had subsequently uncovered via empirical investigation or to reflect the contested political realities that continue to shape this area of law. Increasingly I came to see that the political legitimacy of health and safety regulation as a whole, as reflective of its contested normative status, was central to understanding this issue, and that viewing the new offence as communicative of symbolic messages about legitimacy could assist in clarifying its role and purpose. Regulation is as much about the promotion of a particular set of values and securing commitment to a particular conception of the good society as it is about changing behaviour to conform to prescribed standards and expectations.

On this reading, then, regulation can simultaneously work (in terms of behaviour change) and not work (in terms of promoting particular values) and so can have instrumental effects while it also struggles to communicate the moral messages that underpin its political status and validate its existence. Declining rates of death and injury suggest that compliance-oriented regulation is working on some level. But political opposition, declining enforcement, and the persistence of significant areas of resistance to regulation all signify the failures of regulation and its politically constrained nature. Understanding that regulation can succeed and fail at the same time allows for insights derived from the regulatory studies literature and from critical perspectives on regulation to be reconciled to some degree. This book seeks to understand the successes and failures of regulation and argues that corporate manslaughter reforms can be understood as a means of restating the reasons for regulating that underpin health and safety as a social and legal project. It is hoped that this book will contribute to understandings both of the corporate manslaughter reforms as a solution to the problems that health and safety regulation faces and of the nature and origins of those problems.

Acknowledgements

My thanks go to my colleagues at the School of Law, University of Reading, UK, for providing a collegiate and supportive working environment. Particular thanks go to Thom Koller for research assistance during the project, Dave Hallam for performing numerous IT rescues, and all of the admin team. The thoughts that have been fed into this book have benefited from the input of many people over the last few years, in many different ways, including Sarah Colover, Garry Gray, Fiona Haines, Gavin Leigh, Sally Lloyd-Bostock, Neal Stone, David Whyte, participants of the 2011 Socio-Legal Studies Association (SLSA) 'Criminalising Commerce' stream, and the numerous students and colleagues at Reading with whom I have discussed these issues. Of course, all errors and shortcomings remain my own. Finally, love and thanks are due to my family (especially Sarah, Randy, Lynn, and Derek), who have supported me through life, study, and work. Special gratitude is reserved for my parents, Janice and Peter, whose love and support has always been a great help and is hugely appreciated. Lastly, and most importantly, thanks to my wife Natalie, without whose love, care, encouragement, and friendship this book would not have been written and for which I am eternally grateful.

Series Preface

Paul Almond's book is likely to be of interest to a range of scholars because it examines the law governing organisations that are in some way responsible for people losing their lives (and specifically the Corporate Manslaughter and Corporate Homicide Act 2007) from a range of perspectives. For example, he provides a historical account of regulatory law and health and safety practices. From this we learn that some of the central themes of this book that govern the way the laws on corporate killing were constructed and implemented have their roots in the past. This includes, for example, the competing demands of worker protection and market-driven regulatory approaches; the restrictions of safety rights at work for individuals because of the greater need to support economic and political systems; and the rationale for the low priority given to protecting workers from unsafe practices (including a lack of commitment to taking enforcement action) despite Health and Safety being a reflection of a 'good society'.

Moreover, this book provides an insight into a form of sanctioning that is perceived to sit outside the criminal justice system. Paul Almond discusses the distinction between what is classified as criminal and what is regulatory, looking critically at issues of seriousness, harm, and social impact. He assesses the role of big organisations both in influencing and in some cases controlling the agenda for different types of responses. He discusses the lower priority of regulatory law and how some are 'not universally condemned' and perceived as 'not matters of real crime' despite having extremely serious consequences.

Indeed, the role of law in holding businesses to account is an important one, and Paul tracks the shift towards corporate criminal liability which, he argues, is likely to spread further. A major issue that underpins his analysis is the limited and sometimes arbitrary approach taken to enforcement. In the regulatory environment he critically assesses the dangers inherent in systems of law which seek to appease public demands for 'justice' because of fears that such approaches will lead to mistrust and non-cooperation. He also critically evaluates the different status of criminal and regulatory law in relation to community norms that underpin both legitimacy and effectiveness.

In bringing these themes together he examines a range of issues around work-related death and indeed the death of non-workers, which, he shows, constitute a far greater problem than has traditionally been thought. This is partly because much work is invisible, at least to authorities and those who count the incidents of deaths at work, as well as those who respond to them. He draws upon the theoretical writings of Jürgen Habermas; incorporates international comparative work; discusses the inherent dangers of treating corporate manslaughter as a special case of Health and Safety; and includes a critique of regulation per se, not least as it applies to Health and Safety generally and corporate manslaughter specifically.

Many supporters of the Act and those who seek to criminalise corporations that kill workers will find Paul Almond's critique of its provisions enlightening. For him, while it may be a form of 'penal populism' and the result of 'political expediency', it is also a necessary measure, and one that has the potential to bring very positive benefits. Even then, it must be acknowledged that the new offence is unlikely to be effective in practice and may not constitute the optimal means of responding to work-related deaths.

Martin Gill
Director of Perpetuity Research and Consultancy International (PRCI) and Professor of Criminology at the University of Leicester, UK

An Introduction to Work-Related Deaths

The phrase 'work–life balance' has become increasingly familiar and widely used in recent years as a means of describing the difficulty encountered in managing the competing time demands placed on individual life in the modern world and the encroachment of professional commitments into spaces previously set aside for personal commitments (Tausig and Fenwick 2001). Hochschild (1997) calls this the 'time bind': the diminution of private social relations due to the demands imposed by the economic and cultural value associated with work (also the 'temporal trap': Simon 2010). The way in which the identities of individuals are defined and constructed is increasingly shaped by work. One of the primary indicators used in defining our external identity is our job: what we do, what we earn, how successful we are (Goffman 1969). Those who work are defined by it; those who do not are increasingly socially excluded (Atkinson 1998; Young 1999). The result is the domination of individual life by work, a dominance which, as Richard Sennett (1998) points out, can have corrosive personal and social consequences.

The term work–life balance has another connotation; there are many situations in which the demands of the workplace impact the lives and bodily integrity of workers and members of the public. Occupational ill health, injury, and death resulting from work-related activity constitute persistent social problems and bring about significant economic, personal, and psychological consequences for individuals and for society more generally. High-profile examples include the explosion at the Union Carbide chemical plant in Bhopal, India, in 1984 (approximately 30,000 dead: Sharma 2005; Shrivastava 1987); the sinking of the passenger ferry the 'Herald of Free Enterprise' in Zeebrugge, Belgium, in 1987 (193 dead: Department of Transport 1987); the Piper Alpha oil rig explosion in the North Sea of Scotland in 1988 (167 dead: Cullen 1990); the Kader toy factory fire in Thailand in 1993 (188 dead: Haines 2003); the explosion at a firework factory in Enschede, Netherlands, in 2000 (22 dead: van Kamp *et al.* 2006); the explosion at a BP refinery in Texas City, USA, in 2005 (15 dead: Hopkins 2009); and the explosion on the BP-operated Deepwater Horizon oil rig in the Gulf of Mexico in April 2010 (11 dead: Kerr *et al.* 2010).

These incidents also demonstrate that responsibility for work-related deaths is not simply attributable to the individuals whose actions contribute to causing them; the organisational contexts in which those individuals operate are even more influential in bringing them about. Corporations, employers, and government bodies are all increasingly recognised as actors in their own right and as appropriate bearers of legal responsibility for the harmful outcomes of both systemic organisational failures and the actions of employees. There is also a perception that in many cases this responsibility is sufficiently culpable to fall within the scope of the criminal law, and so corporate bodies should be able to bear criminal liability for these outcomes (Gunningham and Johnstone 1999; Slapper 1999; Wells 2001). The antecedents of corporate criminal liability within Western legal systems stretch back over a 100 years, but for the most part, within this time period, there has been very little effort to develop mechanisms to effectively criminalise corporate bodies. In recent years, however, this has changed, primarily due to the impact of work-related disasters like those mentioned above. In particular, contemporary legal systems increasingly recognise a need to provide a response to these deaths which adequately reflects the gravity of the harms done and the wrongfulness of the actions that cause them.

As a result, the most high-profile issue within this field has been the development in many national jurisdictions of systems of criminal homicide liability for organisational entities, in order to operate in parallel, or in tandem, with other, existing, systems of legal control. Systems of regulatory law governing health and safety, or of civil law liability for death and injury at work, share many of the same contextual origins as corporate criminal liability and have close links to them in practice, but constitute very different bodies of law. In the UK, the first successful prosecution of a corporate body for the general criminal offence of manslaughter occurred in 1994,[1] the same year in which a consultation paper concerning a potential 'corporate manslaughter' offence was published (Law Commission 1994). This was followed by further proposals from the Law Commission in 1996 and the Home Office in

2000 and 2005, and the introduction of the Corporate Manslaughter and Corporate Homicide Act in 2007, which created a specific 'corporate manslaughter' offence to be used in relation to the most serious work-related deaths. This constitutes only the second such offence to be introduced anywhere in the world, the first having been introduced in Australia's Capital Territory (ACT) in 2004 via the Crimes (Industrial Manslaughter) Act 2003 (Sarre and Richards 2005). Other nations (like Australia, Canada, and the USA) have increasingly started to bring prosecutions under the general law of manslaughter since the 1990s, and many more have reformed their existing criminal laws so as to facilitate the criminal liability of corporate bodies (Beale and Safwat 2004; Bittle and Snider 2006; Gunningham and Johnstone 1999: 210; Sarre and Richards 2005). The 2010 conviction for manslaughter of Continental Airlines in France, following the 2000 Paris Concorde air crash (which killed 113 people), demonstrates that corporate homicide liability is an issue of international significance.

This shift has coincided with a public trend towards an increased mistrust of corporations and their motives, particularly in relation to issues of globalisation (Wells 2001). But, at the same time, statistics on work-related injury and ill health show generally downward trends in most developed countries during the same period. So why is it that the last ten years have seen such a trend towards the use of the criminal law as a means of signalling societal disapproval of excessive corporate risk-taking and of achieving regulatory outcomes? In part, these developments seem to reflect the broader trends towards an expanded criminal justice infrastructure identified within the literature on the contemporary politics of law and order, particularly relating to the emergence of a 'culture of control' (Garland 2001) and the climate of 'populist punitiveness' (Bottoms 1995; Hutton 2005) that accompanies it (Lacey 2008; Pratt 2000; Simon 2007; Tonry 2004). Roberts *et al.* link the emergence of punitive penal policies across the Western world to the development of a culture of penal populism, where 'punishment policy [is] developed primarily for its anticipated popularity' (2003: 65). The criminal justice system is used as a mechanism to 'represent . . . the state's willingness to use force against its enemies, to express popular sentiment, and to protect the public by whatever means necessary' (Garland 2001: 138).

It may appear that the shift towards corporate manslaughter could be understood in these terms. But the idea of penal populism seems to be of little relevance to the corporate context, where there is little evidence of any concerted desire to impose genuinely tough criminal liability (Gray

2009; Snider 1991; Tombs and Whyte 2007; Wells 2001), offenders are not marginalised 'others' and are not subject to highly public forms of condemnation, enforcement occurs mainly outside the mainstream criminal justice system, and the criminal law is used as a last resort only (Braithwaite 2003; Hawkins 2002; Wells 2001). Corporate and regulatory offending constitutes a radically different political and legal context to mainstream criminal justice, and a different set of dynamics apply to this sort of crime. This book aims to explain and better understand contemporary trends towards the use of criminal law as a means of holding corporate bodies accountable for work-related deaths. The legal, social, and historical contexts of this movement will be examined, and the book will ask: how do these new 'criminal' tools of regulation relate to other systems of legal control, including regulatory law? What political and social factors account for the differences between national jurisdictions in this area? Crucially, why has the movement towards corporate homicide liability occurred, and what does it signify?

This book will argue that the systems of regulation put in place to control workplace health and safety have had both positive and negative effects, and have proved to be both a blessing and a curse. We are safer now than we have ever been (at least within the Western world), and this is a point which even the most strident critics of safety regulation must concede (Tombs and Whyte 2007: 44). At the same time, we are more concerned about these risks now than ever before. We struggle to relate to safety regulation as a process, and question its status as a socially beneficial activity. State intervention to offset the harmful side effects of industrialisation, in the form of legal regulation, constitutes a powerful advance in terms of social justice, but its bureaucratic nature has a tendency to divorce those areas of regulation from their social contexts (Habermas 1988); work-related deaths become objects of analysis and problems to solve, rather than wrongs in any normative sense. The values that regulation embodied are increasingly obscured as the law loses its communicative power. Regulation, like all law, requires a connection to public values in order to legitimate itself (Almond 2007; Habermas 1973; Haines and Gurney 2003). When minor sanctions are used to signal breaches of 'quasi'-criminal offences which are regarded as merely regulatory by policymakers (Home Office 2005: 58) and the public (Almond 2008), within a political context dominated by economic interests and a lack of government support for regulation (Tombs and Whyte 2007; 2010), how far can regulation be understood as reflective of public values of this kind?

Criminalisation through the development of corporate manslaughter-type offences constitutes an effort to recapture some of this communicative capacity, to secure support for the normative project of safety regulation by demonstrating that the harmful potential of corporate power is subjected to meaningful oversight. At the same time, regulatory scholars have demonstrated that a powerful tool for securing safer working environments is the voluntary compliance that results from a widespread belief in the rightness of the law on the part of those subject to it (Tyler 1990; Tyler and Darley 2000). This book will attempt to demonstrate that 'criminal' responses to work-related deaths demonstrate the shifting requirements of the regulatory system, specifically the need to 're-moralise' health and safety law and demonstrate the normative values that legitimate that system. Imposing criminal liability upon corporations which kill constitutes a movement towards this end; motivated partly by a political need to secure support, partly by a need to demonstrate the legitimacy of health and safety law, and partly by a desire to increase stakeholder commitment to the values of health and safety. Even limited use of the criminal law might assist in signalling the values of social justice and solidarity that underpin regulation.

Yet questions remain about whether this will occur in practice; it is far from clear that the new laws will overcome the political and economic restrictions that attach to the regulation of corporate interests. There are significant obstacles in place which are likely to impede the capacity of the new offences to reshape the profile of the regulatory process as a whole, and the inherent shortcomings of the criminal law are likely to undermine many of the communicative aspirations of the regulatory system. This also explains why not all nations have moved towards criminalisation. In many countries, the development of systems of regulation is tied to the wider process of establishing participatory democratic rights. Where prevailing social and political attitudes and policies explicitly prioritise the same values of social justice and solidarity that underpin regulation, resorting to criminal law as a means of promoting these values proves unnecessary as regulatory laws can perform this role by themselves. Conversely, it is countries where the values of free-market liberalism are most prominent (the common-law jurisdictions of the English-speaking world) that the criminalisation of corporate activity has taken place to the greatest degree. There is also a 'need' for such measures in these societies, as regulation here has been subject to sustained attack in recent decades; communicative laws are needed to underpin the rehabilitation of public discourses about regulation as a legitimate matter of social governance.

Plan of the book

Chapter 1 sets out the immediate contextual background to the problem of work-related deaths, as a social phenomenon, and the movement towards the use of criminal law as a means of responding to this problem. The differences between criminal and regulatory systems of law within the occupational health and safety context will be explained, and the reforms that have taken place in the UK will be reviewed. The Corporate Manslaughter offence introduced in this jurisdiction constitutes the most explicit example of the contemporary international trend towards criminalisation and so will form the basis of much of the discussion within this book. And while the UK reforms signal, in their intention at least, a change in the way in which work-related deaths are framed, the reality of this reform process gives little prospect for significant change. Chapter 2 describes the extent to which this development has been mirrored in other national jurisdictions; four main national positions in terms of criminalisation will be identified: countries with specific corporate manslaughter offences; countries without such offences but which allow for corporate bodies to be convicted under the general law of manslaughter; countries that allow for corporate criminal liability but which do not extend it to include manslaughter; and countries that eschew corporate criminal liability altogether. Corporate manslaughter liability is an increasingly common feature of contemporary legal systems and has come to be so in a relatively compressed period of time. This suggests that we can, to some extent, view these different national developments as a coherent whole, reflective of a particular set of influences which may be identified and understood.

Chapter 3 advances a theoretical understanding of this movement towards criminalisation which centres on the relationship between the law and the public sphere, and the way that the regulation of workplace safety is understood by the wider public. Legal regulation is a communicative process and has a normative component. But the laws that regulate work-related death are defined by a lack of normative content and a failure to elicit outcomes that articulate with wider social values. A Habermasian theoretical approach allows us to understand regulation in both instrumental and communicative terms, as a means of effecting meaningful social change and also fulfilling integrative symbolic socio-cultural functions; it also allows us to identify the potential problems of legitimation that are likely to be encountered by systems of regulation which lack a normative basis. Chapter 4 applies this theoretical lens in order to explore the ways in which health and safety regulation has developed over time, what values it has sought to pursue, and how it came to be the instrumental system of law that exists today. The UK context will be explored as a forum for the development of more general themes. It will be shown that health and safety regulation is a rights-giving legal endeavour which performs a market-constitutive role, maintaining the parameters of the employment relationship and the economic system; as such, its transformative capacity is limited by the constraints of that system.

Chapter 5 addresses the historical movement towards criminalising work-related deaths. This trend will be linked to a public, social, and political awareness of a disjunction between the administrative capacity and the socio-cultural status and legitimacy of the regulatory system and to the development of a contemporary political climate of neo-liberalism. The shift towards criminalisation in the UK is a response to a long-standing ambiguity of status associated with the law in this area; criminal law is pursued as a means of providing a forum for the exercise of moral judgements about work-related deaths and the balance of competing interests, something that regulation has failed to do. Chapter 6 considers the potential impact that criminalisation may have in relation to the normative gap that exists within the sphere of health and safety regulation. These new offences have the potential to reform the nature and quality of public discourses about health and safety law and to legitimate that system of law by demonstrating the fundamental values that it pursues. By showing that health and safety law is about guaranteeing the bases of social citizenship and the protection of individuals from attacks on their fundamental interests, criminalisation can validate regulation via its connection to the values of a deliberative public.

Finally, Chapter 7 sets out a series of caveats and limitations on the effectiveness and communicative capacity of the corporate manslaughter reforms, which together have the effect of bringing their potential impact into question. There are many reasons for scepticism about the effectiveness of the new laws, not least the limited nature of the changes introduced and their capacity to be used as purely symbolic measures to serve the interests of political actors rather than the public. While not all of the objections made in relation to these reforms are as fundamental as might be thought, there are still many reasons to be wary about the use of criminal law as a tool in pursuit of welfarist goals in this context. For these reasons, it is possible to conceive of criminalisation as a second-best solution to the communicative problems of regulatory law. Looking at the national jurisdictions that have not moved towards criminalisation leads to the conclusion that the construction of a system of regulation that is itself deliberative, which provides opportunities for normative input via the involvement of workers in the day-to-day management of health and safety provision, and which reflects a social and political culture that more explicitly recognises and valorises the welfarist goals of the regulatory project allows for a more sustainable communicative version of health and safety regulation to be achieved. But the political context found in the UK and the other neo-liberal nations that have enthusiastically embraced criminalisation makes this highly unlikely in practice, rendering corporate manslaughter a 'crutch' necessary for the legitimation of regulation in the absence of true socio-cultural support.

1
The Shift from 'Regulation' to 'Crime'

On the afternoon of Friday, 5 September 2008, Alexander Wright, a 27-year-old junior geotechnical engineer, was collecting soil samples at a building site in Gloucestershire, UK. He was working alone in driving rain in a specially dug trench approximately four metres deep, which was not supported on either side by timber buttressing. Approximately 15 minutes later, the sides of the trench collapsed inwards, burying him under falling soil. Although buried over his head, he was able to call for help, and despite the efforts of those on site to dig him free, mud continued to fall into the trench faster than it could be dug out and he died of traumatic asphyxia several minutes later. An investigation established that Wright's employer, Cotswold Geotechnical Holdings Plc., had disregarded industry guidance and concerns raised by employees and regulators in the past about safe trench-work, had failed to provide adequate training to employees about the hazards involved in this sort of operation, and had knowingly exposed Alexander Wright to a wholly unsafe system of work. This was an extremely serious, entirely avoidable, and highly culpable example of a work-related death.

Quite apart from being a truly dreadful way to die, and a tragedy for the victim and his family, this incident came to acquire legal significance as the first case in which the offence of Corporate Manslaughter, which became law in 2007, was used to hold a corporate body criminally liable for the death of an employee.[1] Cotswold Geotechnical Holdings was convicted of manslaughter in February 2011 and sentenced to pay a fine of £385,000. This case was important as it finally implemented a piece of legislation that had been on the statute books for several years without being used and that represented the culmination of a lengthy reform process prior to that. The verdict established a precedent for the terms of the new offence and signalled that the relationship between corporate bodies and the criminal law had changed. The Corporate Manslaughter and Corporate Homicide Act 2007 was introduced into English law as a means of extending the censure associated with a serious homicide offence to corporate bodies which kill and of providing a more effective means of constructing corporate liability. It is perhaps the most clear and explicit example of a shift towards the extension of the criminal law into areas previously viewed as 'regulatory' in nature that has been seen in many national jurisdictions. Work-related deaths have increasingly come to constitute a recognised social problem and have prompted official responses that are framed in terms of the criminal law, and, in the UK, the case of Alexander Wright constituted an important step in this process. This chapter will begin by defining the parameters of the problem of work-related death, before moving on to measure the extent of this problem and to explain why it is an issue of such public importance. Once this has been done, the law reform process in the UK will be examined, first by looking at the existing enforcement practices for work-related deaths and then by exploring the new corporate manslaughter offence and the changes to the law that this has brought.

Defining the problem of work-related deaths

This book seeks to explain legal responses to deaths arising from safety incidents that occur as a result of the actions of a corporation, business, or other organisational entity. These cases constitute a subsection of the total number of injuries occurring as a result of 'workplace accidents' or 'safety crimes' (Tombs and Whyte 2007). The defining feature for the purposes of this investigation is the fact of death, which is central to the construction of the legal category of manslaughter, and so our focus necessarily centres on 'one statistically minor dimension of a much more complex problem' (Gobert 2008: 414). By referring to 'work-related' deaths, it is intended that all workplaces be included, not just the manufacturing context as might be implied by terms like 'industrial accident'. Additionally, while these deaths are often referred to as 'occupational' fatalities, only a proportion of them occur in the course of the victim's employment. Many more involve members of the public and individuals who interact with corporations outside of their employment; for example, pollution resulting from the Bhopal disaster killed many more people living near the Union Carbide plant than the explosion killed employees (Sharma 2005), and most of the victims of the 'Herald of Free Enterprise' sinking were passengers (Wells 2001). The term 'occupational fatality' also carries an unhelpful connotation of 'acceptable' risk; an 'occupational hazard' is, in common parlance, something we expect to face when we go to work. In contrast, most work-related deaths result from unacceptable risks which victims do not accept as a normal condition of employment. 'Work-related fatality' is the standard term utilised by the UK Health and Safety Executive (HSE), among other official bodies (Almond 2008), and this category incorporates the deaths of both employees and members of the public when they arise via organisational activity.

The effect of everyday language is even more pronounced in relation to the use of the term 'accident', which is critiqued effectively by Tombs and Whyte, who point out that describing work-related deaths as accidents implies that they are 'unknowable and unpreventable, despite the fact that any examination of a range of incidents reveals common, systematic, foreseeable and eminently preventable causes' (2007: 72). Even 'accidents' within complex systems have discernible causes that allow for the attribution of causal responsibility (Perrow 1984); questions of liability should not be precluded via the definition of an event as accidental. The terminology to be used in this book ('work-related death') is intended to encapsulate the contextual variety and normative significance of these cases. A work-related death involves a worker (employee, self-employed, or other person engaged in work) or member of the public who is killed as a result of an event which has arisen out of or in connection with work activity, whether or not they are at work themselves. The term 'death' is preferred to fatality in order to avoid the implication of inadvertence attaching to the latter term.[2] Conversely, the term also avoids prejudging the issue of criminality (unlike 'safety crime'; Tombs and Whyte 2007: 88), thereby avoiding charges of 'moral entrepreneurship' (Tappan 1947). That said, the definitions of crime and non-crime drawn in this context should not be accepted unquestioningly; it may be appropriate to class work-related deaths as crimes once responsibility for them is identified, but when describing the pre-legal fact of death, we need a terminology which avoids predetermining as well as dismissing the possibility of criminality.

Measuring the problem of work-related deaths

In order to understand the importance of the issue of work-related death, it is important to gauge how many fatalities of this sort actually occur. Attempting to do so illustrates three key points: the sheer volume of harm that occurs as a result of corporate behaviour, the difficulty of measuring this harm, and the key role that statistics play in redefining the issue of work-related death in narrow, technical terms. The statistical information allows us to obtain a partial understanding of social phenomena, but it is also socially constructed; as such, we can also learn about institutional decisions regarding inclusion that set parameters on the issue (Kitsuse and Cicourel 1963). The information made available by Eurostat, the Statistical Office of the European Union (EU), indicates that in 2007 (the last year for which full figures are available) there were 5785 deaths at work across the 27 member states of the EU, or approximately 3.5 deaths per 100,000 workers (Eurostat 2010a: 347). Eurostat's adjusted incidence rate seeks to iron out inconsistencies within the data to provide a nationally comparable rate of work-related deaths by proportionally weighting the national figures to offset the statistical impact of high-risk industries (as such, these adjusted rates vary considerably from the actual rates). This suggests that, against an adjusted rate of fatal 'accident' of 81 per 100,000 workers across the 27 EU member states as a whole, states such as Slovenia (149 per 100,000), Lithuania (117), and Sweden (115) stand out as having particularly high fatality rates, while others, including Luxembourg (37 per 100,000), France (50), and Italy (58), have comparatively low rates. The UK stands exactly on the EU mean rate (81), while the rate for Germany is somewhat higher (95) and for Spain somewhat lower (65).

The difficulties in drawing clear conclusions from these adjusted incidence rates are illustrated by the fact that France, Italy, and Spain have some of the lowest adjusted 'rates' of death at work but comparatively high numbers of deaths (395 in France and 455 in Italy, as compared to 169 in the UK). Another comparison is revealing; Germany and Sweden's high incidence rates for work-related fatalities are offset by relatively low incidence rates of serious non-fatal injuries at work (66 and 64 per 100,000 respectively, against an EU average of 76; Eurostat 2010a: 347). While the UK's rate of 75 serious non-fatal injuries is again close to the mean, many of the highest incidence rates of injury are found in the states of the former eastern Europe (such as Estonia, 120; Lithuania, 101; Romania, 94). This variance between fatal and non-fatal incidence patterns suggests that much of the variation in national work-related death rates is a result of different patterns of coverage, reporting, and inclusion in different countries, a conclusion borne out by the rate of divergence (66%) between actual and estimated fatality rates across western Europe (Hämäläinen *et al.* 2009: 129).

It must be noted that these data are by no means complete. For instance, the EU's incidence rates include only 'core' industries because statistics for other industrial and employment sectors are not measured reliably or consistently across all member states;[3] this rules out public sector workers, mining and quarrying, and some aspects of transportation (EUROSTAT 2001: 26), as the UK and Ireland do not record road traffic incidents as part of their work-related fatality data (they fall under the responsibility of a different domestic recording agency). Further, these statistics do not necessarily include the self-employed, or fatalities to workers while they are working outside the physical confines of the workplace. Finally, some jurisdictions have narrow definitional limits on when a fatality will count as 'work-related'; the Netherlands requires that death must occur the same day as the initial incident and Germany within 30 days, while the standard time limit is between one and one-and-a-half years (Eurostat 2010b). The two main omissions from these fatality rates are deaths from illness and deaths of non-employees. A 2007 Labour Force Survey carried out on behalf of the EU found that 8.6% of workers (approximately 20 million people) reported having suffered some form of work-related ill health in the preceding 12 months (Eurostat 2009). The number of deaths resulting from work-related ill health within Western Europe is estimated to be as high as 139,519 *per annum* (2002 figures; Hämäläinen *et al.* 2009: 130). Around half of these deaths are caused by cancers contracted via work.

In the USA, the Occupational Safety and Health Administration's (OSHA) Census of Fatal Occupational Injuries placed the number of fatal work injuries for 2008 at 5214, or 3.7 deaths per 100,000 workers (OSHA 2010). Unlike the data for most of Europe, this figure includes deaths in road traffic incidents while working, which account for 23% of the total fatality rate, but (like the European data) does not include either fatal work-related illnesses or deaths to non-workers. In Canada, there were 1036 work-related deaths (NWISP 2009), and in Australia, 444 (286 'working' fatalities, 117 out-of-work, and 41 public or bystander fatalities; Safe Work Australia 2011). The latter figure incorporates both road deaths while working and those occurring while commuting to and from work. Japan registered 1268 work-related deaths in 2008 (JISHA 2010). Elsewhere, it is necessary to rely on estimates extrapolated from data reported to the International Labour Organisation (ILO) and calculated according to demographic information by Hämäläinen *et al.* (2009). While the ILO recorded 18,067 fatal occupational 'accidents' in 2003, the actual number is estimated to be as high as 357,948, with a further 1.95 million deaths from work-related ill health (Hämäläinen *et al.* 2009: 129). Of these work-related deaths, the vast majority are accounted for by the developing world, with China (97,248 accidents and 332,454 due to ill health) and India (46,928 accidents and 355,863 due to ill health) featuring prominently. Africa as a whole is thought to account for over 470,000 work-related deaths each year. While these are estimates only, they hint at the true global scale of work-related risk-taking. It must be borne in mind, therefore, that the category of work-related deaths is much broader than the published 'accident' rates imply.

Perhaps just as important for the purposes of this book is the exclusion of non-workers from the fatality statistics. The main reason for this, apart from the narrowing effect of the EU's policy focus on the harmonisation of 'employment' rights, is that there is little comparable data on deaths of non-workers resulting from work-related activities (Eurostat 2001: 13); it is therefore impossible to accurately gauge the true number of victims of work-related activities. At this point it becomes relevant to look to national statistics for the UK, where the RIDDOR reporting scheme requires that the HSE record the deaths of non-workers resulting from work activities.[4] The statistics put the number of work-related fatalities per year at 151 for workers and 393 for members of the public; again, these are partial figures, omitting deaths reportable to other government agencies (such as transport deaths and those occurring in some specific industry sectors that have their own regulators; HSE 2010a). They are also reliant on the classification and reporting of deaths as 'work-related', which can be an inconsistent process in practice because it relies heavily on the judgements of actors such as coroners and doctors in linking the outcome to the initial cause. Tombs and Whyte (2007: 47) estimate that a more realistic rate of work-related deaths per year for the UK might be 1600–1700, based upon the RIDDOR reporting rates, death rates for excluded industries, and the estimated number of work-related road deaths each year. To this must be added the estimated annual 20,778 deaths from work-related ill health in the UK (Hämäläinen *et al.* 2009: 137), increasing the total even further. What this means is that work-related deaths must be considered, by any calculation, a significant social problem that merits regulation in the public interest; the level of harm that is inflicted via workplace safety failures also brings important justice considerations into play.

The public importance of work-related deaths

Work-related disasters have constituted some of the most harmful peacetime events resulting from human activity during the last 30 years. They are 'public' events, in that they go beyond the confines of the workplace and cause death and injury to members of the wider community.

They are also avoidable: sloppy oversight, poor maintenance, failures to invest in safety precautions, and the neglect of basic procedures are all common contributing factors in work-related death cases (Tombs and Whyte 2007; Wells 2001). Steve Tombs has argued for the need to conceptualise deaths in this context as 'criminal', and to recognise that they are 'inflicted' and do not occur spontaneously (2004; also Slapper 1999; Tombs and Whyte 2007). Like other harmful social events, fatal safety incidents also impact on the public and shape legal and political debates about risk, in addition to the serious consequences they bring for the victims they directly affect (Clarkson 2008; Gobert 2005; Haines 1997; Snell and Tombs 2011; Tombs and Whyte 2007; Wells 2001). Research into public attitudes towards crime has demonstrated that a special significance is attributed to events which cause death (Almond 2009a; Hansel 1987; Warr 1989). O'Connell and Whelan suggest that the perceived seriousness of fatal offences demonstrates that the 'individualized violation ... of a person' involved is offensive to common standards of behaviour (1996: 308). The same is true of safety incidents; death is important in determining the seriousness of an event, and multiple fatalities are viewed as particularly serious (Almond 2008; Cullen *et al.* 1982; Rosenmerkel 2001).

The fact of victimisation in work-related death cases demonstrates the costs associated with negligent behaviour and establishes a 'prima facie' reason for intervention (Haines 1997: 41; Tombs 2004). But work-related deaths are also 'public' incidents which transcend their immediate consequences because, by laying bare the existence of deep-rooted social problems, they make hitherto unseen risks 'come to life' (Hutter and Lloyd-Bostock 1990: 418). Psychologists have identified the capacity of harmful events to act as signals of wider danger, particularly where they involve unknown hazards or catastrophic potential consequences ('dread risk'; Breakwell 2007: Ch. 7; Slovic 1987; Slovic *et al.* 1979). An example of this would be the explosion at the Chernobyl nuclear power plant in the Ukraine in 1986, which resulted in thousands of deaths, widespread ill health, and vast environmental damage. This event fundamentally changed public perceptions of nuclear power because it brought into focus the harm potential of the nuclear industry; similar effects have emerged following the meltdown at Japan's Fukushima nuclear power plant in 2011. Much contemporary political debate about nuclear power is shaped by Chernobyl's legacy, and it is still perceived as a disproportionately risky technology (Breakwell 2007: 188–190; Pidgeon *et al.* 2008). Events that 'cross the factory fence' (Tombs and Whyte 2010: 49) can have consequences reaching far beyond their immediate context, acting as 'signal incidents' that indicate an 'absent, weakened or fragile local social order' (Innes 2004: 341), making risks visible, and altering the way that recipients of the signal respond to them.

As well as constituting problematic social events, there are other reasons why work-related deaths must face intervention by the law. Such deaths affect many people, and so may be regarded as an issue of 'social' justice, while their tendency to affect the vulnerable means that they also have a strong social 'justice' component. Framing work-related deaths as public issues in terms of their psychological and social impacts may suggest that the concern is exclusively with disasters, but while 'big cases' grab the attention (Almond 2008; Wells 2001), the majority of work-related deaths do not take this form. HSE estimated that 23% of workplace deaths result from falls from heights, making this the most common single cause of work-related death, ahead of strikes by moving or falling objects (16%) and vehicles (14%), contact with moving machinery (11%), and crush injuries (10%).[5] These trends carry through into the causes of non-fatal injuries as well; 38% of reported major non-fatal injuries result from slips, trips, and falls at work, while another 37% of three-day injuries result from manual handling activities (a trend echoed by Eurostat 2009). The true paradigm case of work-related death, then, is that of an individual who is killed while carrying out an 'ordinary' activity which has an extraordinary (but perhaps not unforeseen) consequence. And while arguments for regulation are made most explicit by disaster cases, the need for regulation is most acute where the risk factors involved are 'routinised' and normal (Glassner 1999; Gray 2006; Silbey 2009: 357; Slapper 1999: 7). This is where decisions about risk-taking are most regularly taken and where the need to employ systems of regulatory intervention to pattern those decisions so as to achieve public-interest goals is most pronounced. As outcomes of 'normal' working practices, work-related deaths reflect a public interest in the control of unacceptable risks to health and safety and demonstrate the potential for the autonomy of workers to be compromised by employers.

There is a tendency for accounts of work-related deaths to focus exclusively on traditional workplaces and employment relationships, overlooking the fact that a significant proportion of work does not fit into this model (Atkinson 1985; Belous 1995; Cappelli 1999; Estlund 2003: Ch. 3). Atypical work accounts for many deaths and injuries each year, often involving some of the most marginalised and disadvantaged people in society (Bardasi and Francesconi 2004; Mayhew and Quinlan

1999; Rodriguez 2002). This underpins a social 'justice' rationale for intervention; the regulation of workplace safety becomes a matter of protecting the vulnerable in the same way as other social welfare interventions (Feintuck 2004: 59). The notion of marginalisation is crucial in understanding where the risks associated with work most commonly fall. Will Hutton characterised Western (specifically British) society as having a 40-30-30 structure, with 40% of the population in relatively secure and stable employment, 30% in insecure fixed-term and temporary work, and a final 30% who are excluded from the legitimate world of work entirely (Hutton 1995: 105; Young 1999: 8). The insecure workers of the middle 30% are not given the same employment protections as the stable 40%, and so often find themselves working in conditions that pose significant risks (Gray 2002; 2006). The regulatory context within which work-related deaths arise is increasingly diverse and this poses important challenges for regulators, such as how best to ensure that adequate resources are devoted to protecting the interests of those most in need. This fragmentation of the workplace is mirrored within regulatory regimes which govern health and safety at work; notions of 'responsive regulation', 'smart regulation', and 'reflexive' regulation have emerged (Aalders and Wilthagen 1997; Ayres and Braithwaite 1992; Braithwaite 2002; Gunningham and Grabosky 1998; Gunningham and Johnstone 1999; Parker 2002; 2006) to characterise a 'pragmatic, flexible, and pluralistic approach to regulation involving the use of multiple regulatory techniques' to address the needs of specific contexts and situations (Black 2007: 58).

Crucially, it is those with the least power within the workplace who disproportionately face risks to their health and safety: they include temporary workers, those in low-paid casual work, and those who work outside the cooperative business–regulator relationships that are central to state regulation (Gunningham and Johnstone 1999; Haines 1997; Hawkins 2002; Hutter 1997; Wells 2001). While some regulators recognise the need for responsive regulatory regimes to facilitate the intensive regulation of 'bad apples' as well as to accommodate self-regulation by organisations who can do so (Ayres and Braithwaite 1992; Hampton 2005), there remains a fundamental challenge in extending the influence of regulatory systems to include marginal workplaces (Gunningham and Johnstone 1999: 4; Quinlan 1999). The final 30% of Hutton's model include, in addition to the long-term unemployed and socially marginalised, those who work within the unregulated black-market economy, which can also inflict serious harm upon workers. An example of this is provided by the deaths of 23 migrant Chinese workers while working as cockle-pickers in Morecambe Bay in northern England in 2004. The victims had been trafficked into the UK and employed illegally by an unregulated 'gangmaster',[6] and drowned when the fast-moving tides in the bay cut them off from land (Tombs and Whyte 2007: 27–29). This case highlighted the risks that affect the large number of people who work in illegitimate jobs on the fringes of the regular economy, and prompted specific legislation to govern temporary-worker employment (the Gangmasters (Licensing) Act 2004).

In addition to illegitimate employment, many other workers are employed in contexts that do not conform to the traditional employment model. There are many legitimate industries that are relatively invisible and ungovernable. For example, the construction industry is notorious for its transient worksites, informal employment practices, and for the high levels of risk attaching to the work undertaken (Hawkins 2002: 124–135; HSE 1988; Tombs and Whyte 2007: 11); agriculture is another industry that poses many of the same challenges. Construction also has one of the worst rates of workplace injury and death of any industry; HSE statistics for 2008–9 showed that there were 106 deaths (and a rate of 254 major injuries per 100,000 workers) in the UK construction industry that year (HSE 2009a). The safety inspectors whom Keith Hawkins interviewed in his study of HSE enforcement practices (2002) spoke of the significant problems caused by the invisibility and transience of many construction firms (also Hutter 1989: 160). These factors made it impossible to build the sort of long-term relationships that are the basis of HSE's normal regulatory approach. As such, the regulation of the construction industry tends to be more prosecution-focused than other areas of health and safety regulation (Hutter 1989: 160). Yet this example is instructive; where regulation is needed most, it is also hardest to implement.

Taken together, these insights help to demonstrate why work-related deaths, and the safety of those affected by corporate activities, can be regarded as a proper subject for regulatory intervention. The severity of the physical harm involved in work-related deaths makes a persuasive case for intervention on a public-interest basis. Further, the tendency is for these incidents to affect individuals who are disadvantaged in comparison to the organisations that inflict those harm, either because they are marginalised citizens, as with the Bhopal case (Tombs and Whyte 2007: Ch. 1), or because, as employees, they are the weaker party in an employment relationship (Gray 2006; Haines 2003). The risks that cause deaths in these cases are not undertaken freely and voluntarily; they are imposed on those affected, whose disadvantage renders them unable to exercise autonomy in the matter of the risks they face. Consumers, passengers, and users of corporate services may not necessarily constitute 'disadvantaged' groups, but information deficits and an inequality of bargaining power can impede their ability to freely self-determine their own risk-taking (Ogus 1994: 38–41). As such, regulation of these areas is consistent with the social justice aspirations of regulatory law.

Regulatory enforcement practices following work-related deaths

Laws to control the risks that cause work-related deaths are a common feature of the legal systems of most Western nations. For the most part, they take the form of wide-ranging workplace safety statutes, which aim to establish basic standards of workplace safety provision and treat work-related deaths as examples of safety breaches in general terms. These laws are not a new feature of those domestic legal systems; they emerged in often piecemeal fashion during the late 19th and early 20th centuries (see Chapter 4) to establish minimum standards of safety within industry. This involved the imposition of penalties where legal requirements were not met and serious or fatal injuries resulted, a role normally fulfilled by governmental regulators as part of the wider job of overseeing workplace health and safety. In the UK, this involves HSE, a non-departmental body which provides guidance to duty-holders, implements regulations, and enforces breaches of those regulations (Baldwin 1987; Dawson *et al.* 1988; Hawkins 2002; Hutter 1997; Hutter and Manning 1990; Slapper 1999). HSE investigates work-related deaths along with the Police, but takes primary responsibility for the enforcement of these cases under ss. 2 and 3 of the Health and Safety at Work Act 1974 (HSWA) as failures to ensure, so far as is reasonably practicable, the health, safety, and welfare of employees or members of the public. Because enforcement is only one of the many roles that HSE fulfils, it has tended to regard enforcement as a secondary component of its operation, and rates of prosecution reflect this (Almond 2006; Dawson *et al.* 1988; Hawkins 2002; Hutter 1986; Tombs and Whyte 2007). In 2009–2010, HSE issued 9734 enforcement notices (statutory notifications compelling improvement or prohibition in relation to a breach of the law), and prosecuted 1026 offences, achieving an average fine of £15,817 per breach (compared to 8054 notices, 1099 prosecutions, and £14,614 average in 2008–2009; HSE 2010a). To contextualise these figures, there were 121,430 work-related injuries reported to HSE during the same period and 152 fatal injuries to workers.

While enforcement figures for work-related deaths are hard to locate, it is estimated that in 2000–2001, HSE secured 120 convictions under health and safety law following 436 recorded work-related deaths, resulting in an average fine of £34,369 (Almond 2006: 894). The enforcement of the law here differs greatly from that found in relation to other areas of criminal law; only a very small proportion of the cases that are reported or investigated result in any kind of enforcement action being brought.

A similar arrangement exists in most other jurisdictions; regulators take primary responsibility for initiating legal action in the event of a work-related death or injury. In the USA, the Occupational Safety and Health Act 1970 (OSH Act) gave individual States the role of implementing legislation which reflected standards set at the Federal level. The OSH Act was created by that legislation as the Federal agency with responsibility for coordinating safety regulation in the USA. It operates in partnership with State-level agencies to enforce a system of monetary civil penalties following breaches of the OSH Act. The imposition of these penalties is relatively non-discretionary, but the average fines tend to be relatively small ($873 for a serious breach and $32,000 for a wilful breach; Rhinehart 2008: 123; Silverstein 2008). Like the UK's HSWA, the OSH Act also allows for the criminal prosecution of defendants who breach the Act, particularly where that breach results in death, and for fines and imprisonment to be imposed in response (see OSH Act s. 17(4)), although these powers are used rarely (Rhinehart 2008: 124). In Australia, health and safety is enforced by State/Territory-level agencies which carry out the duties imposed by the health and safety statutes passed by each individual state. Again, enforcement is a last-resort measure, and fines are the primary sanction used following a breach of the law (Gunningham and Johnstone 1999: 377; Hall and Johnstone 2005: 71; Sarre and Richards 2005). A similar system of Provincial/Territorial enforcement operates in Canada, where different industrial sectors are governed by Federal and Provincial/Territorial labour codes, while health and safety enforcement in New Zealand is the responsibility of the national Department of Labour.

In most European national jurisdictions (including Sweden, France, and the Netherlands), occupational health and safety standards are enforced by unitary labour inspectorates that fall within the responsibilities of State Departments of Employment or their equivalent (Gunningham and Johnstone 1999: 378–379; Walters 1996: 302–303; Walters *et al.* 2011). Some jurisdictions, such as Spain and Italy, utilise localised systems of regulation, while Germany divides this responsibility between Federal and regional (Land) regulators, and between Industry Safety and Standards Inspectorates and Employer's Liability Insurance Associations (Gräbe 1991). The regulatory approach taken in these different national systems shows a degree of consistency, centring on the concentration of resources on high-risk worksites, the pursuit of compliance via the provision of advice and training, and the enforcement of broad duties (Eichener 1997; Walters 1996: 303–304; Walters *et al.* 2011). A significant factor driving this convergence has been the influence of EU health and safety legislation, particularly the 1989 Framework Directive (89/391/EEC) and subsequent Commission strategies aimed at raising and harmonising standards across the EU (Eichener 1997; Walters 1996; Wright 2008). Individual States have been pushed to reform their domestic laws in order to fulfil an overarching EU commitment to a wide-ranging conception of health and safety which incorporates diffuse and process-oriented notions such as employee well-being and psychosocial health. This has resulted in the diffusion of an approach that promotes partnership, cooperation, and the use of 'soft law' techniques that frame health and safety as an issue of well-being, and which (it is suggested) support a shift away from regulatory interventionism (Eichener 1997; Walters *et al.* 2011; Wright 2008: 3).

These systems represent examples of the traditional paradigm of the 'activist' state: a rational, centralised, administrative 'command-and-control' approach to regulation (Gunningham and Johnstone 1999: 6–7). The regulation of health and safety requires implementation via an activist agency with the capacity to make and uphold laws that secure material improvements in standards. This means that enforcement has tended to be bound up with other, more facilitative, functions and is not separated out under the criminal law. In the case of interpersonal violence, the state has relatively little capacity to facilitate future compliance, and so enforcement can normally be handled by the criminal justice system in reactive mode, although there are criminal justice measures, like the UK's Anti-Social Behaviour Orders, which seek to moderate future behaviour (Crawford 2009; Simon 2007). Enforcement within the workplace safety context, on the other hand, is viewed and utilised as a subsidiary of ongoing compliance-seeking processes (Ayres and Braithwaite 1992; Gunningham and Johnstone 1999; Hutter 1997). The enforcement philosophy is one of 'law as last resort' (Hawkins 2002); the costs of bringing a prosecution, in terms of regulatory resources, loss of goodwill from the regulated, and loss of reputation should the prosecution fail or be seen as unreasonable, are taken to mitigate against utilising prosecution except in the most egregious cases.

Prosecution is not a core component of the regulatory process, and convictions, when they do occur, result in sanctions that are less harsh than those found elsewhere in the criminal law. Health and safety violations, even those resulting in death, are rarely treated as matters of criminal law *per se*. Despite this, a number of national jurisdictions also allow for the prosecution of corporate defendants under the law of manslaughter following a work-related death. In particular, the UK, Australia, the USA, and Canada have had legal principles in place to allow for the attribution of liability for an offence of manslaughter to a corporate body (Coffee 1983; 1999; Gunningham and Johnstone 1999; Sarre and Richards 2005; Wells 2001), and several European jurisdictions have also allowed for corporate criminal liability in similar circumstances, including the Netherlands (Field and Jorg 1991) and France (Orland and Cachera 1995). Where this possibility does exist (such as in the UK), it has remained a relatively rare component of a wider regulatory programme.

The last 15 years or so, however, have seen numerous jurisdictions either legislate to introduce new offences or broaden the terms on which a corporate body can be held criminally liable, with the intention of 'criminalising' corporations that kill. The result has been the establishment of a 'two-track' model of corporate liability; systems of regulatory offences and 'criminal' offences such as manslaughter coexist as alternate legal responses to work-related death. Cases are categorised as either regulatory violations or criminal offences depending on their seriousness, harmfulness, and socio-political impact (Almond 2006; 2009a; Hawkins 2002; Slapper 1999; Wells 2001). This distinction, although not clear-cut, tends to be between offences that censure substantial wrongdoing as defined by reference to external, content-dependent, reasons for complying, such as the shared values of the normative community (Ashworth 2000; Duff 2001), and offences which aim to achieve an outcome in pursuit of a common good, but which give only instrumental, content-independent reasons for complying. This reflects the *mala in se/mala prohibita* distinction drawn in criminal law theory between offences that are intrinsically morally wrongful, and those which are wrong as a result of being defined as such in pursuit of some ulterior goal (Lacey 2004: 145; Wells 2001: 7). 'Criminal' offences that apply to work-related deaths frame responsibility in terms of a wrongful act, inflicting or causing death or injury, while 'regulatory' offences frame liability for the same event in terms of a failure to perform activities or fulfil a duty to a required standard (Clarkson 2005: 681). There is also a functional difference; regulatory laws are evaluated instrumentally in terms of their effectiveness, while criminal offences exist in order to censure, but not to achieve any other end (Lacey 2004: 145; though ends like deterrence and retribution may be met as a result). Offences that are criminal in nature are handled via the criminal justice system, and so should adhere to principles of due process, equal treatment, and proportionality, while regulatory offences are not, and so do not necessarily reflect these values in the same way (Ashworth 2000).

Of course, as Wells points out, the 'fact' of differential treatment cannot necessarily be read as establishing anything more than the historical contingencies that led to this state of affairs, and does not demonstrate that offences *should* be differentiated in this way (2001: 21–26). But aside from arguments about how the distinction between criminal and regulatory law should be drawn, it is clear that a *perceived* distinction does exist between the two. Criminal law is regarded as more serious and as carrying a greater degree of moral censure than regulatory law (Almond 2008; Almond and Colover 2010; *forthcoming*). A desire to attach a criminal status to work-related deaths has proved to be a significant factor motivating reform of the law because, while existing systems of regulatory offending such as the HSWA 1974 are formally criminal law statutes, they are *perceived* to occupy a 'quasi-criminal' category below this. The law reform process aims to re-categorise these cases as criminal matters, and so to provide the kind of normative judgement that criminal proceedings are perceived to deliver. The remainder of this chapter will examine the reform process in the UK, which constitutes the most significant development in this direction anywhere in the world. The key features and outcomes of this reform process will be examined, and the way in which this process has attempted to redefine the conceptual status of the worst work-related death cases will be assessed.

Corporate manslaughter reform in the UK

The most explicit means of imposing criminal liability for death on a corporation is via the creation of a specific corporate homicide offence. The UK Parliament legislated via the Corporate Manslaughter and Corporate Homicide Act (CMCHA) 2007 to introduce the new offence of corporate manslaughter, which allows work-related deaths caused by corporate bodies to be treated as a discrete category of manslaughter offence (Clarkson 2005; 2008; Gobert 2005; 2008; Ormerod and Taylor 2008). This is in addition to existing rules allowing for the attribution of ordinary criminal liability to corporate bodies, and to well-developed systems of regulatory liability for breaches of health and safety law. It has been extremely rare for a legislature to introduce an offence of this sort; to date, the UK and the Australian Capital Territory (the Crimes (Industrial Manslaughter) Act 2003; Sarre 2007; Sarre and Richards 2005) are the only two jurisdictions to have such an offence on the statute books. Although these examples are rare, they are significant as the first attempts to impose 'direct' liability on corporate bodies for an offence that involves explicit moral censure rather than indirectly via the actions of an intermediate agent or representative, thereby reframing the nature of corporate criminal liability.

In both jurisdictions, impetus towards reform came from the existing law's failure to hold corporate bodies criminally liable following a work-related death. Charging a corporate body with a homicide offence requires that it should be shown to have satisfied the *actus reus* and *mens rea* elements of the offence; mechanisms of attribution are used to find individuals who fulfil these offence elements, such as intentionality or foresight (which were designed to apply to individual human defendants), *on behalf of* the corporation. This is difficult in practice because a corporate body cannot hold a state of mind in the same way as an individual, particularly in relation to an offence typically predicated on an assault culpably inflicted by one person upon another. In the UK and Australia, difficulties were encountered when applying the common law's traditionally individualistic models of attribution to large corporations because they restricted the ability of prosecutors to convict corporate defendants to cases where the discrete fault of an individual agent could also be proved (Gobert 2005; Sarre and Richards 2005; Wells 2001). The creation of a specific corporate manslaughter offence allows for liability to be constructed directly via more authentically 'corporate' offence elements which relate to collective and strategic forms of action (Clarkson 2008; Wells 2001). This should, in theory, facilitate greater success in the application of that offence within the corporate sphere.

The reform process

The CMCHA 2007 was given Royal Assent by the UK Parliament in July 2007, and came into force in April 2008, marking the culmination of a legislative reform process that had spanned more than 15 years. The first signs of this emerged following the sinking of the 'Herald of Free Enterprise', a British-operated passenger ferry, which capsized outside Zeebrugge harbour (Belgium) in 1987 and caused the loss of 189 lives. This catastrophic event prompted much public concern and was brought about by the 'Herald' sailing out of harbour with her bow doors open, a disastrous error for a 'roll-on, roll-off' ferry of its type as it allowed the car decks in the hull to quickly become waterlogged, causing the vessel to capsize in just a minute and a half. The Sheen Report, outlining the findings of the official public inquiry into the incident, placed the blame at the feet of the operating company, P&O European Ferries (formerly Townsend Thoresen):

> All concerned in management... were guilty of fault in that all must be regarded as sharing responsibility for the failure of management. From top to bottom the body corporate was infected with the disease of sloppiness.
>
> (Department of Transport 1987: para. 14.1)

Following the inquiry, a manslaughter prosecution was launched against the company,[7] citing as causal factors the flaws in the systems of safeguards used, the safety policies and guidelines issued to staff, and the provision of safety equipment, as well as organisational pressures for a quick turnaround (see Wells 2001: Ch. 6 for a review). The failure of this prosecution made the shortcomings of the law plain to see. British law had long utilised the 'identification doctrine' as a means of imputing liability to a corporate body. This requires that a person of sufficient seniority as to constitute the 'directing mind and will' of the company, usually a director or senior manager, must embody the corporation's fault by satisfying the *actus reus* and *mens rea* elements of the offence charged before the corporate body can be liable (Clarkson 2008; Gobert 2005; 2008; Ormerod and Taylor 2008; Ridley and Dunford 1997; Wells 1996; 2001). This means that a specified person has to be found who has *acted as* the company in committing the offence in question and in possessing the knowledge, intention, or foresight required. In the case of P&O, this meant establishing that a recognisable director had acted recklessly with regard to the risk of death present in the case, and had either foreseen that risk before taking it or had not given any thought to it (Wells 2001: 109).[8] This proved to be an insurmountable evidential obstacle and the prosecution collapsed, leaving a perception that the law was unfit for its purpose (Wells 1988; also Field and Jorg 1991; Pearce and Tombs 1990; 1991; Slapper 1993).

It should be noted that the 'Herald of Free Enterprise' was not the only event of this period which influenced the emergence of the idea of corporate manslaughter. A number of disasters within a short period of time, including the King's Cross London Underground fire in 1987

(31 fatalities), the Piper Alpha oil rig fire in 1988 (167), the Clapham Junction rail crash in 1988 (35), the Hillsborough football stadium disaster in 1989 (96), and the sinking of the 'Marchioness' on the River Thames in 1989 (51), although not all classified as matters of criminal liability, all contributed to a growing public climate of concern over the lack of safety of taken-for-granted activities, creating fertile ground for law reform (Gobert 2005: 27; Wells 1988: 791; 2001: 120–122). In 1994, the Law Commission issued a consultation paper on involuntary manslaughter which floated the idea of a 'corporate manslaughter' offence in response to the lessons learned from the 'Herald' prosecution (1994: paras. 4.2; 4.20–4.30). This was followed in 1996 by a full report, which advocated the introduction of such an offence and indicted the identification doctrine as a *de facto* barrier to successful prosecution (Law Commission 1996). The report suggested that it should be possible to show that corporate conduct has failed to reach a certain standard without recourse to an intermediary individual's state of mind, particularly in relation to a fault standard like gross negligence that does not require advertence.

The Law Commission adopted a subjectivist approach, refusing to recommend a vicarious liability standard, which would allow any offence committed within the scope of an individual's employment to constitute an act of the company, as that would broaden the range of acts for which a corporation could be liable to include ones that were not committed *by it* in any real sense (1996: 7.29–7.31). This would also retain the requirement that the culpability of a corporate entity should be contingent on the actions of a single individual. A similar consideration was also thought to mitigate against the 'aggregation model' of liability, which constructs corporate liability via the advertence and actions of a number of individuals (Wells 2001: 108). This approach, the Law Commission argued, would merely put a gloss on the existing identification doctrine (1996: 7.33). Instead, the Commission endorsed a model of 'management failure', whereby the objective conduct of the company as a whole is central to the issue of liability, rather than any subjective fault. Under this formulation, corporate manslaughter is committed where:

> *a) A management failure by the corporation is the cause or one of the causes of a person's death; and*
> *b) That failure constitutes conduct falling far below what can reasonably be expected of the corporation in the circumstances.*
>
> (1996: draft bill, cl. 4)

The systems of work, organisational practices, and management policies of the corporation are assessed against objective criteria to determine whether a failure in these systems caused the death in question and whether that failure was sufficiently serious to make the corporation liable. While this encompassed much of the same substantive content as the general duties of care contained with health and safety law (specifically ss. 2–3 of the HSWA 1974), it would not impose an absolute duty; instead, it would attach liability only to those cases where the failure occurred at the strategic management level. This would lead to the adoption of a test focused upon a 'failure to ensure safety in the management or organisation of the corporation's activities', or more concisely, a 'management failure' (1996: 8.19). So it would be deficiencies in the collective, not in the conduct of an individual, which would make the corporation liable for the offence. The Commission also envisaged that this management failure test would be utilised in relation to a specialist offence broadly equivalent to the individual offence of gross negligence manslaughter.

By the time the Law Commission started contemplating reform, the old law had actually been used to successfully convict a corporation of manslaughter in the 1994 case of 'R v OLL Ltd.',[9] which established corporate liability following the drowning of four school children on a canoe trip in Lyme Bay, Dorset. The company responsible had failed to provide safety equipment (such as life jackets), had not taken adequate precautions (checking the weather, informing the coastguard), and had not laid down safety procedures and training for the instructors in charge. It was also a very small operation and had only one director, who was directly responsible for day-to-day operations as well as overall management, and so no problems were encountered in linking the director and the company for the purposes of the identification doctrine (Ridley and Dunford 1997: 106–107). This decision was followed in 1996 by another,[10] confirming that companies *could* commit homicide offences, but the means of establishing this liability remained problematic. Subsequently, another five small companies have been the subject of successful corporate manslaughter prosecutions (Almond 2007: 288), but despite high-profile efforts, no large corporation has ever been convicted of manslaughter (though no official statistics exist because the Home Office does not differentiate corporate manslaughter convictions from other involuntary manslaughter cases). These cases involving small companies lacked the profile needed to significantly influence the law, but the Law Commission's proposals, and their subsequent endorsement by the New Labour government elected the following year, which had made a manifesto pledge prior to the 1997 election (and again prior to the 2001 election) to introduce the new offence when in power, did move the issue into the legal mainstream.

Once the Law Commission had moved towards a more 'organic' approach to corporate fault (Gobert 2005: 5; Wells 2005: 155), it was the turn of the Home Office to begin putting the idea into practice. In 2000, a consultation document was published which broadly endorsed the corporate killing offence proposed by the Law Commission, albeit with a different name. Critics of the 1996 proposals had highlighted the vagueness of the management failure test, the residual need to identify who constitutes the 'management' of a firm and which of their actions constitute 'the way the company is run', and the lack of any structured connection between corporate and individual liability, which rendered individual directors 'invisible' behind the shield of corporate liability (Clarkson 1996). The Home Office sought to consult on these issues and to gauge how such a change might be accepted by stakeholders and interest groups. Again, it was consulting against the backdrop of public concern over significant loss of life, as the previous year had seen 31 people killed in the Ladbroke Grove train crash, giving credence to Snider's assertion that governments only prioritise health and safety reform 'when forced to do so by public crisis' (1991: 216). Within two years, the Hatfield (2000; four deaths) and Potter's Bar (2002; seven deaths) rail crashes had increased the pressure for law reform, as what had appeared to be isolated events coalesced into a pattern of corporate negligence that seemed to reflect the fragmentation of the newly privatised rail network (Lodge 2002). Although HSWA 1974 convictions (and large fines) were obtained in each of these cases, criminal liability in the form of a manslaughter conviction was avoided.

The most significant subsequent attempt at prosecution, that of Great Western Trains in relation to the Southall crash, collapsed after the Court of Appeal ruled that an identified individual director or senior manager must be guilty of the offence of gross negligence manslaughter before the corporate body they represented could be convicted, despite the fact that liability for that species of manslaughter did not require evidence of a culpable state of mind (Wells 2001: 113).[11] Rose LJ, on behalf of the court, stated (at 191) that the law did not regard either the state of mind or the actions of a corporate body as separable from those of its individual agents and so the corporation could not be held to have acted except through a director or senior manager. In this sense, the 'conduct' of the corporation was not treated any differently from its *mens rea*, but this made the law even more restrictive; while corporate *mens rea* focuses on decision-making and information flows, which can be traced to the boardroom level, corporate conduct is heavily rooted in the actions of those referred to by Lord Denning as the 'hands' of the corporation,[12] operational-level employees who are quite removed from the direct oversight of the directors who constitute its 'brain'. As such, those who act 'as' the company are not normally the same people who are directly involved in dangerous practices at an operational level.

This decision effectively closed the door on the possibility of applying the existing law to a complex corporate body, confirming that the identification doctrine remained in place and increasing the pressure on the Government to legislate. For the most part, the developments in the 2000 Home Office paper were practical, extending the proposed scope of the offence to all undertakings (all businesses and employing organisations, whether incorporated or unincorporated), and specifying that enforcement should be undertaken by HSE, not the Police. Management failure was retained as the basis of liability despite the evidential problems it was envisaged as potentially giving rise to (2000: 3.1.9; Glazebrook 2002; Sullivan 2001: 32). What sort of organisational breakdown or failure constitutes a 'management failure', and how direct a role must it play in causing the death? In endorsing the Law Commission's proposals, the Home Office seemed happy to accept that a degree of legal uncertainty might exist in the interests of addressing the public concern that was cited as justifying the reform process. The Home Office subsequently published a draft bill in 2005 that set out the terms on which the government intended to legislate (Clarkson 2005; Gobert 2005; Pemberton 2005; Wells 2005). In explaining the rationale for the new offence, why they had renamed it 'corporate manslaughter', and why it would be handled by the police rather than by HSE, the Government referenced the symbolic power that the new offence was intended to possess, but did so in language that betrayed a disregard for health and safety law:

> The government recognises the importance of police involvement in clearly signalling the position of the new offence as a serious offence under the general criminal law, rather than an offence that might be characterised as regulatory'.
>
> (Home Office 2005: para. 58)

This admission tacitly acknowledged that social perceptions and patterns of enforcement in relation to regulatory offences meant that they were unsuited to the communication of messages about wrongfulness.

The 2005 proposals explicitly connected the management failure test to the actions of a specified class of individuals in a way which had not been done before (Wells 2005: 155). The offence would be committed if

> *the way in which any of the organisation's activities are managed or organised by its senior managers –*
>
> *a)* *causes a person's death, and*
> *b)* *amounts to a gross breach of a relevant duty of care owed by the organisation to the deceased.*
>
> (Home Office 2005: draft bill, cl. 1(1))

According to this formulation, the failure must be attributable to the senior managers of the firm, the same class of individuals that must be shown to be culpable under the existing identification doctrine. This seemed to constitute a shift away from the organic approach originally envisaged by the Law Commission and towards a more restrictive agency-based model that retained the existing law's insistence on constructing corporate responsibility via reference to specific employees. The evidential concerns raised in the 2000 consultation were resolved in favour of a narrow conception of 'management' in which it is the acts of managers, rather than the policies and systems of the corporation, that bear responsibility. This appeared to constitute a backward step in that it seemed 'unduly restrictive and threatens to open the door to endless argument in court as to whether certain persons do or do not constitute senior managers', thereby losing the focus on the moral status of the company itself (Clarkson 2005: 683–684).

The new offence

In 2007, this reform process culminated in the passing of the CMCHA 2007, which brought the proposed offence into law. The 2007 Act imposes liability on an organisation when 'the way in which its activities are managed or organised' causes a death and constitutes a gross breach of a relevant duty of care (s. 1(1)), replicating the wording of the Home Office draft. Section 1(3) makes clear that this breach of duty must be substantially caused by the way in which those corporate activities are managed or organised 'by the senior managers' of the organisation, thereby confirming that the need for a connection to the actions of specified individuals is retained. Although no 'individual' manager need be shown to have caused the failure which breached the duty, and although the failure of senior management need only be a 'substantial element' contributing to that breach (s.1(3)), meaning that the conduct of other individuals can also play a part, the test as laid out does 'forc[e] the inquiry back onto the issue of identifiable individuals' in a manner likely to prove restrictive in practice (Ormerod and Taylor 2008: 604). Additionally, as many commentators have pointed out, the reference to 'senior managers' is liable to prove evidentially difficult, raising as it does definitional uncertainty over the scope of this class of individuals: is seniority determined according to job title, function performed, or some other legal criteria, and how can the contribution of managers to an operational failure (short-sighted policies and slack oversight) be assessed independent of the negligent actions of other staff, whether caused by inadequate supervision or not (Gobert 2008: 418)? Failures to implement safe ways of working, and to provide adequate support to front-line staff in risk-bearing roles, play a key role in causing many work-related deaths and necessitate the adoption of a relatively broad conception of management's role. There is no clear boundary that can be drawn to compartmentalise the responsibilities of senior management and even where responsibilities for safety have been devolved to junior employees, this should not preclude management responsibility for that state of affairs (Ormerod and Taylor 2008: 605).

In terms of scope, the Act incorporates breaches of a duty of care as owed under the civil law of tort; this include those which have been placed on a statutory footing, and particular reference will be made to those duties contained within the HSWA 1974, particularly ss. 2–3. No new legal duties are imposed by the CMCHA 2007; rather, it seeks to overlay existing legal obligations with the additional threat of criminal proceedings where those obligations are breached in a manner that can be described as 'gross'. The definition of grossness has long proved controversial in English criminal law,[13] not least because of the circularity inherent in the test's specification that negligence becomes criminal when it is so bad that it merits criminalisation. The new offence addresses this problem to some degree, specifying that the breach of duty must 'fall far below' what can reasonably be expected of the organisation in the circumstances. The link to a prescribed duty rather than a general standard of negligence adds a degree of certainty to what might otherwise be a rather open-ended legal formulation (Ormerod and Taylor 2008: 602).

The Act applies to qualifying 'organisations', a term which encompasses corporations (based in the UK or overseas), as well as partnerships, trade unions, employer's associations, police forces, and (specified) government departments and bodies; this coverage removes the possibility of inconsistencies arising because of the legal status of offending organisations, but the inclusion of public bodies can be queried on both practical (it is heavily proscribed by ss. 3–7 of the Act; Ormerod and Taylor 2008: 597) and principled (it exceeds the Act's broad rationale of putting 'safety before profit'; Gobert 2008: 415) grounds. It applies to harm resulting in death taking place anywhere in the UK or its territorial waters (or on a British-registered ship or aircraft), and a company convicted of the offence is liable to an unlimited fine, which the Sentencing Guidelines Council recommended should not ordinarily be less than £500,000, and 'may be measured in millions of pounds' (2010: para. 24; Davies 2010). Finally, the court has the power (under ss. 9–10 of the Act) to issue remedial orders requiring the convicted company to take specified steps to address the causes of the breach, and publicity orders requiring the company to publicise its conviction in a specified manner. In many ways, these publicity orders represent the most innovative development in the whole Act.

Overall, the Act takes a concerted step towards the criminalisation of companies that kill. It improves on the old common-law offence in many ways and offers a more flexible basis for the attribution of responsibility within a complex organisation. But the offence has been criticised for its conservatism, and the reluctance of the government to entertain the idea of independent fault seems to indicate a lack of commitment to the notion of organisational liability (Gobert 2008; Wells 2005). The management failure tests are sufficiently imprecise to allow for significant uncertainty to remain about whether it will actually succeed in imposing liability on large companies. By retaining the connection to senior individuals, the offence does not deliver on the Law Commission's original aim of instituting a genuinely collective approach to corporate fault (Wells 2005: 155); at the same time, however, the focus on corporate fault precludes any 'individual' liability from arising, whether as principal offenders or as accomplices (Gobert 2008: 414). This means that the mechanisms of individual deterrence which commentators had hoped to harness (Gobert 2005; 2008; Tombs and Whyte 2007) were ignored in favour of an emphasis on the corporation as a whole. In a sense, this is the Act's principal failing; it is too corporate in nature to impact meaningfully on the individual decisions of directors and not corporate enough to herald a true sea change in the law.

The CMCHA came into force with some fanfare in April 2008. Since then, it has been utilised only once, in the Cotswold Geotechnical Holdings case referenced earlier. It remains essentially untested, given the relatively straightforward nature of that case. The Home Office, in its Regulatory Impact Assessment of the proposed offence (2006: 13), estimated that there might be ten to 13 additional prosecutions brought under the new law each year. The hope was for a wide-ranging, effective, powerful offence that would fundamentally redraw the relationship between corporations and the law. The reality has been a much more circumspect piece of legislation, albeit one that has managed to catch the attention of the business world (if not the public; Almond and Colover 2010). The Act steers a 'path between emotion and economic reality' (Davies 2010: 402), in that its symbolic aspirations are curtailed by the concerns of the government with ensuring that business interests are not unduly harmed. The process of law reform in this area points to a deeper set of underlying tensions that constrain the law in its attempts to control corporate behaviour, and the remainder of this book will seek to explore these tensions.

2
The International 'Corporate Manslaughter' Phenomenon

The early 21st century is part of the era of mega-corporate capitalism (Braithwaite 2008: 19), and the increasing dominance of multinational corporations as institutions of economic, political, and social influence has been accompanied by demands for them to be held more accountable for their actions (Wells 2001). The post-2008 global financial crisis, the Deepwater Horizon oil spill in the Gulf of Mexico in 2010, and a host of other events have demonstrated both the centrality of corporations to the new world order and also their power to destroy the lives and livelihoods of individuals. The criminalisation of corporate offending has become a key theme within the debates that follow these events, and there has been a new acceptance of the notion that a company can be criminally culpable. It is no longer the case that deaths at work are universally construed as accidents, which, if they are characterised as forms of wrongdoing at all, are viewed as matters of *mala prohibita* rather than *mala in se*. In this chapter, the trend towards imposing corporate criminal liability for work-related deaths will be explored in an international context, to build on the discussion of the British context in Chapter 1.

Four particular approaches to the criminalisation of corporations that kill will be identified among the developments that have occurred across different national jurisdictions. The first of these is the introduction of a direct corporate liability homicide offence, of which the UK's corporate manslaughter offence, discussed in the previous chapter, is the most high-profile example. The second is the imposition of corporate criminal liability in general terms, via a mechanism of attribution (such as the identification doctrine) which allows a corporation to be liable for a homicide offence aimed at individual defendants; this often creates the 'possibility' of corporate homicide liability but does not lead to the imposition of liability in practice. The third is to have these mechanisms of attribution to facilitate corporate liability, but to exclude this from applying to homicide offences, thereby precluding manslaughter liability. The final approach is to exclude corporate criminal liability altogether, putting corporate wrongdoing into a different legal category (administrative, regulatory, or technical offences) that exists separate from the criminal law. Overall, there has been an international shift towards criminalisation in the last two decades or so, and the regulatory context within which these developments have occurred, and the preliminary drivers of legal change in this area, will be identified in order to better understand the appeal of criminalisation at this moment in time.

Model one: Direct corporate liability for homicide offences

The most direct form of criminal liability for a corporation which causes death is the creation of a specific homicide offence. The UK provides something of a lead on this front, having legislated via the Corporate Manslaughter and Corporate Homicide Act (CMCHA) 2007 (see Chapter 1). But it is not the only jurisdiction to have done so; the Australian Capital Territory (ACT) has also introduced an offence of this sort (Sarre 2007; Sarre and Richards 2005). Both of these legislative developments are relatively new and have been very sparingly used, meaning that both remain essentially experimental in status. Introducing an offence of this sort signals that a positive policy choice has been made about the degree of normative accountability to be directed at a corporation that kills; it is an unequivocal statement that a value judgement has been made and will be acted on. But, as the example of the ACT shows, the legislative act of passing such an offence into law does not automatically mean that it will be used in practice; this can make reform of this sort a purely symbolic exercise. Corporate manslaughter offences are open to this fate because they are new and unusual legal forms that do not map onto any established procedures for implementation and so have no natural pathway into practice; reform can bring false hope to those who wish to see meaningful change.

The ACT's manslaughter offence was, when introduced in 2003, the only specific corporate homicide offence anywhere in the world. The possibility of corporate liability for manslaughter had existed in Australian law for some time (see Model Two, below), but this had been done, as in England and Wales, through the attribution of liability to a corporate body via the *mens rea* of its senior employees. Just as in England and Wales, this test had limited the capacity of the law to hold culpable corporate bodies liable for deaths resulting from their activity (Gunningham and Johnstone 1999; Sarre 2007; Sarre and Richards 2005). A movement towards the use of criminal law as a tool of corporate regulation had begun to emerge in the early 1990s, influenced in no small part by the work of scholars such as John Braithwaite, whose study of occupational fatalities in the coal-mining industry (1985) had demonstrated how many of these deaths were avoidable outcomes of corporate misfeasance. In 1992, the Criminal Law Officers Committee of the Standing Committee of Attorneys-General recommended that new principles for the attribution of criminal responsibility to corporate entities be introduced to facilitate more effective accountability (Hall and Johnstone 2005: 68). At around the same time, prosecutors in several States (Victoria, New South Wales, and Queensland) began attempting to initiate manslaughter prosecutions against corporate bodies, with little success (Gunningham and Johnstone 1999: 210). The first successful prosecution, 'R v Denbo Pty Ltd.',[1] took place in 1994 and seemed to signal a shift in prosecutorial attitudes, though the rates of success when prosecuting corporate manslaughter cases remained poor.

In response, the Australian government legislated in 1995 to liberalise the means by which criminal culpability could be attributed to a corporate body. The Criminal Code Act 1995 allows for corporate bodies to be found liable for harms caused by operational-level employees acting within the scope of their employment, not just the acts of senior managers. The intention, knowledge, or recklessness necessary to make a corporate body guilty could be supplied either by the board of directors or by a 'high managerial agent', or by showing that a 'corporate culture' existed which directed, encouraged, tolerated, or led to, non-compliance with the law (Criminal Code Act 1995 s. 12.3(2)). This constitutes a form of aggregation principle, whereby the acts of diffuse individuals can be taken together as representing the acts of the corporate body (Hall and Johnstone 2005: 68; Sarre 2007: 651). The corporation's express or implied authorisation or toleration of the offence is evidenced via the *mens rea* of directors or senior managers, or the corporate culture of the firm as expressed via an 'attitude, policy, rule, course of conduct, or practice' (Criminal Code Act 1995 s. 12.3(6)). This constituted a significant liberalisation of the rules on attribution, but this reform only extended to Commonwealth crimes, while most offences, including manslaughter, were the legislative responsibility of individual States and Territories, each of which would have to pass enabling legislation in order to bring the Criminal Code Act into force.

The ACT became the first (and to date, only) Australian jurisdiction to implement the terms of the Criminal Code Act, doing so via an offence of 'industrial manslaughter' set out in the Crimes (Industrial Manslaughter) Act 2003. This offence is committed where a corporate body causes the death of a worker and is either reckless as to the risk of serious harm to a worker or negligent as to a risk of death. These fault elements are satisfied if the company 'expressly, tacitly, or impliedly authorized or permitted' the offence via the actions of its directors or managers or its corporate culture (s. 51). The death may result from the actions of any employee, and the corporate negligence required can be demonstrated via aggregation (Sarre 2007: 652–653), although the offence also allows for 'senior officer' liability where an individual's reckless conduct caused the death in question. It was only introduced as a specific offence because when the federal provisions were enacted in the ACT in 2002, they could only apply to offences created after this date, preventing them from applying to existing manslaughter laws. Despite this, the ACT's offence was the first of its sort anywhere in the world.

The unfortunate postscript to this innovation has been the complete ineffectiveness of the law in practice. The ACT is very small territory which encompasses Canberra, the Commonwealth capital of Australia, and is home to the administrative institutions of national government, which together employ 80% of the working population in the territory. It has very little heavy industry or manufacturing and very low rates of occupational injury and death, and in 2004 the Australian government curtailed the application of the Crimes (Industrial Manslaughter) Act further by exempting government employers from the offence (Sarre 2007: 653). To date, no prosecutions have been brought under the Act and none are anticipated. On this reading, therefore, it is hard to draw any conclusions about the value of the offence, except that responding to a problem through legislative reform is not the same thing as addressing it meaningfully. The ACT experiment has been characterised as a 'symbolic' gesture that has not been underpinned by any real commitment to the pursuit of the values that the law seemed to embody (Sarre 2007: 653). As Haines and Hall observe, this 'push for industrial manslaughter legislation ... may succeed in temporarily satisfying the need to blame, but ... deflect attention away from measures that may be more fruitful and instrumentally beneficial' (2004: 271).

Model two: Attributed corporate liability for homicide offences

More common than jurisdictions with specific corporate manslaughter offences are those (such as the USA, Canada, Australia, France, the

Netherlands, and much of mainland Europe) that allow for corporate bodies to be held liable for mainstream criminal law offences, including homicide and manslaughter offences, but do not have a specific corporate manslaughter offence in force (Gunningham and Johnstone 1999; Wells 2001: Ch. 7). Within these jurisdictions, corporate harms may be dealt with either as breaches of the criminal law, with culpability based on the harmful consequences that result, or as breaches of a parallel system of safety regulations, with culpability focusing on the failure to manage risk. The extension of criminal liability to corporate bodies occurs in two ways; in common-law jurisdictions (such as the UK, the USA, Canada, Australia, South Africa, and New Zealand), the law has evolved general principles which dictate how a corporate body can fulfil criminal fault elements and so commit a crime. For the most part, these jurisdictions have long recognised the 'capacity' of corporate bodies to bear criminal responsibility but have wrestled with the problem of how to effectively *establish* liability in practice (Beck and O'Brien 2000; Bittle and Snider 2006; Coffee 1983; 1999; Diskant 2008; Eser *et al.* 1999; Sarre and Richards 2005; Wells 2001).

In civil law jurisdictions (such as France, Belgium, the Netherlands, and Denmark), the process of recognising corporate criminal liability has involved the reform of national Penal Codes. This has tended to involve an explicit policy decision to extend the law to corporations, rather than the piecemeal emergence of such an outcome over time (Wells 2001: 138). For the most part, these jurisdictions have historically been resistant to the notion of corporate criminal liability, regarding corporate defendants as legal but not 'moral' entities (Beale and Safwat 2004; Eser *et al.* 1999; Weigend 2008). In recent years, however, there has been a 'quiet revolution' in corporate criminal liability (Wells 2005: 154), with more jurisdictions moving to extend the criminal law to include corporate bodies. A few jurisdictions, such as the Netherlands, have relatively long-standing corporate criminal liability; the majority have recognised it only recently. In many cases, legislators in civil law jurisdictions are required to specify that a criminal offence can be committed by a corporate body during the drafting process, meaning that crimes must be 'opted in' to the scheme of criminal liability (such as France; Orland and Cachera 1995), while common-law jurisdictions do not normally differentiate between offences in this way.

Once the possibility of liability exists, it becomes necessary to establish exactly *how* a corporate body might be able to fulfil the requirements of that offence, given that it is not able to act or to hold a state of mind by itself. Different jurisdictions use different methods to attribute fault to corporate bodies, often by specifying a particular class of employees or agents who can be taken to be acting 'as' the company, whether this includes all employees (vicarious liability, or 'respondeat superior', as in the USA; Coffee 1983); or only those acting 'on behalf of' the company for a particular purpose (as in New Zealand;[2] Wilkinson 2003); or those whose managerial responsibility marks them as the 'directing mind' of the company (the 'identification doctrine', as in Canada, Australia, and the UK; Wells 2001: 130–136). It is also worth noting that there are significant differences between jurisdictions in the degree to which these legal measures are utilised in practice. While a number of American States have been 'relatively' hawkish in pursuing manslaughter convictions against corporate bodies, and Australia and the UK have both seen a gradual increase in the willingness of prosecutors to bring such charges, in other jurisdictions there is much less practical use of these measures.

The USA

Notions of corporate liability have had a longer history and have been more readily accepted in the US legal system than almost anywhere else. Corporate liability emerged slowly in English law (on which US law was based) during the 19th century, with culpability based on vicarious liability (or 'respondeat superior') where the acts and omissions of corporate employees breached a duty incumbent upon it,[3] but this was understood in terms of an essentially factual responsibility for offences that did not require criminal intent (Coffee 1983; Elkins 1976; Wells 2001). US law changed with the decision in 'New York Central & Hudson Railroad Co. v United States',[4] which held that corporations could be liable for the actions of their agents even in relation to offences which required intention. The case concerned a commercial offence requiring that a specific intent be shown on the part of the defendant; there was evidence of a legislative intention to make corporations liable for it, and this, along with the need for effective sanctioning, was critical to the decision (Brickey 1981: 413; Harlow 2011: 128). This pragmatic approach made further extension likely in subsequent cases (Coffee 1983: 254; Khanna 1996: 1484), and such an approach had already been taken in the earlier case of 'United States v Van Schaick',[5] where the corporate owner of a steamship which sank, killing around 900 people, was held to be properly subject to liability for manslaughter because Congress had not intended that such bodies should avoid liability. Subsequent to this, different State jurisdictions diverged in how they interpreted and applied both Federal- and State-level homicide statutes; so while New Jersey did hold that a railroad company could commit involuntary manslaughter[6] (Harlow 2011: 129), in New York, the decision in 'People v Rochester Railway and Light Co.'[7] held that the offence of manslaughter required the killing of one human being by another 'human' being, and so corporations could not be liable for such crimes (Wells 2001: 133; Swigert and Farrell 1981: 165). The 'Rochester' decision was influential in restricting the spread of corporate homicide liability in other States, and meant that subsequent cases, such as the Triangle Shirtwaist fire in New York in 1911, in which 146 workers in a clothing factory were killed, were initiated against human factory owners rather than employing companies (Reiner and Chatten-Brown 1989: 83).

This presumption against corporate liability was addressed by the Occupational Safety and Health (OSH) Act 1970, the primary piece of legislation governing the regulation of workplace health and safety in the USA. This was intended, like the UK's HSWA 1974, to provide a comprehensive degree of legal protection to workers, via the imposition of broad duties on employers and the use of enforcement to secure compliance (Reiner and Chatten-Brown 1989; Rhinehart 2008; Silverstein 2008). The Occupational Safety and Health Administration (OSHA), the regulator created by the Act, imposes mandatory workplace standards in relation to workplace hazards, issues guidance to those seeking to comply with these standards, and enforces against those who breach them via abatement orders, civil penalties, and criminal prosecution. The civil OSHA penalties extend to a maximum of $7000 ($70,000 for a 'wilful violation'), but in practice average fines are as low as $873 and are only levied in a minority of cases (Rhinehart 2008: 123). This scheme of enforcement has long been criticised as lacking deterrent capacity (Jones 1991; Reiner and Chatten-Brown 1989; Silverstein 2008), although there is some evidence of a positive correlation between OSHA enforcement and subsequent compliance (Gray and Scholz 1993). The OSH Act allows OSHA to refer a case to the Department of Justice for criminal prosecution where the wilful violation of a specific OSHA standard results in death of an employee (29 U.S.C. ss. 666(e) (2000)), and such a conviction can be punished by up to six months imprisonment and a $250,000 (individual defendant) or $500,000 (corporate defendant) fine. This can also occur where advance notice of an OSHA inspection is given, and where statements or documents supplied to OSHA are knowingly falsified. These offences are intended to be the pinnacle of the enforcement model but, in practice, OSHA has not used these powers with any regularity; in 2008 it was calculated that there had been 68

OSHA prosecutions in the 28 years that the statute had been in force (Rhinehart 2008: 124). At the same time, however, rates of work-related death and serious injury remained significant. Part of the reason for OSHA's failure was the erosion of the agency's political legitimacy in its early history (Bardach and Kagan 1982; Silverstein 2008). A highly proactive enforcement strategy was adopted in the 1970s which antagonised employers, but the lack of priority attached to serious violations also alienated supporters of the regulatory project. Political constraints and business interests narrowed the parameters of notions of 'acceptable' levels of regulatory activity, and as moral and practical leverage was lost and resources were cut, OSHA found that the political risks associated with bringing criminal proceedings were just too high, resulting in an 'enforcement gap'.

The result was that OSHA was effectively usurped as a criminal law enforcer by State-level prosecutors, who stepped in to utilise general homicide laws to pursue those responsible for work-related deaths (Jones 1991; Reiner and Chatten-Brown 1989). From the late 1970s onwards, the 'Rochester' approach to criminalisation was rolled back, with legislative reforms (widening the meaning of the term 'person') and judicial decisions in many States determining that corporations can be liable for manslaughter (including California, Illinois, Indiana, New Jersey, New York, Pennsylvania, Texas, and Wisconsin: Harlow 2011: 133; Swigert and Farrell 1981: 165; Wells 2001: 132). One of the landmark cases was the prosecution of the Ford Motor Co. in relation to road traffic accidents involving its Pinto subcompact car (Dowie 1977). This model had a defective fuel tank design which was prone to explode in the event of a rear-end collision; investigations showed that Ford knew of this design flaw and had determined that paying out damages to victims was more cost-effective than a product recall. A recall was eventually forced, and Ford had to pay damages in numerous costly civil negligence cases. The company also went on trial in Indiana on three counts of reckless homicide following a fatal accident which killed three passengers; although a Grand Jury determined that a crime had been committed which Ford might properly be called to answer for, the trial jury acquitted the company (Becker *et al.* 2002; Dowie 1977; Harlow 2011: 133). The significance of the case lay in the fact that it had been brought at all; the 'notion' of corporate manslaughter was established, and this facilitated the more proactive approach being taken by state prosecutors across the country (Becker *et al.* 2002). Corporate homicide prosecutions became a new component of State-level prosecutors' roles, and in some places (Los Angeles, for example: Reiner and Chatten-Brown 1989: 94) cases of this sort have been pursued proactively.

State jurisdictions have adopted systems of corporate criminal liability that are broadly in line with the American Law Institute's Model Penal Code (MPC), which imposes corporate criminal liability in three ways. First, where no legislative intention to make the law apply to corporations is evident, the identification doctrine applies (American Law Institute 1962: para. 2.07 (I) a–c). This requirement that the criminal act be 'performed, authorised, or tolerated in a reckless manner by a high-ranking managerial agent or member of the board of directors' brings with it many of the same evidential limitations found in other jurisdictions (Coffee 1983: 255; 'Developments' 1979: 1251). Secondly, where a legislative intent to apply the offence to corporate bodies is evident (for example, in relation to antitrust offences), a version of the federal 'respondeat superior' system applies, subject to a due diligence defence. This holds that '[A] corporation may be held criminally responsible for [crimes] committed by its employees if they were acting within the scope of their authority, or apparent authority, and for the benefit of the corporation'[8] (Coffee 1983: 255; 'Developments' 1979: 1247). This means that it is possible for one individual to supply the relevant *mens rea* while another committed the *actus reus* of the offence, so a worker may fatally injure another, but the supervisor may be the one who overlooked the danger of the act (Coffee 1983: 256). It is also possible to aggregate the liability of more than one individual employee to compile the required corporate liability, using the 'collective knowledge' doctrine (Coffee 1983: 256; Walsh and Pyrich 1995: 625),[9] although these provisions have proved more effective in convicting small rather than large corporate bodies (Coffee 1999). Finally, strict liability offences are assumed to apply via the 'respondeat superior' rules unless a legislative intention to the contrary appears. In practice, most States have tended to adopt version of this model which closely mirror the federal attribution rules.

In the 30 years since the Pinto case, the willingness of prosecutors to bring homicide prosecutions against corporate defendants has increased, although definitional, policy, and resource issues have all constrained the use of these measures (Harlow 2011: 145–149). The use of criminal sanctions following work-related deaths is perhaps more commonplace in the USA than anywhere else in the world, yet the impetus for this came from the failures of existing systems of regulatory enforcement; a lack of resources and institutional legitimacy rendered the pursuit of criminal enforcement politically and practically difficult.

Criminal prosecutions at State level have addressed this problem to a degree, but even where criminal sanctioning is accepted, enforcement is rare and occurs against a backdrop of under-enforcement that is at odds with notions of a punitive regulatory state. Even in the jurisdictions where criminal law is most widely resorted to, its use remains an anomalous and statistically rare occurrence.

Other common-law jurisdictions

Legal developments in Australia have already been reviewed in discussing the reform process in the ACT (see Model 1, above). Australia's Criminal Code Act 1995 states that for offences of intention, recklessness, and knowledge, *mens rea* must be 'attributed to a body corporate that expressly, tacitly, or impliedly authorised or permitted the commission of the offence' (s. 12.3(1)). Three means of doing this are provided for: firstly, by proving that the directors of the company possessed that *mens rea* when committing or permitting the offence (a variant of the identification doctrine); secondly, by proving that a high managerial agent had the *mens rea*; and thirdly, by proving that 'a corporate culture existed within the body corporate that directed, encouraged, tolerated or led to non-compliance with the relevant provision' (s. 12.3(2)c). This reformulation of common-law principles required the legislatures of the individual Australian States to ratify it before it could apply to offences like manslaughter; so far, only the ACT has done so (Sarre and Richards 2005). Other States (including South Australia, Victoria, and New South Wales) have rejected or forestalled efforts at introducing similar offences, and others have shown little inclination towards reform (Sarre 2007: 653–654).

For the most part, this has reflected an unwillingness to disrupt existing workplace safety systems and jeopardise what are perceived to be productive safety management arrangements between employers and trade union representatives (Johnson 2008: 358). It also reflects a latent conservatism among lawyers and legislators and the influence of corporate interests over the legislative process. That said, many Australian States have moved instead to beef-up offences and penalties under existing occupational health and safety legislation (often as a means of scuppering manslaughter reforms: Sarre 2007). The preferred approach has been to differentiate occupational health and safety from homicide, so successful manslaughter prosecutions remain a rarity. Each State jurisdiction in Australia has its own regulator with responsibility for the enforcement of health and safety laws, and these bodies inspect workplaces, conduct audits, and investigate incidents in order to assess compliance (Gunningham and Johnstone 1999: 347; Johnstone 2004; Walters *et al.* 2011: 81–84). They are also empowered to issue prohibition and improvement notices and to bring prosecutions where necessary. As in the UK, this is usually done as a last resort, with inspectorates preferring to utilise cooperative approaches wherever possible (Gunningham and Johnstone 1999: 377; Walters *et al.* 2011: 82). While the penalties issued can be significant (up to $1.65m in New South Wales), fines of this magnitude are rarely levied, and can in fact be very low, thus mirroring the reality of enforcement practices in the UK and the USA. Yet in practice the occupational health and safety system is the only means by which corporations that cause death are prosecuted.

In Canada, the criminal liability of corporate bodies became an issue of debate following the Westray mine disaster of 1992, when 26 miners were killed by a fireball which erupted when a methane cloud in a mine-shaft was sparked by defective machinery. The subsequent investigation found evidence of serious negligence on the part of supervisors and managers of the mine-owning company, as well as the company itself (Curragh Resources Inc.), including inadequate risk management, training, and safety provision. Crucially, it also found that the mine owners had received numerous warnings about safety violations at the mine site from regulators and safety representatives but had failed to act in response to those concerns (Bittle and Snider 2006; Johnson 2008; MacPherson 2005; Richard 1997). Criminal charges of manslaughter and causing death by negligence were brought against two managers who bore direct responsibility for the event (the company was also charged with numerous health and safety offences); however, no convictions were ever secured. Despite this, the Westray prosecution was a significant turning point in that it prompted a significant backlash from trade unions, an array of political actors, and victim and pressure groups, and this (along with the damning evidence that emerged from the official inquiry) motivated the federal government to push through reforms to the Criminal Code of Canada. Bittle and Snider make the point that, as with reform elsewhere (particularly the UK), it took the confluence of a significant tragedy and an emergent public culture of mistrust of corporate actors before the reform movement gained the political traction required to succeed (2006: 475); the specific and the general highlighted significant corporate accountability deficits, and this made criminalisation politically feasible.

Prior to this reform process, the law in Canada relating to corporate criminal liability was governed largely by the terms of the identification doctrine (Ferguson 1999). The case of 'Canadian Dredge and Dock

Co. v The Queen'[10] had confirmed that a corporate body could only be liable where the fault element required for the offence was fulfilled by a senior manager or director who constituted the directing mind of the company. Under Canadian law, the class of people who could fulfil this role was narrower than in the UK and elsewhere. This fed into a more formalised distinction between criminal and regulatory offences than exists in most common-law jurisdictions, with the latter operating on a negligence basis that does not pose the same problems of identification as the former. Of course, homicide offences such as manslaughter fall into the former category, and so in order to convict a corporate body it would be necessary to prove that the action of the directing mind in committing the offence '(a) was within the field of operations assigned to him; (b) was not totally in fraud of the corporation; and (c) was by design or result partly for the benefit of the company' (*per* Estey J. at 713–714). In essence, this allowed for a high-level individual with responsibility for a particular purpose to fulfil the role of directing mind (so an area or branch manager, or person with authority for a particular area of operation). The same problems were encountered here as elsewhere when applying the identification doctrine, particularly those relating to the drawing of robust connections between high-level directors and operational-level failings.

The legislative response was Bill C-45, known as the 'Westray Bill'. This redefined the bases of corporate criminal liability on two fronts. Firstly, it established that an organisation (a broader category than 'corporation') could be liable for a criminal offence when a senior officer (a broader category than 'directing mind') either (i) is a party to an offence while acting within the scope of their authority; or (ii) possesses the requisite mental state to be a party to an offence and directs other employees or agents to do the act or omission involved; or (iii) knows that an employee or agent will be a party to an offence and does not take reasonable measures to stop them (Criminal Code of Canada s. 22.2). C-45 did not broach the issue of 'corporate culture', retaining instead a focus on individual liability as the basis of corporate fault. In many ways, it is similar to the American notion of 'respondeat superior', in that knowledge of the criminal behaviour of an employee will render the organisation liable but not as inclusive, a 'classic Canadian compromise', according to Bittle and Snider (2006: 478). Additionally, C-45 introduced s. 22.1 into the Criminal Code of Canada to govern offences of negligence, which established that an organisation would be liable if its employee committed an offence, and the relevant senior officer(s) departed markedly from the standard of care they might be expected to demonstrate. This represents a much more collective approach to fault; C-45 allows for liability to arise where several individuals have acted negligently, but each has not been so negligent as to depart markedly from the standard of care expected (or in English law's terms, is negligent but not grossly so), on the basis that the totality of these decisions might satisfy this requirement (MacPherson 2005: 207). Cases like Westray typically involve a multitude of bad decisions which are each relatively limited in significance but which combine to form a systemic failure that has serious consequences.

Bill C-45 seems to liberalise the process of fault attribution, ostensibly making it easier to convict culpable corporations, but many are sceptical about the approach taken, pointing out that liability remains tied to essentially indeterminate notions of individual responsibility within the corporation – who is a senior manager? What is the extent of their authority? What constitutes a relevant standard of care? (MacPherson 2005: 205–208). Additionally, the emphasis throughout the Bill on identifying lower-level employees as 'parties' to the offence in question opens the door for the 'responsibilization' of workers who commit safety violations (Bittle and Snider 2006; Gray 2006; 2009), suggesting that it is they, rather than the employer, who is principally responsible for things going wrong. Further, the corporate provisions within C-45 are buttressed by schemes of individual liability which relate to employees, producing a culture of 'joint responsibility' which has shifted the focus away from corporate bodies, not towards them (Gray 2009). The last critical point to note about C-45 is the lack of impact it has had in terms of corporate criminal liability; one successful prosecution (that of Transpavé Inc., which entered a guilty plea) took place in 2007, but there have been few charges brought in the seven years since C-45 (two prior to 2010, and three in 2010). At the same time, there has been no real sign of a more proactive prosecution approach emerging in relation to occupational health and safety regulation (Walters *et al.* 2011: 238).

Europe's 'quiet revolution'

European jurisdictions have traditionally been resistant to the notion of corporate criminal liability. Civil law penal codes have tended to draw rigid distinctions between criminal and administrative law and to conceive of the former as only applicable to natural persons, in line with Kantian ideals of individualism (Weigend 2008: 929); as legal fictions, corporations cannot be said to possess any moral capacity in their own right, separate from that of those individuals who constitute it (Orland and Cachera 1995: 112; Weigend 2008: 937). For continental jurists, the punishment of the corporation is, by definition, the punishment of a class of persons as a whole, something which violates fundamental principles of criminal law. In addition, civil law systems do not allow for the kind of piecemeal legal development that has characterised the emergence of corporate criminality in common-law jurisdictions (Wells 2001: 138). In recent years, however, this resistance has reduced and many European jurisdictions have moved towards recognising corporate criminal liability, a move driven by international legal influences (European Union (EU), United Nations (UN), and Organisation for Economic Co-operation and Development (OECD) conventions on bribery and corruption), as well as a growing recognition of the ever-increasing power that corporations wield in the modern world (Beale and Safwat 2004: 108). Some jurisdictions have well-established histories of corporate criminal liability. Denmark has recognised corporate liability since 1926, and reformed its Criminal Code in 1996 to introduce a general principle of liability, but this did not extend to core offences such as manslaughter (it did include financial offences: Nielsen 1999: 190). This was rectified in 2002, when the Criminal Code was again reformed, this time to allow legal persons to be liable for all offences contained therein (Beale and Safwat 2004: 111). The Danish Code states that the 'criminal liability of a legal person is conditional upon a transgression having been committed within the establishment of this person by one or more persons connected to this legal person or by the legal person himself' (1996, s. 27(1)), establishing 'respondeat superior' or direct corporate negligence as the basis of liability (Beale and Safwat 2004: 112).

A more inclusive tradition of corporate criminal liability has existed in the Netherlands since 1976, when Article 51 of the Criminal Code was reformulated to state that 'offences can be committed by human beings and by corporations' (Beale and Safwat 2004: 110; Field and Jorg 1991: 157; Keulen and Gritter 2011). Almost any criminal offence may be committed by a company, even those involving moral culpability such as involuntary manslaughter (as evidenced by the conviction of a hospital for negligent homicide in 1987).[11] Corporate liability under the Dutch system is contingent upon the policies, practices, and capacities of the corporation, as reflected in the test laid down in the 'Ijzerdraad' case.[12] This stated that an employee's acts are only 'corporate' if it was within the company's power to determine whether the employee acted this way, and the employee's act was accepted by the corporation as part of normal business operations ('power and acceptance': Field and Jorg 1991: 164; or 'disposal and acceptance': Keulen and Gritter 2011: 182). These criteria were subsequently applied to *mens rea* offences in the

'Kabeljauw'[13] case, which established that liability is predicated upon the degree of diligence exercised by the corporation in monitoring risk-causing behaviour and responding via supervision. If there is evidence that the requisite degree of diligence was not exercised, then the corporation will be liable; like the 'gross negligence' standard applied in English law, the conduct must have fallen below an expected standard (Beale and Safwat 2004: 111). Rather than engaging in debates about the metaphysics of the controlling mind, the Dutch test is more 'open' (Keulen and Gritter 2011: 183) and bases responsibility on the practical ability to prevent the harm. In the 'Hospital' case, poor record-keeping and equipment maintenance, and a culture of non-compliance, made the hospital liable for manslaughter; it *ought not to* have allowed the failure (Field and Jorg 1991: 165–167). It should be noted, however, that the vast majority of breaches of health and safety violations are dealt with under the administrative system of regulation, rather than under the criminal law (Aalders and Wilthagen 1997). This is done by centralised safety regulators (the Dutch Labour Inspectorate) who pursue a broadly self-regulatory, accommodative, and cooperative mode of regulation, and who enforce the law via prosecution as a matter of last resort. Manslaughter prosecutions in these cases, although possible, have remained something of a rarity.

The most significant development in recent years, however, has been a shift towards criminalisation in a wide range of jurisdictions. Rules allowing for or broadening corporate criminal liability have been introduced in quick succession in Norway (1991), France (1992), Finland (1995), Belgium (1999), Italy (2001), Switzerland (2003), and Austria (2006), among others, suggesting a shift away from the doctrine of *societas delinquere non potest* ('a legal entity cannot be blameworthy') (Beale and Safwat 2004; Kyriakakis 2009). Not all of these jurisdictions allow for corporate criminal liability in relation to offences against the person or 'non-economic' crimes, and some have yet to test how far corporate criminal liability might extend in practice. Nevertheless, many do allow liability to extend to offences like manslaughter. For example, France changed its Penal Code in 1994 and again in 2004 so as to allow for corporate criminal liability, having maintained fidelity to the notion that criminal fault was a purely individual concept since the introduction of the Napoleonic Code (Beale and Safwat 2004: 115; Deckert 2011; Orland and Cachera 1995: 114). But principled arguments about the nature of criminal, as opposed to administrative, wrongdoing, and the normative status of criminal punishment, failed to influence the form that the law took (Orland and Cachera 1995: 121). Instead, the reforms recognised both the legal precedent set by existing administrative penalties for corporate financial wrongdoing and the policy arguments for reform highlighted by several high-profile cases.

The new Penal Code states: 'Legal persons, with the exception of the State, are criminally liable for the offenses committed on their account by their organs or representatives ... in the cases provided for by statute or regulations' (Article 121–122; translation from Orland and Cachera 1995). Article 221–227 goes on to specify that a legal person may incur criminal liability for the offence of manslaughter by 'Causing the death of another person by clumsiness, rashness, inattention, negligence, or breach of an obligation of safety or prudence', and may be subject to a fine or other penal sanction (including professional prohibition, judicial supervision, and publicity sanctions: Article 131–139). In order for the company to commit the offence, the individuals who perform the act in question must do so in the course of their duties and for the benefit of the corporation, or must act negligently, for example by failing to observe a safety law (Orland and Cachera 1995: 147). Negligence here means that the defendant must have ' "broke[n] the rules" with his eyes open' and therefore have an advertent but unintentional state of mind (Spencer and Brajeux 2010: 8). This negligence must be on the part of a high-ranking officer or manager, even if the immediate act causing death is committed by a non-senior employee, for instance where the manager has been negligent in implementing safety policies (Beale and Safwat 2004: 117–120). Again, in fact, it is only very occasionally that these negligence offences are used to criminalise employers following safety violations (Spencer and Brajeux 2010: 23); as in the UK and elsewhere, action has arisen primarily in relation to exceptional events such as the Concorde air crash of 2000 in Paris, which resulted in 113 deaths and led to the conviction in 2010 of Continental Airlines under this 'causing death by negligence' (manslaughter) offence. As elsewhere, this operates alongside a more established, centralised system of safety inspection and regulation which is broadly conciliatory, operates under heavy political and resource constraints, does not prosecute often, and lacks a degree of perceived social importance and political legitimacy (Walters *et al.* 2011: 251, 255).

Similar developments have taken place elsewhere in Europe; Belgium provides an example of a jurisdiction that has a mixed historical relationship with this idea. Belgian law acknowledged as long ago as 1934 that corporations could be the subjects of criminal statutes, but did not allow that such a body could actually commit a crime until 1948, and even then did not allow that such an entity could be criminally sanctioned for such an offence (Stessens 1994: 498–499). The outcome of this was that it was not unusual to find examples of the prosecution of ten or more directors standing trial together as individuals for an offence that might sensibly be classed as 'corporate', leading to significant rule of law concerns (Faure 1999: 106). In 1999 the Belgian Penal Code was reformed to allow for corporate liability for offences committed for its benefit by senior management (similar to France). Finland reformed its Penal Code in 1995 to allow for a negligence-based form of corporate criminal liability to be imposed where a senior officer who represents the company commits an offence or is complicit in its commission, or where the corporation's actions do not demonstrate the degree of diligence necessary to prevent an offence (Penal Code of Finland, ch. 9 s. 2(1); Beale and Safwat 2004: 113). This was extended in 2003 to encompass all criminal offences, not just those which specified application. Norway has also reformed to impose corporate criminal liability (including for a manslaughter offence) where an offence is committed by an employee or agent on behalf of an enterprise and as part of that person's work (Nielsen 1999: 190).

Many jurisdictions have struggled with the conceptual and constitutional problems that accompany corporate criminal liability, leading some to impose a *de facto* criminal system that is officially classed as 'quasi-administrative'. Italy introduced measures in 2001 (Legislative Decree no. 231/01) to make corporate entities directly responsible for criminal offences committed pursuant to the interests of the company by directors, executives, and employees, but had to do so in a way that would not violate a wider constitutional principle limiting criminal liability to human defendants. Italy had, for a long time, maintained fidelity to the doctrine of *societas delinquere non potest,* regarding criminal law as something that applied to natural persons only and utilising administrative sanctions to regulate corporate behaviour (de Maglie 2011; Gobert and Mugnai 2002; Militello 1999). The shift in approach embodied in Decree 231/01 was a direct response to the requirements imposed by the EU, including the 1999 Convention of the Council of Europe on Corruption, that corporate crimes be effectively controlled. Initially, the Italian legislature limited the application of the Decree to areas of fraud against the State, corruption and bribery (de Maglie 2011: 260; Gobert and Mugnai 2002: 625). But subsequent legislation has extended the scope of the Decree to include other economic crimes such as money laundering, terrorism, and, via Law no. 123 of 2007, crimes against the person, including manslaughter committed in violation of safe working practices (de Maglie 2011: 261). Companies can avoid liability if they can show that the individual was not acting in pursuit of the company's interests, or if they can produce evidence that they have a compliance programme in place in order to prevent the offending in question and so were not 'structurally negligent' in how they ran their operations and managed safety (Gobert and Mugnai 2002: 626). This comes closer than most other domestic legal systems to using notions of corporate culture (Wells 2001) and internal decision-making systems (French 1984) as means of attributing responsibility. This constitutes a bold legal innovation and, although classed as a form of quasi-administrative liability, suggests a significant change of position in relation to corporate criminal liability (Beale and Safwat 2004: 107; de Maglie 2011: 269). This does not necessarily translate into practice, where a more cautious approach to implementation is expected. There has been some indication that the idea of corporate homicide might be gaining traction in practice; however, this has occurred in relation to the prosecution of individual directors.[14]

Model three: No attributed corporate liability for homicide offences

The third approach to the criminalisation of corporate activity is to allow for the imposition of liability, but to limit this to a range of specific offences which excludes manslaughter and other fatal or non-fatal offences against the person. This approach reflects the tentative position of corporate criminal liability in many jurisdictions, as well as the fact that these developments originate in policy contexts far removed from corporate manslaughter reforms. The extension of corporate criminalisation via the liberalisation of models of attribution is not driven by a desire to criminalise work-related death cases and does not necessarily mean that such cases will be handled differently as a result. Much of the impetus behind this development has come from bodies such as the OECD and the EU and reflects the emergence of a transnational regulatory regime which is intended to facilitate the growth of the international regulatory capitalist system (Braithwaite 2008; Levi-Faur 2005). The result of this tends to be that corporate criminal liability is constrained to principally economic forms of offending, such as antitrust and corruption or bribery, and is not envisaged as applying in relation to areas of social regulation like occupational health and safety. In some cases, the rationale behind the limitation of corporate criminal liability can be due to issues of practicality rather than principle. In many jurisdictions, the process of reform is undertaken via the introduction of new legislation which sets out the terms on which corporate criminal liability can be attributed. This piece of legislation must specify which offences within the criminal law it will apply to, or enabling legislation is required to make it apply to existing offences. Additionally, some jurisdictions with established systems of corporate criminal liability find that they cannot hold companies liable for homicide offences due to definitional issues; for example, under the law of New Zealand, homicide offences are defined by the Crimes Act 1961 s. 158 as requiring 'the killing of one human being by another'. As such, this precludes a non-human defendant from being able to commit this offence (Wilkinson 2003). So although New Zealand recognises corporate criminal liability and utilises a relatively liberal version of the identification doctrine,[15] and although s. 29 of New Zealand's Interpretation Act 1999 confirms that the phrase 'legal person' does include corporations, it does not have a law of corporate manslaughter.

In other countries, corporate criminal liability has been limited as a matter of principle to economic forms of offending such as bribery, and it is not extended to interpersonal offending. This reflects a purposive model of law reform, whereby change is introduced as a way of addressing specific problems. An example of this is provided by Brazil, where resistance to corporate criminal liability has been set aside by two constitutional provisions relating to economic (Article 173) and environmental (Article 225) offences but not to other crimes. And Portugal first acknowledged that there may be exceptions to a general rule restricting criminal responsibility to human defendants in 1983 (Penal Code Article 11), but these exceptions relate to economic offences only (Serra 1999). Instead, work-related deaths in these jurisdictions are treated as matters for regulatory law to resolve, even while other forms of corporate wrongdoing may be handled as crimes. Finally, there are nations in the developing world where systems of occupational health and safety regulation, and corporate criminal liability, are still in their relative infancy, and where issues of corporate criminalisation in the sphere of health and safety have not yet been addressed. Chinese criminal law does allow for corporate liability, but this is limited to primarily economic forms of offending, and to 'intentional' wrongdoing, not offences of negligence (Jiachen 1999). The Labour Law of the People's Republic of China was introduced in 1995 to update regulation in this area, and Chapter 12 of that statute places the primary responsibility for health and safety (and the main liability to sanctioning) onto individuals within organisational settings, not onto organisations themselves (Pringle and Frost 2003). Chinese regulation has been hampered in practice by a significant lack of clarity and some pronounced shortcomings in terms of enforcement; in part, this is because in the scramble for traction in the new world economy, the maximisation of economic growth has taken precedence over the enforcement of effective regulation. Chinese industry seeks to undercut production costs elsewhere and, in doing so, 'sets the floor' for workplace conditions in competing developing nations (Brown and O'Rourke, 2003). In other jurisdictions, such as Japan, Korea, India, and Israel, corporate liability has also been recognised for certain categories of criminal offence (Pieth and Ivory 2011: 12–13).

The economic focus of corporate criminalisation can be traced back to the nature of the primary driver behind reforms; the pressure exerted by the OECD in demanding, as set out in Article 2 of the 1997 Convention on Combating Bribery of Foreign Public Officials, that nation states must have some form of 'effective, proportionate, and dissuasive non-criminal sanctions' to ensure against bribery, corruption, and corporate wrongdoing means that individual nation states that were entirely without corporate criminal liability have had to introduce legal measures to allow for it in this context (Kyriakakis 2009: 349; Wells 2010). This does not necessitate a blanket application, and indeed, jurisdictions such as Portugal and Brazil have limited themselves to applying these measures *only* to economic crime. In some ways, these offences are more easily accommodated within a sceptical jurisdiction because they are essentially technical in nature and do not explicitly involve issues of social justice or welfare (which might be considered political in nature). The use of criminalisation as a regulatory measure here can be characterised as 'market-constituting' (Braithwaite 2008; Harcourt 2010; Levi-Faur 2005) in that it establishes the rules and boundaries of the economic marketplace, rather than structuring its operation or outcomes. Bribery and corruption laws ensure that entry to economic markets is contingent upon confirming to the rules of that market, and those who do not (or cannot) compete fairly are excluded as they are liable to subvert its efficient operation.

The second factor driving this trend towards criminalisation, and which also explains its limitations, is the influence that human rights discourses have wielded in attempting to hold companies responsible for transnational rights abuses (Clough 2008; Kyriakakis 2009). Corporations have been implicated in the commission of human rights offences since the Nazi atrocities of the Second World War (Weigend 2008: 927); in recent years, multinational corporations have been implicated in human rights violations in the developing world, usually as complicit actors in relation to breaches committed by domestic governments, for example, via the installation of oil and gas extraction facilities for governments which engage in genocide, murder, and forced displacements in order to facilitate development (Clough 2008: 901). These international considerations have played a part in shaping international legal conventions and have also brought pressure to bear on domestic governments to make corporations based within their jurisdiction criminally liable for human rights breaches committed overseas. While this has not yet had a direct impact in terms of criminal liability for occupational health and safety, it has contributed to the development of national corporate liability regimes and a culture, at least in the West, of questioning the ethics of corporate activities overseas, including in relation to employment practices.

Model four: No corporate criminal liability

The final approach to corporate criminal liability is to exclude it from the law altogether, instead dealing with wrongdoing under regulatory law. *Societas delinquere non potest* remains a fundamental principle of many legal systems, particularly those influenced by German law (Weigend 2008). This reflects the influence of Kantian notions of moral responsibility, under which corporations are accorded the status of 'fictions' and so are incapable of bearing moral fault. The German system has influenced many of the jurisdictions discussed already, including Portugal and Brazil, which retain some connection to the notion that corporations cannot commit crimes; in addition, it has influenced jurisdictions such as Greece, the Czech Republic, Mexico, and Argentina, which remain resistant to corporate criminality (Kyriakakis 2009: 342; Pieth and Ivory 2011). In Germany itself, there has been much debate about the possibility of introducing corporate criminal liability (Hefendehl 2000; Meyer 1999; Schneider 2009; Weigend 2008), but the assumption against liability has remained so central to the basic principles and logic of the criminal law that the Criminal Code has not needed to spell it out explicitly (Schneider 2009: 32).

Since 1968, German law has adopted a compromise solution by allowing for a class of administrative offences, known as *Ordnungswidrigkeiten* (OWiG), to be applied to corporate bodies. This allows for an administrative fine (of up to €1 million) to be levied against a corporation if it can be shown that a relevant individual committed an offence; there is not necessarily a need to establish exactly *who* that is, so long as it can be shown that *someone* must have done so (Weigend 2008: 130). Corporate liability for an OWiG offence is intended to be purely descriptive of factual responsibility, rather than delivering any normative judgement about the corporation in question (Böse 2011: 230). The most important example is s. 30 of OWiG, which provides for a form of accessory corporate liability to apply when an individual with organisational control functions commits an offence that breaches an obligation incumbent upon the corporation (Schneider 2009: 33; Weigend 2008: 929). The breach of a duty of supervision by a senior manager, in not preventing the error of a low-level employee (which directly causes an offence), can constitute an offence in itself under s. 130 of OWiG, and the company can be liable under s. 30 as an accessory to that offence. In theory, this could provide a basis for a corporate conviction in a negligent homicide case (Böse 2011: 233); in practice, the evidential hurdles involved mean that this rarely occurs. Schneider, in discussing the Wuppertal rail crash of 1999, demonstrates that the OWiG offences struggle to link senior managers to operational failures in the same sort of way as common-law notions of identification (Schneider 2009: 34–36). Furthermore, OWiG offences are rarely, if ever, invoked in relation to negligent homicide cases; fining corporate bodies in these circumstances is viewed as undesirable by prosecutors and at odds with the proper purpose of administrative penalties, given the inherent moral component of a negligent homicide charge.

Germany remains wedded to the notional separation of criminal law from corporate wrongdoing. The fundamental objections that German lawyers have to corporate criminal liability are threefold: firstly, that acting is a matter of volition and it is individuals and not collectives who possess the moral and cognitive capacity to *choose* to offend; and secondly, that corporations cannot exercise the kind of moral self-determination required by German criminal law (Weigend 2008: 934), that is, by consciously choosing to violate moral norms, because they cannot meaningfully comprehend the moral norms being violated. The third objection best helps in understanding the occupational health and safety context; corporations cannot be punished under criminal law because the purposes of punishment (the inculcation of moral reasons to obey the law) hold no traction in relation to corporate bodies. For them, punishment is purely an issue of deterrence and it makes no sense to use criminal law to achieve this end when administrative penalties are capable of delivering the same outcome without necessitating the kind of hard metaphysical work that criminal liability requires. The instrumental work of redressing the harm done by occupational safety failures is done by the co-managed government public insurance system, one half of the dualist regulatory system, which imposes costs on employers and provides redress to victims of occupational safety injuries, as well as regulating practices within firms (Gräbe 1991). The second component, the state Industry Safety and Standards Inspectorate, enforces the terms of the Industry Act as a last resort, preferring to utilise cooperative measures where possible. These offences are non-criminal and are utilised rarely; the primary mechanisms of regulation are cooperative systems of worker involvement in safety management and insurance schemes for when things go wrong.

The non-criminalising jurisdictions have had to introduce laws in order to satisfy the OECD's requirement that they have 'effective, proportionate, and dissuasive' laws to ensure against corporate wrongdoing in the commercial and financial spheres (Kyriakakis 2009: 349). Germany has been able to point to the OWiG laws as satisfying this requirement; other jurisdictions have had to innovate to reach a solution that is compatible with their domestic jurisprudence. Spain excludes corporations from bearing 'direct' criminal responsibility on the same principled grounds as Germany, but does allow for a corporate body to be criminally punished as an accessory to an offence if it is used as a means of offending by an agent (so-called ancillary consequences; Bacigalupo 1999). Similarly, Sweden does not allow for corporate criminal liability, but it does allow a kind of 'quasi-criminal' liability to arise where a natural person commits an offence which entails a 'gross disregard for the special obligations associated with the business activity' and the 'entrepreneur' fails to do 'what could reasonably be expected of him for prevention of the crime' (Swedish Penal Code, Ch. 36, s. 7). This is essentially a form of secondary responsibility for failing to prevent the crime of another; aside from this, Sweden uses non-criminal sanctions to enforce against occupational health and safety breaches, such as those contained within the 1977 Work Environment Act. This establishes enforceable general duties which are regulated via a tripartite health and safety system, which prioritises the use of trade union representatives (the country has a very high union membership rate) and worker involvement in the management of health and safety in the workplace (Frick and Walters 1998; James and Walters 2002; Kelman 1984; Walters 1995; 1996).

Swedish safety regulators have long been wedded to a highly discretionary, consensual, and cooperative model of regulation (Walters *et al.* 2011: 120–127); the regulatory system has not historically allowed for the routine imposition of fines or for first-instance sanctioning, instead it has only progressed towards sanctioning once notices given of problems are not complied with (Kelman 1984: 105). Despite this, there has been more of a shift towards the use of regulatory penalties, such as injunctions backed up by contingent administrative fines, in recent years; around 220 such cases per year are referred for potential prosecution (Gunningham and Johnstone 1999: 378; Walters *et al.* 2011: 133–135). This has coincided with a shift away from consensual welfare-oriented values within the regulatory system, reductions in the resources and political support given to regulators, and a generalised decline in the influence of organised labour in this time period. There are also special administrative sanctions that can be imposed onto employers who violate specific provisions, meaning that resort to the 'criminal' law, even in the sense in which health and safety offences in the UK are criminal, is avoided. The Swedish Penal Code was amended in 1991 to create specific occupational safety-related offences to hold liable those employers who negligently default on their obligations and cause an injury or death; but these are classed as 'consequences' of penal liability, not criminal punishments *per se*, because corporations cannot commit crimes.[16] These measures are used relatively rarely; approximately 20 cases per year are brought under these penal provisions, of which maybe eight will involve work-related deaths (Gunningham and Johnstone 1999: 379; Walters *et al.* 2011: 135).

Conclusion

There has been a significant shift towards the development of corporate criminal liability in recent years. The notion of corporate homicide has taken hold in a range of national jurisdictions, and the spread of corporate criminal liability as a conceptual tool of supranational market constitution makes it likely that it will spread further in future. But specific offences for this purpose are a rarity, and although many countries allow corporations to bear criminal responsibility, this does not necessarily extend to offences against the person, such as manslaughter. But the notion of corporate homicide is, at least in theory, a feature of many more national jurisdictions than was the case 15 or 20 years ago. In identifying this trend, we are led to several important conclusions. Firstly, almost no country eschews corporate liability completely; many national jurisdictions have an explicitly criminal system, and others have systems which perform 'criminal' functions but are conceptualised as 'administrative' or 'quasi-administrative'. The practical distinctions between criminal and non-criminal systems are often very fine indeed; there are administrative penalties (such as those in operation in Italy) that are criminal in all but name, and there are systems of regulatory offences (such as those in operation in the UK and USA) that are formally classed as part of the criminal law but which are not popularly regarded as such due to the way they are enforced. A lack of criminal law does not mean a lack of law, and criminal laws do not necessarily signify tougher legal controls. The ambiguity of status associated with occupational health and safety law permeates contemporary legal systems now as much as it has done in the past (Carson 1979; Haines and Sutton 2007).

Secondly, even where the criminal law is formally made available for application in the corporate context, there is a significant gap between having those laws and enforcing them. There are no countries where corporate manslaughter convictions are common, and even nations that are proactive in terms of criminalisation have low rates of prosecution for these offences. Many countries that allow corporations to be liable for manslaughter offences do so only notionally; these laws remain 'on the books' only and as such are hard to interpret as evidence of any shift towards a new 'punitive regulation' (Baldwin 2004). At the same time, the regulatory systems that govern occupational health and safety are also characterised by an overriding commitment to the use of formal enforcement as a 'last resort' technique. As Braithwaite observes, nowhere do regulators adopt aggressive 'policing' enforcement strategies, 'not even the Sherriff of Nottingham had tried to enforce zero tolerance' in relation to corporate offending (2003: 14). So although there has been a shift in terms of the introduction of criminal laws, this does not necessarily translate into a shift towards punitive regulatory 'practices'; this leads to the conclusion that the reasons for introducing these laws are not necessarily linked to their prospective practical impact. If there is an instrumental driver behind these reforms, it is the spread of economic regulatory requirements imposed by transnational organisations in order to establish the rules of the international marketplace. So the irony is that the emergence of corporate criminality has, to a large extent, been driven by the needs of business. But this alone does not explain why the new laws have been extended to allow homicide liability in occupational health and safety contexts. We are left to conclude that the purposes of these new laws must in fact be symbolic and relate to what they say about the relationship between business and the state.

Thirdly, the most pronounced shifts towards corporate criminal liability, and the only examples of a sustained commitment to using these laws, have come from the common-law jurisdictions of the UK, the USA,

Australia, and Canada. The nature of lawmaking and the pragmatic (critics from civil law traditions would say unprincipled) attitude to the criminal–administrative law divide in these nations are important in explaining this tendency; there is more scope to take a 'problem-solving' approach to law reform. But it is also possible to suggest that something about the nature of these countries explains this trend; they are jurisdictions with long traditions of market-centred, economically liberal politics, and relatively minimal traditions of social welfarism and multi-level representation within workplaces and government (Lacey 2008). On the other hand, nations that continue to reject corporate criminal liability (for instance, Germany and Sweden) do have traditions of social welfarism and worker representation, and practices in health and safety regulation seem to bear this out (Walters 1996). It is suggested, and subsequent chapters will explore this further, that the economic and political contexts of regulation in neo-liberal nations undermine the legitimacy of health and safety regulation in a way that does not occur in social democratic nations, and this process creates a need for criminal laws to buttress this legitimacy by moralising the issue in hand. Corporate manslaughter laws are, therefore, introduced as a means of symbolically addressing the deficits of regulatory regimes in this regard. The next chapter will begin to explain how and why regulation must show that it matters.

3
Work-Related Deaths as Symbolic Events

This chapter provides a theoretical overview of how and why issues of regulatory law are enforced, and what considerations shape this process. It will position this book in relation to existing approaches to this issue, aiming to build on both the critical literature influenced by Marxist theory and the work of scholars writing within a broadly pragmatic 'regulatory studies' tradition. These often conflicting approaches are reconciled via the notion of regulation as a communicative endeavour which incorporates normative and instrumental components. While regulatory systems tend towards instrumentalism, in terms of a focus on technical issues and compliance with the law, work-related deaths have a communicative power which instrumental systems of regulation struggle to respond to. A Habermasian theoretical framework will be used to explain how the moral and instrumental components of this issue interact, and why the latter predominates within the context of health and safety regulation. It will be argued that corporate manslaughter reforms can thus be understood as a reaction to this instrumentalism and a primarily communicative response to the normative demands of wider society.

Theorising the role of regulatory enforcement

Enforcement is just one element of the role fulfilled by regulatory agencies, along with the issuing of guidance and advice to regulated companies, the creation of legal standards, the proactive monitoring of compliance, and the coordination of self-regulation. Regulation is defined in terms of the 'sustained and focused control exercised by a public agency over activities that are valued by a community' (Selznick 1985: 363); this definition identifies the 'directive' nature of regulation in compelling certain behaviours in pursuit of desired outcomes (Ogus 1994: 7), as well as the constraint of this compulsion by virtue of the nature of the acts regulated. Baldwin *et al.* (1998: 3) suggest that the defining feature of 'regulation' is that it encourages activities that are defined as desirable, such as wealth generation, employment, and the provision of valued services, rather than prohibiting purely anti-social activities. The latter, it might be argued, involves a different moral agenda and should be left to the criminal law (Gill 2002: 532; Richardson 1987: 299). Regulation is, therefore, primarily concerned with the 'management' rather than the 'prohibition' of conduct, with the result that enforcement action is utilised relatively rarely in practice (Hawkins 1984; 2002; Hutter 1997; Kagan 1984; Scholz 1984; Tombs and Whyte 2007). Despite this, enforcement is the most high-profile form of regulatory activity, capable of communicating with a wide audience, and is often invoked in response to incidents that may have had very serious consequences.

There are numerous ways of thinking about regulation: as a matter of correcting markets (Breyer 1982; Ogus 1994; Veljanovski 1983), pursuing procedural public interest goals (Baldwin 1995; Feintuck 2004; Sunstein 1990), and enacting certain values, such as the pursuit of social solidarity and freedom from domination (Braithwaite 2008; Prosser 2006; 2011). These differences of purpose make regulation a politically contested activity, and enforcement represents the most controversial part of the process – why enforce, and when, and in pursuit of what outcome? Much of the literature has identified two main 'schools' of thought on these issues: the 'compliance school' and the 'deterrence' or 'punishment school' (Ayres and Braithwaite 1992; Baldwin *et al.* 1998; Gray 2006; Hawkins 1984; Hopkins 1994; Pearce and Tombs 1990; Reiss 1984; Tombs and Whyte 2007), and while these terms have been used pejoratively in the past (Hawkins 1990; 1991; Pearce and Tombs 1990; 1991), the discussion here merely aims to explain the continuum along which regulators position themselves as 'proactive or reactive, as an educator or a policeman, or as providing persuasion or punishment' (May and Burby 1998: 161). It should be noted that 'enforcement' is a broad term, covering a wide range of different measures, from verbal warnings (Eckert 2004) and conversations about compliance (Black 1998), to bargaining and the threat of sanctions (Hawkins 1983; 1984; Hutter 1989), to administrative penalties such as enforcement and prohibition notices (Hawkins and Thomas 1991), to prosecution for regulatory and criminal offences. There are many debates about enforcement; for now, the question is 'why enforce?'

Compliance-focused enforcement

The general consensus within the literature on occupational health and safety regulation is that rates of formal enforcement action are low across different national jurisdictions and regulatory regimes, when compared to rates of violation of the law (Almond 2007; Gunningham and Johnstone 1999; Hawkins 2002; Hutter 1997; Tombs and Whyte 2007; Wells 2001). Enforcement via prosecution occurs, for the most part, as a 'last resort', a measure to be utilised when all alternatives have been exhausted and no other course of action is feasible (Hawkins 2002: 14). This has long been the preferred approach of safety regulators in the UK at least, reflecting the high costs associated with prosecuting, in terms of time, money, and disruptions to regulatory relationships (Almond 2006; Hawkins 2002; Hutter 1986; 1989; Hutter and Manning 1990). The widespread use of formal enforcement powers constitutes a less efficient use of regulatory resources than a programme of cooperation because it focuses sustained attention onto a small number of cases, leaving many others untouched, and imposes higher procedural demands than confrontational methods. Enforcement should only be used sparingly, with an eye on the relative costs and benefits, principles usually ingrained in prosecution policies such as Health and Safety Executive's (HSE's) Enforcement Policy Statement (2009b: para. 7; Hawkins 2002: 91).

And yet this pragmatism is only part of the rationale for limited enforcement action, reinforcing preferences for a last-resort enforcement strategy which is characterised as compliance-centred, accommodative, or self-regulatory in nature. Within this broad approach, enforcement activity is only justified where it serves the wider utilitarian goals of securing a greater degree of compliance with regulations and lower levels of death and injury. Regulation is instrumentalist in nature, focused on changing things, and enforcement action occurs pursuant to this agenda; in Hawkins' terms, '[l]aw is there…to achieve some practical end, to make a difference…the legitimacy of the act of prosecution inheres in instrumental claims about action in the public interest' (2002: 4). Regulation is forward-facing, centred on influencing what *will* happen in the future and the subsequent behaviour of regulated actors. This understanding has two outcomes: firstly, it conceives of legality as a continuum rather than a binary (legal/illegal) state, with regulated companies moving from non-compliance towards the goal of compliance through a series of prescribed or managed regulatory steps and processes (Hutter 1989; 1997). Secondly, rather than being a state of full accordance with the law, compliance is a state that is negotiated by the regulator and the regulated; in most cases this is contingent upon what can reasonably be expected in the circumstances (Hutter 1997). Because of this, the compliance approach tolerates a degree of non-compliance, viewing safety management as a 'work in progress' rather than as a matter of substantive illegality.

The emphasis on collaborative safety management highlights another component of this approach: the notion of self-regulation as the primary route to compliance. Regulators facilitate businesses in managing their own compliance, offering advice and guidance, and seeking to maintain productive relationships with the regulated. Enforcement within a compliance-based model tends to be responsive and structured around the progression of the regulatory relationship towards adversarial measures like prosecution over time (Aalders and Wilthagen 1997; Ayres and Braithwaite 1992; Baldwin and Black 2008; Black and Baldwin 2010; Braithwaite 2002; Gilad 2011; Gunningham and Grabosky 1998; Gunningham and Johnstone 1999; May and Burby 1998; Parker 2002). Within these approaches, adversarial enforcement occurs only once efforts at regulating cooperatively have failed to secure compliance; regulators then progress to the use of more punitive measures to try and prompt engagement. The enforcement pyramid model advanced by Ayres and Braithwaite (1992: 35) provides an example of this hierarchical approach:

> our presumption should always be to start at the bottom of the pyramid, then escalate to somewhat punitive approaches only reluctantly and only when dialogue fails, and then escalate to even more punitive approaches only when the more modest forms of punishment fail.
>
> (Braithwaite 2002: 30)

This notion of escalated enforcement underpins many different variations of enforced self-regulation, including Gunningham and Johnstone's 'two-track' model, where 'track one' is adversarial and enforcement-led and applies when companies do not maintain an effective 'track two', regulated company-led and self-regulatory safety management system (1999: Ch. 4), versions of economic game-theory-based tit-for-tat regulation (Scholz 1984), and responsive regulatory strategies, where the actions, attitudes, and contexts of regulated companies all provide a basis for the reactive setting of regulatory interventions (Baldwin and Black 2008; Black and Baldwin 2010; Braithwaite 2002). The threat of enforcement alters the costs of non-compliance, incentivising the maintenance of effective safety management systems.

Corporate manslaughter, and offences of this sort, would perform this role, sitting at the top of the enforcement pyramid and exerting a downward pressure towards compliance (Gunningham and Johnstone 1999: 213). But the 'big stick' must be used sparingly because, as adherents of the compliance model argue, over-enforcement tends to produce mistrust and non-cooperation (Ayres and Braithwaite 1992; Bardach and Kagan 1982; Haines 1997; Hampton 2005; Parker 2006; Scholz 1984; Tyler 1990; Tyler and Darley 2000). In Braithwaite's terms:

> ...by resorting to more dominating...forms of social control only when more dialogic forms have been tried first, coercive control comes to be seen as...more legitimate, more procedurally fair, [and] compliance with the law is more likely.
>
> (2002: 32)

The primary criticisms of this approach relate to the conception of voluntary compliance that it rests upon. There is an assumption that law-breaking is exceptional and limited to a few 'bad apples' (Bardach and Kagan 1982), but there is evidence that elements of regulatory offending are pervasive (Braithwaite 1985; Gray 2006; Pearce and Tombs 1990; Tombs and Whyte 2007; 2010; Wells 2001). An essentially rational, law-abiding commitment to legality is assumed to be the default position, and breaches of the law are taken as lapses from this. This overlooks the fact that corporations sometimes act irrationally because they possess a 'bounded rationality' (Ayres and Braithwaite 1992: 29; Gunningham and Johnstone 1999: 69; Parker 2002: 66; Scholz 1997; Wells 2001: 74) or because they rationally calculate that breaching the law carries a greater prospect of gain than of loss. Critics reject the 'consensus-based' approach's understanding that offending is an unfortunate by-product of legitimate activity (Tombs and Whyte 2010: 49), asserting instead that there is no widespread commitment to lawfulness, that the negotiated nature of compliance allows for the 'bargaining away' of legal standards (Ashworth 2000; Handler 1992), and that this approach allows business interests to define legality. Underfunded regulators employing non-confrontational approaches to technical transgressions of negotiated standards are unlikely to challenge the pervasive causes of injury and death to workers and the public.

Punishment-focused enforcement

The counterpoint to compliance-based enforcement is the 'punishment school', sometimes also termed the 'sanctioning' (Hawkins 1984) and 'deterrence' (Parker 2002; Reiss 1984) model. For writers in this tradition, regulatory law should use rigorous enforcement and sanctioning in order to redirect the behaviour of the regulated population, who tend to operate as 'amoral calculators' (Kagan and Scholz 1984; Pearce and Tombs 1990). Corporations only comply with the law when it is in their interests to do so; it will only be in their interests when the punishments associated with non-compliance outweigh the benefits. This is because corporations exist for one overriding reason: to maximise profit. This economic rationality manifests itself in two distinct approaches to deterrence-based enforcement. The first is a law and economics-based model of deterrence regulation which emphasises the need for enforcement to correct market failures by imposing sanctions to counteract the savings associated with non-compliance, according to a utilitarian calculus of cost and benefit (Baldwin and Cave 1999; Breyer 1982; Francis 1993; Ogus 1994; Scholz 1997; Veljanovski 1983). This approach is avowedly instrumental; enforcement exists in order to allow for the redistribution of the costs of non-compliance, and deterrence is a means of shaping rational decision-making rather than as a matter of moral conscience.

The alternative form of deterrence theory is more critical and sees corporate actors as 'immoral' rather than non-moral actors; decisions are made on the basis of economic criteria, and 'moral' criteria are actively extinguished by the profit-seeking imperative of business. This approach sees regulatory offending as a necessary outcome of capitalism; society is structured so as to facilitate the pursuit of profit by business, and the infliction of harm is an inherent and accepted part of the accumulation process (Bittle and Snider 2006; Carson 1970; 1979; Pearce and Tombs 1990; 1991; Slapper 1999; Snider 1991; Tombs and Whyte 2007). To this end, the role of regulatory enforcement is to act in direct opposition to this self-interest, providing a reason to refrain from harmful risk-taking. Aggressive and punitive enforcement of protective laws such as those governing health and safety prevents regulatory crime (and 'crime' rather than 'non-compliance' is the preferred terminology; Gray 2006: 877) by deterring these amoral calculators from harmful courses of action. This approach necessarily comes to the conclusion that systems of safety regulation currently fail to provide this deterrent effect due to their compliance orientation. The 'law as last resort' strategy leads to routine under-enforcement, and this reflects a political and systemic unwillingness to impose meaningful sanctions upon powerful corporate actors. It is issues of political economy, with underfunded regulators seeking to apply laws in the 'public interest' to an immensely powerful business lobby that has the capacity to effectively shape what the law is and how it should be applied, that fundamentally define the regulatory sphere. Regulatory enforcement is characterised by its ineffectiveness, with low rates of prosecution and relatively trivial sanctions applied in response to widespread offending behaviour; as Tombs and Whyte (2010) illustrate, rates of enforcement in relation to safety offences are in decline, and this is linked to a declining political commitment to the regulation of corporate activity.

This critical perspective has been criticised in turn. Firstly, many of the objections to compliance-based enforcement put forward are normative rather than descriptive, in that they do not engage with the reality of regulatory practices (Hawkins 1990); pursuing a deterrence-based enforcement strategy in practice would necessitate a much greater investment from central government, something which is unlikely to be forthcoming given the prevailing political context of opposition to state intervention (Hawkins 2002). Realistically, it is argued, such a system would prove unsustainable given the potentially divisive effects of less discriminate enforcement activity (Bardach and Kagan 1982; Kagan and Scholz 1984). Aggressive criminalisation may be a desirable strategy in relation to an unequivocally wrongful form of offending, but breaches of health and safety law, being both a side effect of socially desirable activities and often a matter of degrees of non-compliance, may not be conducive to a zero-tolerance enforcement approach. Furthermore, it is suggested that there is evidence that simple deterrence-based enforcement does not work (Simpson 2002); Scholz (1997) and others have demonstrated that the 'amoral calculator' model of corporate deterrence is flawed because obedience to the law is underpinned by the combined effects of deterrence and voluntary compliance, and it is bounded by the information that regulated companies actually possess (Thornton *et al.* 2005).

Similarly, as a concept, deterrence is not as simplistic or narrow as these accounts suggest; the effects that enforcement can have are much more wide-ranging and include many forms of behavioural impact beyond a simple rational aversion to offending (Gray and Scholz 1993; Mendeloff and Gray 2005). It should be noted as well that critical commentators regard the empirical value of compliance-based approaches as similarly unproven and intangible (Pearce and Tombs 1990; Tombs and Whyte 2007). The prevailing regulatory orthodoxy is that while deterrent-based enforcement plays a part, this is as a 'back-up' to more significant processes of voluntary compliance, demonstrating that breaches of the law are not ignored, and highlighting the moral costs of non-compliance (Gray and Scholz 1993; Parker 2002: 69; Scholz 1997). As with other areas of offending, it is a belief in the legitimacy of the law that motivates compliance, not fear of getting caught (Tyler 1990; Tyler and Darley 2000). Theorists have pointed out that elements of corporate virtue, or commitment to law, can more sustainably motivate compliance in the absence of punishment because they reflect elements of morality and conscience (Braithwaite 2002; Genn 1993; Haines 1997; Parker 2002). As such, it is argued, they should be nurtured and enforcement action, which has the potential to erode this voluntary commitment, curtailed. Deterrence is incapable, in and of itself, of successfully motivating law-abiding behaviour.

Reconciling different approaches to enforcement

The result of this debate has been that scholars and regulators have tended to see a role for both cooperative risk-management and adversarial punishment within regulatory regimes (Aalders and Wilthagen 1997; Ayres and Braithwaite 1992; Gilad 2011; Gray 2006; Gunningham and Johnstone 1999; Hopkins 1994; Parker 2002; Sinclair 1997). The 'responsive' and 'two-track' regulation scholars recognise that there are limits to voluntarism and that these necessitate the use of enforcement action where there are serious and wilful breaches of the law. As Sinclair (1997) points out, all regulatory schemes feature four key variables to varying degrees, namely, 'regulatory compulsion', 'regulatory flexibility', 'industry design input', and 'win-win outcomes'. While deterrence models may rely mainly on compulsion, and self-regulatory compliance models on industry input and flexibility, in reality, no system can function without elements of all of these features. Even Bardach and Kagan (1982) advocate the prosecution of bad apples, and even Tombs and Whyte (2007) envisage a role for rehabilitative and compliance-led regulatory engagement within a mixed sentencing strategy. As such, the distinction between these two broad theoretical approaches is one of degree rather than of intractable difference.

Contemporary health and safety regulation tends to draw more heavily upon the compliance rather than the deterrence approach; UK safety regulators have always prioritised the provision of guidance and advice over prosecution (Carson 1970; 1979; Hawkins 2002), and the same can be said of regulators elsewhere (see Chapter 2). The current tendency is for versions of 'risk-based' regulation to be used, whereby enforcement resources are targeted at those regulated actors who are deemed to pose particular risks to regulatory objectives (Black 2005; Black and Baldwin 2010). Approaches of this sort are enshrined in statements of regulatory principle, such as the UK's Hampton Review of regulation (2005) and Macrory Report on regulatory enforcement (2006), which together advocate a more flexible, less burdensome system of regulation which utilises inspection and formal enforcement more infrequently, something that critics categorise as broadly deregulatory (Tombs and Whyte 2010). Although the use of prosecution is advocated in relation to the most egregious cases, this remains a small proportion of a 'streamlined' enforcement profile (Hampton 2005: 2.73). Discussion of the liability of corporations for manslaughter must be understood against the backdrop of a regulatory system where enforcement action is utilised as an exception rather than a rule.

On the one hand, there are significant gains to be made in terms of securing obedience to the law via the use of a consensual and compliance-seeking regulatory strategy. Nurturing law-abiding tendencies and corporate virtue in a way that adversarial enforcement sometimes fails to do can bring about improvements in safety performance (Braithwaite 2002; 2008; Gunningham and Rees 1997; Haines 1997; Parker 2002). Indeed, in the developed world, we are safer now than we have ever been; rates of death and injury at work are historically low, most employers attend to their legal requirements, and many employees enjoy levels of protection unheard of even 20 years ago. Safety professionals proliferate and, along with trade unions, have played a vital part in campaigning for safety provisions at a regulatory and organisational level. There have been significant benefits associated with the regulation of safety through a cooperative system, and these successes cannot be overlooked. On the other hand, there is no doubt that breaches of regulatory law are under-enforced, and that many egregious failures to control safety risks go unpunished and unregulated. Regulatory law fails to prevent a significant number of deaths and injuries each year, and there are enough bad apples among employers to suggest that more needs to be done to secure effective and widespread compliance with the law (Tombs and Whyte 2007; Wells 2001). While it is necessary to recognise the political factors that constrain the achievement of justice in relation to work-related deaths, it is also important to recognise the facilitative nature of the law and the capacity of workers, employers, and regulators to affect change. How is it possible to make sense of these two divergent but persuasive sentiments regarding safety regulation? How can we explain the progress made as well as the significant constraints put upon that progress?

The instrumentalism of regulatory enforcement

The first step towards reconciling the perspectives sketched out above involves recognising that regulation is, under both views, a matter of 'instrumentalism', that is, of affecting some form of measurable change in the external regulated environment. Instrumentalism relates to a conception of law as a medium for the achievement of particular policy outcomes, whereby decisions in individual cases are made in pursuit of substantive goals rather than on the basis of the application of legal rules in a formalistic sense (Unger 1975: 89; also Nonet and Selznick 1978; Tamanaha 1997; 2006; Teubner 1987: 401–405). Law is 'consciously viewed by people and groups as a tool or means with which to achieve ends', which may include personal interests, ideological causes, and public policy goals (Tamanaha 2006: 6). This view of the law as a route through which individual actors may pursue their own interests as against those of others emerged in the early 19th century (2006: Ch. 2); as Chapter 4 will demonstrate, this is also the period in which safety regulations emerged in the UK and elsewhere. These laws are instrumental in that they exist in order to alter phenomena and change behaviour in pursuit of public interest goals (Gusfield 1981; Haines 2011: 23–28; Hawkins 2002: 4), reflecting what Teubner terms 'the unstoppable rise of "purpose in law" ' (1987: 403). The success or failure of a regulator is determined by reference to demonstrable changes: Have rates of injury and death declined? Are employers engaging with the law to a greater degree? Are the costs of safety failures reduced, and allocated appropriately? To return to Selznick's definition of regulation as a matter of focused control over valued activities (1985: 363), we can see that the concept is itself instrumental in nature, being irreducibly tied up with utilitarian, goal-oriented, and strategic notions of oversight, problem-solving, and performance enhancement. As Hawkins points out, enforcement is important in this instrumental conception of regulation:

> to prosecute in the regulatory arena is to invoke the criminal process so that the rule-breaker is not minded to violate rules in the future, or so that others who might also be tempted to break rules choose to do otherwise, for fear of an unpleasant fate.
>
> (2002: 4)

Both economics-based and critical approaches to deterrence accord with this instrumental logic, viewing enforcement as a way of producing compliance with the law by rendering the costs associated with offending so great as to outweigh the benefits. Rates of injury, illness, and death also provide a basis against which we can evaluate the relative failure of compliance-based regulatory policy to fulfil this instrumental goal (Tombs and Whyte 2007; 2010). The theoretical basis on which this critical tradition is based is also instrumental; law and regulation are viewed as tools through which the interests of business and capital are fulfilled (Pearce and Tombs 1990; Slapper 1999; Snider 1991; Tombs and Whyte 2007). The weakness of safety regulation thus reflects the ability of dominant economic elites to shape the legal system in accordance with their own interests; any initiatives which appear to be in the interests of workers are merely part of a 'confidence trick' which creates a false impression of democracy (Sargent 1989: 44). But this instrumentalist tendency has a narrowing effect, viewing all questions of law as matters of class relations which are reducible to economic relations. If safety regulation exists merely to manage the interests of business, by providing a veneer of respectability to exploitative employment practices (Carson 1979; Snider 1991; Tombs and Whyte 2007), then we are unable to understand the countervailing trends towards the granting of meaningful legal protections which are too significant to be dismissed as a sleight of hand or manifestation of false consciousness. Law is not merely a tool of domination, but also a forum through which it is possible for individuals to act pursuant to their own self-determinative interests. It provides a means for the emancipation of individuals from structural constraints, and it is this potential that justifies the interest taken in regulation as a source of social justice. Critical approaches to regulation tend to reduce law to the status of an implement or tool wielded solely by those with economic power (a class which their analysis suggests is entrenched in that position), so rendering impotent the efforts at reform of the law. Why change the law if it will continue to be used in this way by these groups? If we view law instrumentally, then accepting that it is wielded purely in the interests of a ruling class means that we deny the possibility of effecting meaningful change (Tamanaha 2006: 122).

Similarly, the compliance-based approach to regulation is instrumental in outlook, being fundamentally concerned with increasing levels of compliance with legal rules. On this approach, law is a means of fulfilling regulatory goals in a facilitative way. An instrumental rationality informs the emphasis placed upon working towards compliance; by negotiating over levels of acceptable compliance and seeking future change rather than punishing past violations, compliance-based regulation is, in Unger's (1975) terms, concerned with substantive (progressing towards a designated social goal or outcome) rather than legal justice (upholding established rules and principles). For Teubner, this represents a shift away from 'rule-orientation' and towards 'purpose-orientation', whereby upholding ill-defined, need-driven standards in pursuit of results takes priority over maintaining fidelity to precisely defined, principled legal norms (1987: 403). Responsive and risk-based approaches to regulation both aim to change regulatory performance, and their value is assessed according to how far compliance is improved, and to what effect; outcomes are more important than fidelity to the letter of the law (Ashworth 2000). As Hutter (1997) points out, compliance with the law is contingent and marks a point on a continuum running between total compliance and total non-compliance, and the law aims to produce an effect in terms of this continuum. As such, it is important to understand how this logic of instrumentalism informs current safety regulation regimes.

Instrumentalism in regulatory rationales

Systems of regulation are often justified in terms of the need to correct market failures and economic inefficiencies (Baldwin and Cave 1999; Breyer 1982; Francis 1993; Ogus 1994); monopolies, externalities, price-fixing cartels, and informational deficits all create an economic case for regulation in order to correct the efficient functioning of a market. In short, 'regulation is necessary because social and private costs and benefits, and hence incentives, are misaligned' (Stiglitz 2009: 13). This is the primary rationale for intervention; while other public policy goals may be served, the presence of a market failure acts as a *de minimis* threshold for intervention (Breyer 1982: Ch. 1). In instrumental terms, the law serves the interests of specified parties by ensuring that costs are distributed so that prices reflect risks accurately. There is a link here to the economic deterrence school, in that the threat of regulatory sanctions corrects the market failure that arises when the benefits of causing harm outweigh the costs; a lack of deterrent effect would mean that the market was failing to allocate the costs associated with safety breaches effectively (Ogus 1994; Veljanovski 1983). Considerations of market failure are augmented by assessment of the costs and benefits of regulation for those involved via processes of decision-making that are heavily dependent on the analytical methods of the social sciences and economics (Teubner 1987: 405). Regulation, it is argued, is only justified when the benefits of the law outweigh the costs associated with it according to the economic calculation of the monetary impact of regulation. An example of this is provided by the British Government's 'Better

Regulation Executive' (BRE), the body responsibile for the design and reform of government regulations, who justify regulation in terms of the economic costs of market failures, including a lack of standards, anti-competition, and crises of investment (2009: 1.7–1.14), which together provide 'the economic rationale for government intervention' (2009: 23). While some role is envisaged for consideration of 'social inequality problems' in justifying regulation, this is conceptualised in economic rather than normative terms.

This economic framework carries through into the evaluation of regulatory strategies, with the BRE stating that 'where it is possible and cost-effective to do the analysis, costs and benefits should be monetized' in order to facilitate an instrumental assessment of economic impact (2009: 21). This approach downplays non-monetary rationales for intervention, including the emotional, cognitive, and social impacts of organisational wrongdoing, and overlooks the (less easily quantified) symbolic and normative goals of regulation (Helm 2006; Hood *et al.* 2001; Prosser 2006; 2011), privileging the interests of those who can represent their position in economic terms. The economic approach to regulatory evaluation is prevalent (Hampton 2005; Macrory 2006; Prosser 2011) and reflects the essentially market-based nature of many regulatory systems. Further, in the UK, Regulatory Impact Assessment (RIA) tools were introduced in 1998 in order to formalise the evaluation of the costs and benefits of proposed regulations and to entrench this mode of thinking even further.

These tools allow for the systematic consideration of the likely impact of new legal measures but tend to privilege a deregulatory agenda because the benefits of a regulatory regime are much harder to demonstrate than its costs (Helm 2006: 178; Tombs and Whyte 2010: 50). The costs of industrial incidents also tend to 'spillover' into wider society (Breyer 1982), creating what economic models of regulation refer to as 'externalities' (Baldwin and Cave 1999: 11; Ogus 1994: 35–38) or costs accruing to parties not directly involved in the underlying exchange. So while costs located within the production process and direct benefits that accrue to others (protection from injury) can be quantified, the diffuse costs associated with risk, such as those attaching to pollution or other widely distributed outcomes (the health costs associated with Chernobyl or Bhopal, for example), are not included. As critics of HSE have argued, these economic modes of regulatory thinking result in enforcement strategies that privilege consideration of the financial implications of regulation rather than the moral case for action and render regulatory systems vulnerable to degradation in the face of economic pressures such as recession (Bain 1997; Tombs and Whyte 2010). It should be noted, however, that this economic instrumentalism does not constitute an explicit reason for regulating, as envisaged by the HSE itself, and that HSE does not formally rationalise or make policy on economic terms (Prosser 2011: Ch. 5). It does, however, apply the language of economic analysis when determining strategy and approach. Additionally, an instrumental, economic framework for regulation is of only limited value in defining the importance of regulation; it is the 'nature' of the economic costs and the circumstances in which they arise that provide reasons for intervention in the public interest.

Instrumentalism in regulatory approach

As discussed, compliance-based regulatory strategies prioritise the development of systems, policies, and procedures that produce concrete, measurable improvements in compliance. This outcome is pursued via the provision of advice and guidance to duty-holders, the monitoring and coordination of risk management systems and policies, the use of scientific evidence and quantifiable risk assessments, and mechanisms of audit and self-reporting. Attention is focused on duty-holders and hazards that are assessed as posing the most significant risk, and resources are allocated to areas where they are able to bring about the greatest difference in terms of compliance. Enforcement action is undertaken on instrumental grounds as well; on a formal level, when there is a realistic prospect of securing conviction and fulfilling the public interest (Code for Crown Prosecutors: DPP 1985); and on a policy level, when it offers a means for regulators to shape future behaviour in a particular case (Hawkins 2002: Ch. 9). The problem is, of course, that the instrumentalist framework requires that some evidence of measurable effect be demonstrated in order to assess the value of enforcement action, and this is sometimes hard to achieve in practice. It is hard to measure something that does *not* happen (injuries and offences that are prevented), and there are many unquantifiable impacts associated with enforcement which defy measurement, such as public reassurance and the promotion of the regulator's profile (Hawkins 2002: 285). The challenge for regulators, therefore, becomes one of presenting persuasive evidence of instrumental effectiveness.

The result is an increasing regulatory preoccupation with the pursuit of tightly defined goals, measured through quantifiable outcome indices, and the targeting of resources at high-impact areas of risk (Black 2005; Black and Baldwin 2010; Gilad 2011; Hampton 2005; Hood *et al.*

2001; Macrory 2006; Mendeloff and Gray 2005; Rothstein *et al.* 2006). Notions of economic rationality are used to guide the implementation and delivery of policy within the health and safety sphere, although such considerations are only indirectly related to actual policy formation (Prosser 2011: Ch. 5). For example, in the UK, HSE has focused regulatory enforcement upon key areas of concern via its 'Revitalising Health and Safety' strategy, which started in 1999 as a relaunch of the health and safety agenda some 25 years after the HSWA 1974 (DETR 2000). 'Revitalising' aimed to achieve improvements in core areas of health and safety provision, identified via the use of actuarial analysis of the causes of workplace injury and ill health. These are high-volume, but *relatively* low-impact, workplace hazards, including 'slips, trips and falls', 'lifting accidents', 'workplace stress', and 'hand-arm vibration injuries' (DETR 2000). It was intended that, by targeting the most common forms of accident, injury rates could be reduced and regard for health and safety could be effectively inculcated in the workplace; the responsibilisation of duty-holders and the improvement of the working environment are envisaged as the primary means of improving the management of these hazards (DETR 2000: 18). The success of this strategy was to be measured with reference to overall rates of ill health and injury, underlining the actuarial logic of this regulatory intervention. High-risk hazards, in terms of potentiality for death and disaster, are not central to these approaches. 'Revitalising' aimed to use an economic methodology to promote the 'business case' for regulation and give duty-holders the tools to effectively self-regulate pursuant to a set of clearly defined goals; within this approach, enforcement takes a back seat to more preventative interventions (Tombs and Whyte 2010: 51). But 'Revitalising' has failed to have the anticipated impact upon fatality and injury rates while, at the same time, rates of formal enforcement action have declined dramatically (Dyer 2003; Tombs and Whyte 2010). The imposition of value-free statistically driven targeting judgements appears, as a matter of course, to produce a non-confrontational regulatory approach; instrumentalism is intrinsically bound up with the pursuit of business-oriented regulation.

'Actuarial justice' is a concept utilised in criminological literature to describe the tendency towards instrumental, regulatory modes of crime governance. Writers such as David Garland (2001) have identified the development of a bifurcated criminal justice system, which combines an 'instrumental' strategy and an 'expressive' strategy. On the one hand, modern penal practices are characterised by the imposition of harsher sanctions, politicised penal policies, and the expansion of the penal infrastructure. At the same time, however, the criminal justice system incorporates a broad array of preventative and adaptive strategies (such as closed-circuit television (CCTV)), partnership-based approaches (such as community policing), and techniques of offender regulation (such as electronic tagging), all of which reflect the instrumental logic of risk regulation (Ericson and Haggerty 1997; Hudson 2003; Loader 1996; Norris and McCahill 2006; Simon 2007). This shift towards actuarialism places an emphasis on the management of risks of offending (Bottoms 1995; Feeley and Simon 1992; 1994; Loader 1996) and has three features: the emergence of a language of crime risk and probability, the limiting of the objectives of the criminal justice system to internal goals such as efficiency rather than external social goals, and the aggregation of populations into categories for the purposes of targeted intervention. The result is a criminal justice system that is preventative in its aspirations and that reflects the influence of a pervasive economics-based language of rationality, efficiency, and choice.

A preoccupation with actuarial risk measurement also drives health and safety enforcement. HSE uses enforcement databases to target those duty-holders who are regarded as unable or unwilling to manage the risks that they create (Almond 2006; Hawkins 2002: 222). This is the essence of risk-based regulation, the notion that regulation should 'involve the development of decision-making frameworks and procedures to prioritise regulatory activities and the deployment of resources... [via] assessment of the risks that regulated firms pose to the regulator's objectives' (Black 2005: 516). Such strategies operate in terms of pre-emptive risk, as quantified through the risk assessment tools at the regulator's disposal; such approaches can be responsive and dynamic, reacting to changes in behaviour, context, and outcome, and participatory, in that they co-opt the regulated into assessing performance (Black 2005; Black and Baldwin 2010). This version of risk-based regulation informs the Hampton (2005) and Macrory Reviews (2006), both of which advocated the streamlining of regulatory burdens, the focusing of resources onto high-risk duty-holders, and the restriction of adversarial enforcement to the very worst cases. Because it is aggregate performance that acts as a measure of effectiveness, deserts-based enforcement that seeks to do justice in individual cases is only pursued insofar as it helps achieve broader, instrumental goals via deterrence or persuasion. Regulators must focus intensively on those posing a high degree of risk, while leaving those assessed as posing a low level of risk to self-regulate.

But, as Black acknowledges (2005: 546), problems arise when the concerns of the system and the individuals within it conflict. Risk-based regulation is not about moral or normative desert. It aims to systematise the production of better outcomes, rather than censure specific examples of bad outcomes, because fulfilling the public interest trumps the pursuit of individual justice as a goal of the system. This raises questions about the political decisions that determine how these goals are defined: who decides which goals should take priority and what risks it is in the public interest to tolerate (Black 2005: 547)? Additionally, while prudent regulation requires that efforts be focused where they are likely to produce tangible outcomes, the result is that certain offenders are identified as particularly deserving of control. By targeting coercive enforcement on 'risky' groups in an evidence-led way, while also maintaining proactive relationships with others who are not defined as such, the regulatory system applies different standards of supervision and control to smaller and less economically powerful duty-holders, mirroring the 'othering' of marginalised individuals under the criminal law (Ashworth 2000; Braithwaite 2003; Garland 2001; Gray 2009). At the same time, larger duty-holders who are regulated as responsive partners within a risk-based regime receive the benefits of this approach via less invasive regulatory oversight. Actuarial practices can be profoundly exclusionary, but they are also inclusionary in that they allow the establishment of populations who are insulated against risk (Simon 2007). Actuarialism results in a regulatory system that is instrumental in its pursuit of change, but which also takes place on the terms of those being regulated; it constructs the regulated market by excluding rogue elements and standardising practices, but it is also conservative in terms of the use of enforcement action (Braithwaite 2008). Risk-based regulation strategies are diverse, innovative, and able to produce tangible changes in the regulated sphere, but they take place within accepted boundaries and so maintain established social relations.

Instrumentalism in the definition and measurement of work-related death

The work-related death rates constructed by health and safety authorities exist in order to provide a reliable basis for the comparative analysis of trends over time, between jurisdictions, and across industrial sectors (Eurostat 2001; HSE 2010a). In order to evaluate whether a particular regulatory intervention is effective in controlling safety risks, a stable system of comparative measurement is required; changes in recorded work-related death rates can be used to demonstrate whether this intervention works. This necessitates statistics that are robust enough to underpin such comparison; including work-related deaths involving people, places, and causes that fall outside a tightly defined sphere of paid employment (the public, accidents on the road, deaths from illness) may be more valid as a measure of the full extent of the social phenomena, but would be less reliable as a measurement tool. This 'instrumental' approach to statistics stems from a managerialist and actuarial audit culture within government (Bottoms 1995; Feeley and Simon 1992; 1994). This scaling back of ambition has a deflationary effect on the statistics, and it obscures the problem of work-related death, contributing to its political marginalisation (Tombs and Whyte 2007: 65). But what it really signals is the 'divergence' of the regulatory system from its social context: '[S]uch technocratic rationalizations tend to insulate institutions from the messy, hard-to-control demands of the social world' (Feeley and Simon 1992: 456). Lowering the statistical rate becomes the goal, not achieving social change *per se*, and the regulatory system is insulated from political threat so long as it demonstrates adequate instrumental performance on these criteria. But regulation is also increasingly left with only an 'attenuated connection with the social purposes' of regulation (Feeley and Simon 1992: 457), and this disjunction causes many of the challenges that regulators face, and explains the shift towards criminalisation.

Towards a communicative understanding of enforcement

Regulation is an explicitly social act and involves the use of law in order to fulfil particular public interest goals concerning rights, values, justice, and morality (Feintuck 2004). Regulation occurs in pursuance of a vision of the good society, and while there are conflicts in terms of the substantive form that this may take (Haines and Gurney 2003; Ogus 1994: 46; Prosser 2011), regulation nevertheless provides a means through which the law seeks to communicate a set of meanings to a range of different audiences. While regulatory enforcement and law tend not to invoke the subjective notions of normative responsibility found elsewhere in the criminal law, relying instead on 'normatively irregular' notions of objective fault (Lacey 2001: 354), they remain fundamentally concerned with the job of allocating moral 'responsibility' for outcomes arising from risk-bearing activities (Honoré 1999). The instrumental goals that a regulator pursues must be demonstrably serving the public interest if they are to be regarded as legitimate. The use of enforcement action by a regulator highlights its core values: 'prosecution is a ritualistic encounter which formally identifies the existence of a problem ... the agency publicly aligns itself with the sick and injured ... victims' (Hawkins 2002: 417). This perceived agency alignment is a crucial factor shaping the positive trust profile of safety regulators; they are seen as being on the side of the public (Walls *et al.* 2004: 139). Regulation thus promotes public interest goals by communicating a moral message about the rightness of compliance with the law.

Symbolic and expressive enforcement practices

A crucial component of a communicative understanding of regulatory law is the notion of enforcement as a symbolic process. Regulatory enforcement aims to build moral commitment on the part of the regulated; when regulatory goals are accepted as the right thing to do, they come to be regarded as valid, and so compliance is more likely (Braithwaite 2002: 32; Gunningham and Johnstone 1999; Hawkins 2002; Parker 2002; 2006; Tyler and Darley 2000). Regulatory enforcement thus takes on the role of medium for the transmission of information, and prosecution in particular cases is used to publicly express the concerns of the regulator. Enforcement is 'symbolic' in that specific cases are invested with meaning as representative of the wider normative values of the regulator; prosecution of a culpably negligent employer is not only about the specific deterrence and moral censure of that employer but also about stating that 'this sort of behaviour is not acceptable'. Perhaps the most important statement of a symbolic conception of regulatory enforcement is provided by Keith Hawkins (2002), who provides a detailed account of prosecution decision-making within the HSE. As well as documenting the 'essentially different, if related... enforcement goals' that distinguish prosecution from other forms of enforcement action (2002: 171), and HSE's limited use of prosecution as a last-resort measure, Hawkins focuses on the expressive value of prosecution. Prosecution 'is at once a public and dramatic act, one carrying with it various meanings. It is a formal and newsworthy means of announcing the enforcement of the law and the defence of public interests... The symbolic statement conveys a moral message that has a substantive content' (2002: 206).

As a form of expressive action, prosecution communicates a number of important messages about HSE and its legitimacy as an institution of social control, demonstrating that HSE is fulfilling its political, public, and legal mandate and is thus legitimate. These elements are vital in creating a positive public image of HSE. A regulator with a poor public profile and which is perceived as unreasonable will struggle to secure voluntary compliance from a resistant regulated population (Bardach and Kagan 1982). In this sense, the expressive content of enforcement assists in securing more effective fulfilment of a regulator's goals and institutional interests. This self-serving symbolism is the dominant form of expressive legalism identified by Hawkins: '[O]rganizations can turn the law to display not the law's, but their own presence; their activity, their responsiveness to the concerns of the public, and their ability to make a difference' (2002: 5). So, as an example, Hawkins identifies that HSE will not prosecute in cases where there is a risk of failure, even if it is deserved, because failed prosecutions undermine the image of invincibility that underpins HSE's 'law as last resort' strategy (2002: 298). This version of symbolic enforcement has elements of instrumentalism to it, in that public policy goals are advanced when regulators are well-regarded. This is particularly important given that health and safety regulation can appear to have a politically and legally ambiguous status (Hawkins 1984: Ch. 6; 2002; Hutter 1989: 168).

But organisational interests are not necessarily the same as instrumental public policy goals; while expressive enforcement occurs in pursuit of organisational demands, symbolic regulation acts in pursuit of a moral agenda, using enforcement to further particular conceptions of what is acceptable and desirable. From Hawkins' work, it becomes apparent that the 'morality play' of regulatory enforcement (2002: 444) is just as much about the communication of information about the institutional legitimacy of the regulator as it is about the pursuit of wider social values. This is clear from the ways in which Hawkins' discussion shifts between the two, so that 'endorsing...the symbolic constitution of social and business life' becomes a matter of 'announcing the enforcement of the law and the defence of public interests' (2002: 417). Prosecution aims at setting the instrumental behaviour of the regulator in some normative context, but this context is essentially secondary to the instrumental goals of the regulator. The alignment of regulatory activities with social values, and the imbuing of enforcement with moral meaning, is a way of enhancing the standing of the regulator, not of furthering those values *per se*. Hawkins' methodological approach is non-normative in tone, reflecting a concern with understanding the 'internal' process of decision-making, rather than evaluation of the 'external' politics of regulation, a difference of purpose that underpins some heated exchanges between Hawkins and other, more critical, scholars (Hawkins 1990; 1991; Pearce and Tombs 1990; 1991). This is an instrumental approach to symbolic regulation, where reference to moral ordering strengthens the means rather than defines the ends of the regulator.

It is submitted that there is more to be gained from a consideration of regulatory enforcement as a moral endeavour than a straightforward endorsement of the regulator's normative credentials. While responding to 'political risks' is an important part of what regulators do (Haines 2011), and demonstrates the importance of undertaking regulatory activity that legitimates the law and those who enforce it (Almond 2007), there is a deeper level of meaning here. The enforcement of safety regulation is not simply a matter of demonstrating that steps are being taken to address public concerns; it also represents a set of choices which are constitutive of, and pursuant to, an underlying set of values. It is one thing to consider whether regulators can justify their actions by reference to social understandings of right and wrong; it is another to assert that they are acting *in pursuit of* those understandings. There is a significant difference between what enforcement means in immediate terms, and what it connotes in a wider sense; a focus on institutional meanings limits our focus to the former and overlooks the latter (Gusfield 1981). This is important in explaining why the law seemingly fails to pursue these values most of the time for, as we have seen, enforcement action is used as a last resort and is not regarded as particularly significant when it is used, and many examples of illegal behaviour are neither investigated nor prosecuted. Regulatory law does not enforce moral values as actively as might be suggested. Attempting to provide an account of the substantive link between regulation and social values allows for consideration of the reasons for this lack of moral effect, as well as the substantive basis of the law's normative claims.

Habermas and communicative rationality

In seeking to understand the symbolic role of regulatory law, and why it struggles to fulfil this role, the work of Jürgen Habermas will be used to provide a theoretical basis for an account of regulation as a communicative process. Habermas' social theory presents a critical account of the rationalising tendencies of contemporary societies which sees the route towards social emancipation emerging from the establishment of more democratic and participatory decision-making structures. This 'radical democracy' provides a means of freeing individuals from capitalist domination, while also respecting the agency of individuals (Outhwaite 1996: 18). Such an account can help us in reconciling the aspirational goals and political limitations of regulatory law, as well as its communicative potential and instrumentalist tendencies. Habermas' social theory is structured around two core concepts; the first of these is the notion of 'communicative rationality', or the establishment of value-pluralistic decision-making as a basis for legitimate government. Rather than rooting rationality and truth in ideological, religious, or moral precepts, Habermas sees rationality as emerging through a process of open and rational debate and agreement within the public sphere of society. When individuals enter into discussion over matters of social importance, they do so based upon certain presuppositions about the truth, sincerity, and appropriateness of their 'speech-acts' (Habermas 1984; 1987). Individuals explain and discuss their positions, and this process of deliberation results in a rationally motivated consensus over general interests which provide a valid and reasoned basis for the decisions made. It is democratic and deliberative communicative engagement that underpins the legitimacy of social decision-making processes, not individualistic interest claims.

The implication of this approach for public policy-making in an area such as criminal law is that all decisions taken in pursuit of public interests should seek to give effect to deliberative processes; social practices are legitimate when they reflect the preferences of the wider public, as established through rational debate. So rather than justifying a policy on the basis of its substantive content such as adherence to community values (a process which is disputed in pluralist societies and abused in totalitarian ones), Habermas sees the legitimation process in 'procedural' terms. It is the connection to public processes of rational–critical debate, the 'will of the people', that renders an outcome valid. Because Habermas requires that stringent criteria be met before public debate can be regarded as deliberative (it must be 'rational', 'open', and inclusive, and 'ongoing' or revisable), his approach retains a commitment to principles of civil rights and bureaucratic legal norms even as it acknowledges the value pluralism that postmodernists regard as undermining truth claims (Simon 1994: 949; Weaver 2009: 15). It is possible to recognise the autonomous freedom of individuals to determine outcomes in line with their own values and interests, while also requiring that basic principles of rationality, reason, and civil rights be observed and retaining a commitment to the truth of the justifications provided for social action. In this way, contemporary policy-making can continue to be guided by Enlightenment values of reason.

The second core theme of Habermas' work is the notion that modern societies are divisible into two component parts, the 'system' and the 'lifeworld', distinct spheres which together form the social world. By 'lifeworld', Habermas refers to the everyday mutual understandings, values, and interactions that form the basis of informal social relations (1987: Ch. VI/1). Institutions such as the family, community, culture, and media all constitute the sphere of shared experiences, beliefs, cultural knowledge, and values (Weaver 2009: 11). As such, the lifeworld is the sphere of social action where forms of communicative rationality should predominate, given its emphasis on shared meaning. In contrast, Habermas uses the term 'system' to connote the established social sub-systems of instrumental activity, such as those of money (the capitalist economic system) and power (the formal political system), which stand alongside, and overlay, the lifeworld (1987: Ch. VI/2). These system imperatives are 'steering' media, functionally independent components which facilitate integration by coordinating action, allowing for the successful completion of day-to-day activities where deliberative discussion is not practical or desirable (for example, the coordination of traffic on the motorway system: Simon 1994: 948). The sub-systems of money and power are integrative in that they structure patterns of behaviour so as to serve the interests of the economy and ensure the material reproduction of society. But while the lifeworld is based on communicative action, the system is independent, functional, and strategic. Rather than seeking mutual agreement, the system aims to intervene effectively in a state of affairs or the decisions of others; it is fundamentally instrumental in nature.

Habermas also diagnoses a particular malady in the development of modern societies, namely, the colonisation of the lifeworld by system imperatives (1987; 1988; 1992). In complex societies, maintaining the required functional social integration becomes increasingly difficult. The lifeworld struggles to perform this role alone; shared conceptions of morality fail to provide good reasons to wear seatbelts, for instance, so system imperatives prompt the development of bureaucratic rules and regulations, providing an additional basis for social coordination. What concerns Habermas is the tendency for system imperatives to become disembedded and uncoupled from their social lifeworld contexts (echoing Polanyi's analysis of the disembedding of self-regulating markets: 1944). This uncoupling allows systems of instrumental action to increase in density and complexity and to expand into areas of social action previously governed by the lifeworld, such as family, culture, media, and leisure. The instrumental rationality of the system removes decision-making from the hands of a deliberative public and passes it to bureaucrats and market forces. Accordingly, 'in modern societies, economic and bureaucratic spheres emerge in which social relations are regulated only via money and power. Norm-conformative attitudes and identity-forming social memberships are neither necessary nor possible in these spheres' (1987: 154); systemic rationality predominates, to the exclusion of the processes of mutual understanding that underpin social solidarity. This colonisation occurs as a form of crisis-management; when the 'padding of capitalist modernisation wears through' (Habermas 1988: 215), conflicts emerge which threaten the future of the economic and political systems. The pacification of these conflicts requires that contentious issues be reframed as problems of rationality, which can then be resolved via the application of instrumental reasoning. The appropriate outcome is, therefore, the one that is bureaucratically most correct and economically most efficient.

This results in the reduction of social actors to instrumental roles as consumers, employees, and subjects of decision-making processes rather than participants in them (Habermas 1988: 217). Decision-making becomes the preserve of professional elites, and public policy is reduced to a series of technical questions for experts to resolve (Loader 1996: 33). Individuals become passive, demoralised, and alienated from decision-making processes; for example, Habermas describes how social security systems provide support to disadvantaged people, but at the same time categorise and means-test them, and conceptualise their needs in purely monetary terms. Individuals are distanced from decisions made about them, and social support networks are replaced by bureaucratic systems that treat individuals as consumers or users rather than participants or citizens (Habermas 1988: 208–213; also Carlsson 2002: 84). The pacification of a potential conflict results in the pathologising of the lifeworld and the disintegration of social life. The systems of money and power are predicated upon principles of instrumental reasoning; they are strategic, seeking to serve the economic and political interests embedded within their operation. As such, they require that all decisions be justified in terms of instrumental economic rationality, profitability, and bureaucratic efficiency. But these instrumental goals relate to the interests of specific actors, not values agreed by all via a process of communicative action. This is hazardous; in Habermas' terms, 'the lifeworld ... gets cut down more and more to one subsystem among others. In the process, system mechanisms get further and further detached from the social structures through which social integration takes place' (1987: 154). The colonisation of the lifeworld becomes self-fulfilling, as further areas must be instrumentalised in order to divert potential crises of legitimacy. But this is unsustainable; for Habermas, the result is the perpetual expansion of the state infrastructure and the legitimatory burdens that are placed upon it, and a further increase in the potential for crises of legitimacy.

So, to summarise, Habermas posits the need for the creation of radically democratic political processes in order to root the bureaucratic power of political and economic systems in the shared values of the lifeworld. The alternative is for these political and economic systems to operate independently, dominating human activity in pursuit of their own interests. By recognising the capacity for system imperatives to allow the interests of economic and political power to dominate the lives of individuals, Habermas acknowledges the conflicts that underpin critical theory. Society is a system that constrains individuals, as it is for Marxist theory, structuring outcomes for those subject to it. But Habermas' approach to these issues of domination moves beyond the determinism of traditional Marxist theory, focusing on normative structure and the influence of the spheres of mass democracy, the welfare state, and government intervention, in shaping class conflicts (1984: Part IV). Contemporary capitalism must be understood as a system whose meaning is socially constructed via more sophisticated means than simple hegemonic domination. The same bureaucratic social institutions that constrain individuals also have the potential to emancipate them through the development of stronger forms of democracy.

Habermas and regulatory enforcement

Several efforts have been made to use Habermas' theory to establish the case for a deliberative approach to criminal justice (Dzur and Mirchandani 2007; Hudson 2003; Loader 1996; Weaver 2009). Law exists, for Habermas, as a system of positive and coercive norms which have an integrative function in allowing complex societies to reproduce themselves, even in the face of conflicts between the individuals who constitute it (Habermas 1992: 8; Fraser 2001: 366). Law is uniquely placed to integrate the system and the lifeworld because it is a system of both coercive and positive norms; it constitutes a series of commands backed up by sanctions which prompt strategic compliance, constrain action, and provide good reasons to obey. At the same time, however, law is legitimate because it gives effect to rational agreements, based on communicative action, which provide a democratic basis for those constraints (Habermas 1992: 447). Within a complex and fragmented society, law generalises the normative principles that arise from deliberative face-to-face agreement and applies them universally to 'everyone', even those who were not party to the original agreement (Carlsson 2002: 90). Law supplies the administrative capacity required to give effect to the democratic deliberative impulses of the public sphere, legitimating the economic, bureaucratic, and regulatory systems (Habermas 1992: 169). Law can do this because it 'removes the task of social integration from the actors and, at the same time, sets the medium through which communicative action can become operative in the context of highly differentiated social environments' (Palti 1998: 1021). Laws are perpetuated by the communicative norms that inform their creation; lawmaking must therefore be rooted in a communicative ethic because 'only those statutes may claim legitimacy that can meet with the assent of all citizens in a discursive process of legislation that has in turn been legally constituted' (Habermas 1992: 110). By imposing legal coercions and also identifying moral reasons to justify those coercions, law connects the rules governing social order to citizens' value orientations.

Habermas and criminal law

Scholars have drawn on Habermas' social theory in the criminal law context in two ways (Hudson 2003), highlighting, firstly, the need for policy to have a deliberative basis in the lifeworld and, secondly, the need for outcomes to reflect communicative action principles. A significant body of literature analysing the contemporary politics of law and order has asserted that public attitudes display an increasing tendency towards punitiveness (Garland 2001; Lacey 2008), emotiveness (Pratt 2000), and intolerance, and that these attitudes fundamentally influence criminal justice policy-making (Bottoms 1995; Roberts *et al.* 2003; Simon 2007). Habermasian conceptions of deliberative lawmaking have been applied to demonstrate that these punitive sentiments do not reflect the kind of open, rational debate that constitutes communicative action (Bal 1996; Deflem 1994; Dzur and Mirchandani 2007; Loader 1996; Weaver 2009). A system that pursues democratically grounded action is required (Deflem 1994: 368) to ensure that agencies such as the police act as 'moral institutions' (Loader 1996: 158) concerned not only with instrumental crime control but also with the protection of democratic values of justice, civil rights, and legitimacy. Secondly, the criminal justice system can be understood as an instrumental system in the Habermasian sense; it has an increasingly ends-oriented culture, reflected in the use of performance indicators, a problem-oriented approach to crime, and the status of bureaucratic efficiency as a core virtue (Bottoms 1995; Feeley and Simon 1992; 1994; Loader 1996). This is a corollary of the punitiveness identified above (Garland 2001) and can be attributed to the process of juridification that Habermas identifies. This issue extends to disposals in particular cases; Weaver (2009) argues that deliberative input is required to counterbalance exclusionary sentencing practices, and punishment should aim to communicate both with those being punished and with wider society about the nature of the wrongdoing in question (Duff 2001). Communicative sentencing would utilise principles associated with restorative justice to move the focus away from the instrumental control of offending and towards the facilitation of law-abiding behaviour via deliberative, participatory, communicative action.

Habermas and regulatory enforcement

Regulation also provides fertile ground for the application of Habermasian notions of communicative action because it involves normatively motivated intervention in areas of economic activity that are dominated by system imperatives. In Hawkins' terms, 'regulatory agencies must... preserve the sometimes fragile balance between the interests of economic activity on the one hand and the public welfare on the other' (1984: 9). Regulatory law is a system of rules which play an important social coordination role, ensuring standards of behaviour and reciprocal rights-recognition within a complex society, and using the threat of sanctions to generalise these obligations to all (Habermas 1992). As such, regulation is a core component of the administrative, managerial, rationalising modern state (Teubner 1987). Regulation is also instrumental. It operates as a steering mechanism, coordinating the operation of sub-systems of money and power (employment, financial markets, and business activity) so as to manage structural risks[1] and ensure the future reproduction of those systems (Habermas 1988: 212). Regulation diverts economic and political issues that might provoke conflicts into the social and legal spheres, where they can be mitigated via socialised welfare provision and resolved through reference to legal norms (Habermas 1976: 186). This process of juridification, or the extension of regulation to an ever-wider range of policy areas (Habermas 1992; Teubner 1987), has seen regulatory governance emerge as a key means of state intervention.

It has been suggested that the period since the early 1980s has seen neo-liberal governance assuming dominance across much of the Western world (Harvey 2005), including in criminal justice (Garland 2001; O'Malley 1999) and regulatory contexts (Tombs and Whyte 2007; 2010). Neo-liberalism preaches the need for economic freedom and limited governmental intervention into markets, and a state which protects the integrity of property rights via social and political security (the 'free economy and the strong state': Gamble 1994). But this period also saw a proliferation of regulatory agencies and a significant increase in the amount of regulation being passed into law within these jurisdictions (Braithwaite 2008; Levi-Faur 2005). Majone (1997) argues that a shift has occurred from the post-war ideal of the 'positive state', characterised by redistributive policy-making, welfarism, and macroeconomic management, to a new 'regulatory state' paradigm, where economic liberalisation, policy integration, and delegated government are the dominant goals (also Baldwin and Black 2008; Bartle and Vass 2007; Black 2000; 2001; 2005; Levi-Faur 2005). The growth of regulation is a direct outcome of these policy choices; if governments are not running industries, providing services, or holding administrative responsibility centrally, then regulation, an arms-length method of coordination, becomes a natural policy choice. Crucially, the factors that Majone highlights also link to Habermas' thesis about lifeworld colonisation. The regulatory state is characterised by a high degree of institutional complexity, a commitment to administrative efficiency, a central decision-making role for experts, and the predominance of economic rationality (Majone 1997: 150–162). Regulation-at-a-distance allows for the exertion of arms-length control rather than direct intervention, and for the coordination of action in pursuit of defined goals. It is insulated from the normative influence of the social sphere, appears less intensive than direct government (Bartle and Vass 2007), and does not require substantive justification because it is procedurally justified by the legality of the process through which it is constituted.

The problem, though, as Habermas points out, is that the goals of the state, in this formulation, are defined with primary reference to the interests of systems of money and power (1988; 1992). And the fact that validation is internalised (on procedural grounds) rather than externalised (on substantive grounds) means that regulatory systems can become dominated by the instrumental rationality of system imperatives, resulting in a demoralised system of law which is increasingly distant from the interests of the community. When this happens, law can no longer legitimate itself because it cannot justify the constraints it imposes via reference to a process of communicative action (Habermas 1992: 33). In Habermas' terms, 'every effective belief in legitimacy is assumed to have an immanent relation to truth ... that can be tested' (1973: 97); the law's legitimacy relies upon this demonstrable connection back to the normative structures which sustain it (Habermas 1992: 461). A form of 'legitimation crisis' (Habermas 1973) results when government is unable to represent the steering role taken in relation to the economic and political system as being in accordance with general social interests. As a result, it is necessary for the instrumental functions of law to be rooted in a process of democratic value-formation within the lifeworld if it is to remain legitimate.

Systems of regulation such as those governing workplace safety are instrumental and rational in nature, providing a degree of managerial oversight of standards through the establishment (via legislation such as the HSWA 1974) of enforceable requirements. This occurs in order to mitigate the negative side effects of industrialisation and employment, specifically risks of workplace death, injury, and ill health. The basis of this project can be traced back to an emergent commitment to the extension of protective coverage to a wider enfranchised citizenry in accordance with collectivist ideals, as well as the pragmatic legitimacy concerns of government (Almond 2007; Carson 1979). An instrumental approach to regulation is the only way to ensure that these obligations, values, and commitments are generalised to all. But this will not suffice on its own because such a system of law does not possess the normative foundation necessary to legitimate it. This link should be provided via processes of communicative action, deliberative democratic input into the creation of safety laws that establishes that they reflect the will of all citizens. This may take the form of a 'thick' proceduralisation (Black 2000; 2001), participatory processes that promote mutuality, consensus, and understanding between all subjects. But they also need to engage in activities that give expression to the moral values of the lifeworld. Only by demonstrating their centrality to regulatory processes can the law be legitimated as a valid expression of the public will. Law must be normative and must *be seen* to be normative.

This is where enforcement activity comes in. Enforcement constitutes the most direct way in which a regulatory agency can communicate moral messages, and safety regulators are particularly attuned to prosecution's potential as to express their commitment to a particular normative position (Almond 2007; Gunningham and Rees 1997; Hawkins 1984; 2002; Parker 2006). It also allows for the fulfilment of public interest goals which are not purely instrumental in nature and which go beyond the scope of market correctives (Feintuck 2004). Regulation occurs in pursuance of a vision of the good society (Haines and Gurney 2003; Ogus 1994); this is more wide-ranging than Hawkins' institutional version of symbolic regulation because the advertisement of the regulator's position is of secondary importance to the advancement of the values that underpin that position. The outcome is the establishment of the moral rightness of the law itself, not the enhancement of the status of the regulator (although the two may coincide; Almond 2007; Haines and Gurney 2003; Hawkins 2002; Parker 2006).

If regulation is to be viewed as action in pursuit of normative values, the next question to be asked is what these values might be, or whether they are a contingent 'black hole' into which political preferences can be slotted (Prosser 2006: 377). Many accounts of regulation frame the process in procedural terms, as a way of fulfilling legislative mandates, ensuring accountability and due process and giving effect to expertise (Baldwin 1995; Baldwin and Cave 1999: Ch. 6; Sunstein 1990: Ch. 5). As with the correction of market failure, *some* regulatory interventions reflect these procedural considerations, but not *all*; regulation goes beyond safeguarding the economic interests and procedural rights of citizens and promotes the sort of collective community concerns that the liberal-democratic state marginalises (Feintuck 2004: 59). For Habermas, the process of democratic will-formation that underpins law-creation is of primary importance (1984; 1987); as long as the principles that guide the exercise of power emerge via deliberative discourse, and can be agreed to by all citizens, it does not necessarily matter what those principles are. Enforcement practices should reach outcomes that are consistent with the substantive preferences that communicative action arrives at.

Consequently, many scholars argue for versions of responsive regulation which prioritise positive communicative interactions and 'regulatory conversations' (Black 2002) between regulator and regulated (Aalders and Wilthagen 1997; Ayres and Braithwaite 1992; Baldwin and Black 2008; Black and Baldwin 2010; Braithwaite 2002; Gunningham and Grabosky 1998; Gunningham and Johnstone 1999; May and Burby 1998; Parker 2002). A thickly proceduralised system of regulation, which brings participants together in deliberative dialogue, will be more democratic and consensual and less open to domination by system imperatives (Black 2000: 598). This will make it more able to facilitate 'the permeability of private organizational systems and social power directly to civil society and the public sphere' (Parker 2002: 40), thus rendering the economic sphere answerable to the lifeworld. Such an approach can foster a greater degree of internalised corporate responsibility and virtue and moral commitment to the law (Ayres and Braithwaite 1992; Black 2001; Gunningham and Rees 1997; Haines 1997; Parker 2002). The influence of the social sphere acts as a check on the dominance of economic interests within a 'demoralised' system of regulation, and as a driver of 'good' regulation, in instrumental and normative terms (Haines 2011: 14–20).

The second component of a communicative approach to regulation is to establish a substantive normative basis for enforcement action in pursuit of a particular goal. Although Habermas' theory is notionally procedural in nature, and so value-free, both the qualifying conditions placed on communicative action (that it be rational, open, and ongoing) and the role given to law (as a medium for the generalisation of deliberative norms) prioritise an integrative, solidarity-building conception of law. Law functions as medium of a socio-normative endeavour which is progressive, inclusive, and pursuant to the goal of social justice (Simon 1994). Writers within the 'civic republican' tradition view regulation as occurring in pursuit of substantive goals, including ensuring equality of citizenship, tackling social subordination, and strengthening procedural principles such as the rule of law, with the overarching goal of increasing freedom as a form of non-domination (Braithwaite 2008; Feintuck 2004; Sunstein 1990). There are disagreements about how far different regulatory regimes act pursuant to these goals (Gilboy 1995; Hawkins 1984; 2002; Hutter 1997; Hutter and Manning 1990) but, while it may be realised to varying degrees, the overarching goal of much regulation is the advancement of social interests, particularly those relating to the participation of individuals within social structures.

Regulatory enforcement is the means through which this commitment to social justice is made explicit. Because it involves the delivery of a declarative moral judgement, enforcement action brings the moral basis of regulation to the fore, restating that the law matters, that breaching it is wrong, and why this is so. When regulatory law cannot give effect to these values, it lacks legitimacy, and this undermines its standing (Almond 2007; Haines and Gurney 2003). Enforcement action links the regulatory system back to the basis of public will-formation which underpins it, and so 'moralises' it, demonstrating that it is responsive to the legitimating input of public will-formation. Enforcement action is a public act and brings issues of risk to life in the public sphere (Hutter and Lloyd-Bostock 1992; Walls *et al.* 2004), signalling disruptions to the ordinary course of events and reflecting public concerns about the risks inherent in modern society. At the same time, enforcement action has another level of meaning. Because it tends to be reactive in focus, it does not take place in order to achieve some future state of affairs; rather, it occurs in order to say something about that which has gone before. This sets it apart from most regulatory activities, which tend to be future-focused, and this means that while it *can* be used to fulfil instrumental goals via deterrence or incapacitation, it can exist independently of any consideration of future outcomes. Enforcement action occurs because it is deserved as a response to conduct which is wrongful and breaches the shared values of society (Ashworth 2000; Duff 2001: 58). It declares past conduct as wrong and imposes a penalty that reinforces this moral judgement independent of any consideration of future outcomes. It is a form of purposive communication, censuring past offences as well as reconciling the offender with reasons to obey the law which reflect the values of the normative political community (Duff 2001: 88).

Existing accounts of regulation have a tendency, regardless of their position along the 'compliance/deterrence' continuum, to conceptualise the enforcement action in instrumental, ends-driven terms; it occurs *in order to* deter offenders or *in order to* buttress compliance with the law. They lose sight of the need for enforcement to communicate the censure which the normative political community perceives as appropriate. It happens because it *should*, not because it serves a wider purpose. This is important if regulatory enforcement is to aspire to the status of criminal law, which health and safety offences do, although they are not necessarily perceived as such (Almond 2008; Almond and Colover 2010; Home Office 2005: para. 58; Walls *et al.* 2004). Andrew Ashworth argues that the instrumentalism of responsive regulation (such as the version advanced via John Braithwaite's work) has the potential to 'lead to an unacceptably distorted system in which the prospects of effectiveness and prevention, not the seriousness of the wrongdoing, would determine decisions to criminalise... the aim should be to produce a set of criminal laws that penalise substantial wrongdoing and only substantial wrongdoing' (2000: 250).

As such, enforcement action cannot be represented simply in terms of what it achieves; it matters because of what it *means* as an expression of shared values. Of course, not all regulatory laws can be understood in this way; many possess a purely instrumental rationale. It would be counterproductive to frame these rules in communicative terms because the moral leveraging of offences only makes sense when the law is backed up by social norms confirming that the conduct in question is morally unacceptable (Parker 2006: 604; also Ayres and Braithwaite 1992: 36). But where there is a license to regulate in moral terms, regulatory enforcers must incorporate considerations of substantive legitimacy into their decisions. It is action at the top of the enforcement pyramid, where the law gives direct effect to the judgements of the public sphere by enforcing 'because it should', which legitimates the regulatory system as a whole (Almond 2007: 304; Ayres and Braithwaite 1992; Braithwaite 2002: 30; Parker 2006: 617) and so advances the overarching goals of the regulatory project.

Conclusion

A. Habermasian framework helps us to understand the competing tendencies encountered in the field of regulatory enforcement and the communicative nature of enforcement action. Regulatory systems impose coercive obligations in order to achieve measurable outcomes relating to the protection of workers and the public, but they are dominated by an instrumental rationality that reflects the dominance of systems of money and power in shaping and constraining regulatory practices. While instrumental systems of regulation serve wider social interests by securing outcomes that benefit the economy and society as a whole, the nature of that system distances it from the normative basis in communicative action it requires to sustain it. Enforcement action expresses these normative values in a communicative form; it restates the moral reasons for regulating and places the instrumental regulatory system in some form of normative context. Visible enforcement in cases where justice dictates that action be taken legitimates the regulatory system, linking it to the socio-cultural lifeworld in a manner that renders it democratically valid. While regulatory systems can be made more effective in their instrumental commitments to compliance, this must be accompanied by the rooting of those systems in their normative context. Enforcement activity, the symbolic restatement of a defendant's actions as wrongful and the moral basis for regulation, performs this role.

4
Regulating Work-Related Death – A History

As the previous chapters have demonstrated, work-related deaths have become important objects of legal regulation. This process has been piecemeal and shaped by context-specific considerations and events, including particular work-related deaths. This book aims to establish that the regulation of work-related 'death', as a specific component of the criminal law, is a distinctive contemporary development which reflects the socio-cultural limitations of established regulatory systems. This makes it necessary to explore where the sources of those limitations, and of this instrumentalism, lie within the history of safety regulation. This chapter will overview the development of safety regulation within the UK as a case-study, partly because safety regulation emerged there first but also because the UK has subsequently been the site of the most decisive contemporary development towards the use of criminal law as a regulatory tool. It will show that while much of the impetus towards the development of health and safety regulation was provided by welfarist political concerns, it was also a response to the needs of a free-market economic system. The regulatory system that was constructed succeeded in addressing these issues via centralised structures of oversight and control, but lacked the capacity to communicate effectively the normative reasons for regulating that underpinned it.

In setting out this account, two thematic schemas have been used. The first is a 'three-wave' model of regulatory development, which posits that safety regulation passed through three distinct stages as it progressed towards its current form (Braithwaite 2008; Tucker 1995): market-based regulation by individuals, weak command-and-control state regulation, and participatory self-regulation. It has been suggested that there is now a shift towards a 'fourth wave', which moves the burden of regulating away from the state and towards the regulated

(Bartle and Vass 2007; Black 2005; 2007). This model allows us to identify how the reform of safety laws has been driven by systematic patterns of economic need, democratic expansionism, and political pressure. The second organising principle is the model of juridification or expansion of law's role in the organisation of social relations, advanced by Habermas (1988). He identifies four loose historical stages through which the expansion of law has passed; the 18th-century bourgeois state, the early-19th-century constitutional state, the late-19th-century democratic constitutional state, and the 20th-century social and democratic constitutional state (1988: 205). Habermas' framework reconciles critical accounts of regulation as an outcome of economic power relations (Carson 1979; Tombs and Whyte 2007; Tucker 1995) with others portraying it as a progressive movement of collective advancement (Bartrip and Hartwell 1997; Braithwaite 2008; Hutter 1997: 30–34). The emphasis on the densification of law also links to the literature on regulatory proliferation as a component of the neo-liberal state (Black 2000; Braithwaite 2008; Levi-Faur 2005; Majone 1997).

The first wave: Regulation and legal personhood

While the emergence of the regulatory state is typically linked to the Industrial Revolution (Bartrip and Hartwell 1997: 45; Braithwaite 2008: 14; Dicey 1914), its antecedents go back much further. For example, the Statute of Labourers of 1351 was introduced to alleviate labour shortages resulting from the Black Death by limiting labourers' bargaining power and imposing wage restrictions, with similar measures introduced elsewhere in Europe (Cohn 2007; Lewis 1976). But the emergence of true regulatory government came later; Ogus (1992) describes a strong regulatory tendency within 16th- and 17th-century England, when statutes were passed governing trade, agriculture, and employment. The bulk of this early regulation was economic in nature and concerned the protection of the emergent mercantile sphere. This was the period in which national markets were beginning to emerge, making state-level regulation necessary to replace the local controls that existed previously; despite this, it was left to private prosecutions and local bodies (parishes and Guilds) to enforce regulations (Braithwaite 2008: 12; Harcourt 2010; Holdsworth 1938: 163; Ogus 1992: 15–17; Polanyi 1944: 67), and this localised model endured until the end of the 18th century (Emsley 1987: 138). This was what Habermas (1988: 205) referred to as the 'absolutist' bourgeois state, a political order that facilitated the transfer from feudal to capitalist economy by regulating relations between commodity owners and guaranteeing the liberty of legal persons as autonomous beings. Additionally, regulatory oversight was part of the general policing function of the day. It was the general constables and local watches who oversaw the conduct of commerce, along with the protection of property and prevention of violence (Harcourt 2010; Zedner 2006). This is referred to by Braithwaite as the 'police economy', a period when the governance of markets and the moral disciplining of the poor were not treated as distinct functions (2003: 10).

By the late 18th century, the economy had moved towards industrialism on a grander scale, with a significant increase in the number of people employed in heavy industries such as mining, iron and steel production, and textile manufacture (Briggs 1959: 21–25), and the rapid expansion of cities as the population moved to work in the new factories. While earlier regulations such as the 1351 Statute and the Statute of Artificers of 1563 had addressed work, these measures were designed to force people *into* work and dictate the terms of that employment, not to ensure their wellbeing once working (Hutchins and Harrison 1911: 2; Ogus 1992: 10; Polanyi 1944: Ch. 8). The first 'protectionist' regulatory interventions did not occur until the 1780s when Acts of Parliament gave legal protection to children and apprentices who had been ill-treated by their employers (Hutchins and Harrison 1911: 9; Ward 1962: 19). Young workers were regarded as 'the cheapest raw material on the market' (Kydd 1857: vol. 1, 16; Thomas 1948: 7), and suffered appalling conditions, with death, disease, and cruelty rampant.[1] The market in child labour was a direct outcome of the Poor Laws of the preceding 250 years, which had placed the burden of supporting paupers and their children onto parish rate-payers, who were only too keen to pass this financial liability onto private enterprise by shipping children into the factory system (Carson 1979: 39; Thomas 1948: 7). Similarly, the market in apprentices was created by the protectionist stipulations of the Statute of Artificers, which established and safeguarded apprenticeship as the route into employment in skilled trades, which in turn created a ready supply of cheap labour (Polanyi 1944: 86). This underlines the role played by regulation in *constituting* the market in labour, aiming to ensure the stable supply of employable workers. Governments of this period saw no problem in intervening in the market to restrict the bargaining rights of workers; it would take time before they felt able to also restrict the demands that employers made of workers in return.

The regulation of workplace safety was not really a legal issue before 1800. While civil law allowed members of the public injured by the actions of employees or tradesmen to obtain damages under the tort of trespass to the person (Gregory 1951; Stein 2008), and an employer could be liable for the negligent actions of his employees, it was not until 1837 that a worker managed to sue his employer for work-related injury.[2] Prior to this, the employer–employee relationship was purely governed by the terms of the contract of employment; Tucker identifies this as the first wave of regulation, whereby employees were assumed to be freely contracting agents, and therefore capable of voluntarily undertaking the hazards associated with work (1995: 246). As Alger puts it,

> if the dangers created by . . . the master's indifference to the safety of his men, were in the eyes of the latter too great to be endured with prudence, then, being under this theory a 'free agent' to go or to stay, if he chose to stay he must take the possible consequences of personal injury or death.
>
> (1900: 397)

This is the basis of the maxim *volenti non fit injuria*, which defined the employer–employee relationship. Not only did this approach assume that employers and employees shared the requisite knowledge to allow free contracting (Banks 2009: 131), it also ignored the pressures to enter into work that resulted from the Poor Laws, which offered very little support to unwaged paupers. As a result, risk was a commodity to be priced and distributed between contracting parties rather than a social evil to be controlled.

Industrialisation and urbanisation led to significant problems of integration within these new urban environments as the informal mechanisms of social control that facilitated local policing were lost. This led to an increase in crime in the cities; the response was the creation of an increasingly formalised police force, focused on thief-taking and disorder (Emsley 1987: 175; Zedner 2006), and this marked the first step in the differentiation of regulatory offending from the 'disciplining of the poor' (Braithwaite 2008: 13). This was reinforced by the emergence of a dominant *laissez-faire* conception of the state as safeguarding the conditions within which markets could exist but avoiding interfering in their operation. As such, the policing of social order and the protection of property rights were legitimate avenues for state regulation, as these issues affect the ability of citizens to engage freely in the economy, but the restriction of the terms of that engagement was not (Braithwaite 2008: 13; Dicey 1914; Polanyi 1944: 111). Workplace safety regulation was *laissez-faire* in the sense that market forces were left to regulate risk, and the state avoided assuming any responsibility in relation to the labour market except ensuring the stability of its social context (Alger 1900: 397; Bartrip and Hartwell 1997: 45; Ward 1962: 8). Habermas identifies this bourgeois state as guaranteeing legal personhood but not granting substantive rights to citizens beyond ensuring security and the ability to compete for scarce resources; this is why regulation in this period limited itself to the establishment of rules that safeguard the market and provide for the 'institutionalization of money and power' (1988: 206). The non-regulation of safety reflects the limited nature of citizenship at this stage in the shift from feudal to industrial society; workers were autonomous legal persons, but not possessors of protected rights.

The early second wave: Regulation and the state

By common consensus, the start of workplace safety regulation can be traced to the Health and Morals of Apprentices Act 1802 (Bartrip and Fenn 1983; Carson 1979; Hutchins and Harrison 1911; Ward 1962). The new legislation reflected a growing recognition of two factors; first that workplaces as harsh as the factories of the early Industrial Revolution were a direct cause of illness, injury, and death (reflected in the Manchester Board of Health's inquiry of 1796: Thomas 1948: 8). This led to pressure from social reformers, including clergymen, medical practitioners, magistrates, and others, for controls to limit the excesses of the factory system (Dicey 1914: 109; Ward 1962: 19). The influence of these moral concerns was relatively limited (although see Kydd 1857: vol. 1, 33); Sir Robert Peel, in creating the new Act, ignored the influences of 'people who, in his opinion, were governed more by humanity than by a knowledge of the business' (Thomas 1948: 9). The second factor was the impact of these harms upon the availability of a healthy workforce. Peel recognised that the injury rates in his own factories (he employed 1000 children) were liable to have a negative effect on the productivity of his business (Carson 1979: 39; Thomas 1948: 9); this explains the 1802 Act's focus on maintaining health rather than guaranteeing safety. The Act limited the working day of apprentices to 12 hours and made employers liable for the provision of clothing, accommodation, education, and medical treatment. Factories were inspected by external visitors, who would assess conditions and compliance with the Act; these visitors were usually Justices of the Peace and clergymen, and reported to the Quarter Sessions (courts). Failure to fulfil the terms of the Act would result in a fine of £5 and £10, and employers were entreated to 'act in strict conformity to the said rules and regulations' (Bartrip and Fenn 1983: 203; Thomas 1948: 11).

Taken together, however, the terms of the Act gave only limited protections to workers and did not improve safety *per se* (Bartrip and Hartwell 1997: 51). The Act was not enforced with any degree of rigour and failed to change the behaviour of employers to any great extent. The system of inspection put in place proved wholly inadequate, with the visitors proving unable or unwilling to perform their duties with any thoroughness, partly from fear of antagonising mill-owners, and partly because they had little real power (Bartrip and Fenn 1983: 203; Hutchins and Harrison 1911: 18; Thomas 1948: 12; Ward 1962: 20). In practice, few factories were ever inspected, and the law was little known; by 1816 the Act had withered on the vine. In addition, the Act did not apply to anyone other than apprentice workers in large textile factories. The right to employ children in dangerous roles was not challenged, and no questions were raised about the issue of liability for harm. The 1802 Act was, in many ways, not a real piece of factory legislation, but rather an extension of the existing Poor Laws (Mess 1926: 3; Dicey 1914: 110). By 1815, the earlier Act was obsolete; innovations in steam-power meant that factories could be erected in towns and cities and a new urban labour force was suddenly available for employment. This meant that the apprentice workers covered by the 1802 Act had been replaced by a new workforce who were not protected (Carson 1979: 40; Hutchins and Harrison 1911: 19; Thomas 1948: 16–17). Additionally, the dominance of the textile industry was being surpassed by other manufacturing industries, meaning that the 1802 Act's focus needed extension.

Peel's suggested reforms, including the imposition of minimum age requirements and maximum hours of work for all child labourers, and the introduction of a formalised inspectoral system, were blocked by representatives of business, who claimed that child workers would be impoverished if their employment was limited, that there was no conclusive evidence that such employment was bad for them, and that to interfere in such matters was an unjustified restraint of free trade (Carson 1979: 40; Kydd 1857: vol. 1, Chs. 3–5; Thomas 1948: 21; Ward 1962: 24–28). These employers succeeded in ensuring that the subsequent Cotton Mills and Factories Act 1819 was limited in scope (Hutchins and Harrison 1911: 20–24). Crucially, the resistance of capital to these reforms was the first sign of coordinated opposition to intervention; this was the start of the 'unregulable liberal economy' and the 'militant creed' of *laissez-faire* that underpinned it (Polanyi 1944: Ch. 12; Braithwaite 2008; Dicey 1914). The 1819 Act highlights the constraint of legislative ambition in relation to health and safety, and the limits of the benevolent Tory paternalism to which Dicey (1914) attributed the success of the 1802 Act. Subsequent legislation, in 1825 and 1831, limited itself to addressing working hours and the welfare of child workers within the mill system. These Acts did begin to establish a communicative and publicity-oriented role for law, requiring that copies of the Act be displayed in workplaces and increasing the penalties that could be imposed for breaches of the law. However, as Carson observes, 'What is important... is the fact, unanimously agreed upon by historians who have addressed the question, that they were almost uniformly ineffectual' (1979: 40). And yet, at the same time as these Acts were being passed, there was an emergent sense that the seriousness of the problems associated with the factory system justified the giving of protective rights to workers; commentators identified moral justifications for intervention to ensure that industry served society's interests, and not vice versa.

The rights-based nature of this development is evident from the comparisons drawn between factory workers and slaves, particularly in the context of the abolitionist movement of the time (Hutchins and Harrison 1911: 33; Kydd 1857: vol. 1, 95; Mess 1926: 3; Thomas 1948: 28; Ward 1962: 30).[3] This was an early sign of the emergence of a conception of the state as a rights-granting executive power, taking a protective role in relation to the rights of individuals in accordance with Habermas' (1988) notion of the bourgeois constitutional state. The granting of rights-based protection to workers within the sphere of health and safety fitted this model, but it would be some time before worker rights were effectively protected under the second wave of regulation (Tucker 1995: 246). This conception of the state as a protector of rights is evident in the terms of the Factory Act 1833, which increased restrictions on working hours for children and introduced a new system of criminal penalties for breaches of the law (Carson 1979: 42). These penalties ranged up to a maximum £20 fine, which could be set aside where an offence was not wilful. The Act also made provision for four national Factory Inspectors, each with a team of superintendents, who were empowered to enter factories and implement the terms of the Act, thereby establishing a general template for enforcement action that remained largely unchanged until the 1970s. This has been described as 'the turning point of factory legislation' because of the vast improvement in administration that resulted (Hutchins and Harrison 1911: 40) and was a key step in the development of an administrative state; by undertaking to inspect and enforce via the executive authority of the state, rather than through the localised 'police economy', there was the beginning of the creation of a system that was more compatible with a free-market capitalist system (Hay 1975; Ramsay 2006: 42).

The Act was concerned with the establishment of public (the Act had to be displayed prominently in factories) and rational (greater record-keeping requirements, clearer penalties) justice, and the creation of a centralised, external authority to administer it. This reflected prevailing Benthamite ideals, in that the Act's *laissez-faire* non-interference in the employment relationship was offset by a determination to create the legal machinery through which rights could be upheld in the public interest (Dicey 1911: 185); it 'made possible a great advance in administrative efficiency', bringing aspects of the factory system under legal control for the first time (Hutchins and Harrison 1911: 40). As with many other regulatory developments, this 'Benthamite' approach was concerned with central coordination to facilitate the operation of the market system; employers could only operate as free economic agents within a market system that guaranteed legal equality (Carson 1979: 44). Similarly, employees had to be constituted as freely contracting individuals in order to create a free market in labour (a 'fictitious commodity'; Polanyi 1944: Ch. 6) which would validate the price-driven rationale of *laissez-faire* economics. This development mirrored trends in other areas of criminal justice, where the individual subjectivity and equality of subjects before the law was emphasised in order to obscure and legitimate underlying differences in social condition (Hay 1975; Garland 1985; Norrie 2001). Regulatory inspection was, from its earliest stages, a matter of legitimating the economy.

However, the use of inspection as a regulatory tool was by no means uncontroversial at the time. While many employers recognised the commercial benefits of a measure that would constrain unfair competition by the unscrupulous and by smaller competitors, the general reaction was one of mistrust (Thomas 1948: 78; Ward 1962: 115). While the substantive content of the 1833 Act was hotly contested, the first factory inspectors reported that factory owners initially constituted a receptive audience who appreciated the value of the measures within the Act and were keen to comply with it. But when opposition to the Act hardened and inspectors found themselves confronting resistant employers and suspicious employees, the Inspectorate responded by adopting a conciliatory approach, promoting the terms of the statute to a sceptical audience through negotiation, providing advice to employers in conforming with the Act, and avoiding 'a rigorous execution of conformity to all its details', in the words of Robert Rickards, the Midlands inspector.[4] While it was undoubtedly an uphill struggle to establish the legitimacy of safety regulation within a previously unregulated context, this approach was unsuccessful in securing compliance. The inspectors admitted later to having felt that discharging their duties fully would seriously harm employers, and so they held back from upholding the law with any thoroughness (Thomas 1948: 94). Certainly, prosecution was a little-used measure; by 1835, 177 convictions had been obtained across the 1948 factories registered as in operation (Kydd 1857: vol. 2, 83).

While further Acts adjusting the limitations on hours to be worked and extending the protections given to women as well as children were passed into law in 1841 and 1850, the final significant component of the early 19th-century regulatory movement was the Factories Act 1844, which introduced the first substantive safety limitations on working conditions (Mess 1926: 17). The act stipulated that flywheels, hoists, gears, steam-engines, and water-wheels all had to be securely fenced to protect workers from injury; failure to comply with these requirements carried a penalty in the form of a £5–20 fine. Employers were required to report all injuries resulting in lost working time to a certifying surgeon, who had to investigate the causes; inspectors were also empowered to bring action for compensation on behalf of injured workers (Thomas 1948: 236). This was noteworthy because it was the first time that 'health and safety' as an explicit end had been directly regulated, and it was also the first time that adult workers had been provided any form of legislative protection. Employers were now being prosecuted for failing to provide safe conditions for workers; government was now imposing 'obligations' upon them that directly impacted upon how they ran their production operations, not just the terms and conditions of employment. Government was beginning to transcend the idea of *laissez-faire* and intervene more directly in the affairs of the private sphere, and the ineffectiveness of the enforcement practices adopted highlighted that this was a state still 'learning to regulate' (Braithwaite 2008: 15) even as the legislation passed significantly extended the legal protections given to vulnerable workers.

The backdrop to much of the legislation passed in this period was the extension of the franchise by the Reform Act of 1832, the rationalisation of poverty relief and the workhouse system by the Poor Law Amendment Act in 1844, and continued opposition to legislation restricting free trade, notably the Corn laws, repealed in 1847 (Ward 1962: 302). These trends all contextualise the Factory Acts that were passed in this period; they slowly extended protective rights to a wider class of people, gradually systematised the infrastructure of an interventionist state, but also entrenched the logic of the free market. This was Habermas' bourgeois constitutional state in action: rights-giving, juridifying, but also serving the needs of the economic system (1988: 207). What Habermas recognised, and what much commentary on the development of regulation overlooks, is that these rights were not *solely* side effects of private commerce; law, through the efforts of humanitarian reformers (Ward 1962), was beginning to protect the private interests of individuals. While the 1802 Act established the 'idea' of government intervention, and the 1833 Act the scientific, rationalising 'logic' of government, by 1844 health and safety was providing the first area of 'substantive' intervention with the freedom of businesses, reflecting the expanding moral legitimacy of the state.

The late second wave: Regulation and the public interest

At the core of Tucker's 'second wave' of regulation, and Habermas' notion of the constitutional state, is the idea of law as a mechanism through which the state grants and then protects the rights of its citizens. Yet the provision of effective rights-protection remained limited during the first part of the 19th century. As we have seen, the process of introducing regulatory controls over workplace safety was slow and occurred only in reference to very narrowly defined problems. The idea of rights-protecting regulation was beginning to take hold but was very much a work in progress; there were still no general provisions, as the law did not extend beyond the textile industry, and adult workers received few of the protections extended to children and young people. After the innovations of the early 19th century, the process of extending the scope of regulation continued, with the passing of further Acts in 1847, 1850, 1853, and 1856 to limit the working day and require the fencing in of mill gearings. Various pieces of more specific legislation were introduced in industries allied to the textile trade, such as bleaching and dyeing. The main developments during the latter part of the 19th century fall into two parts: the passing of Factory Acts that were general in application and continued debate over the enforcement of the law.

General legislation

The Factory Acts (Extension) Act 1864 expanded the scope of the legislation passed in relation to the textile industry, extending it to other industries including earthenware production, match-making, and explosives manufacture. In 1867, the legislation was again extended to include forges and foundries, copper, steel and iron-works, machinery, paper, glass and tobacco manufacture, any premises employing more than 50 people, and then to workshops. By 1878, the number of regulations had increased to a point where consolidation was needed. There was also a concern that the specificity of this legislation was inappropriate, both because the textile industry no longer dominated the economy as it once had (Hobsbawm 1975: 41) and because the restriction of child labour was creating an increasing number of adult-dominated workplaces where most existing regulations did not apply (Mess 1926: 9). The law still had little to say about the conditions within which adults could be employed. The specificity of existing legislation reflected the issue-driven nature of regulation up to that point; the organised power of textile workers and the humanitarian focus of campaigners meant that certain specific risks were controlled in the absence of any unified legislative policy (Bartrip 2002; Bartrip and Hartwell 1997; Thomas 1948: 223).

The Factory and Workshop Act 1878 extended the factory codes to all industries and workplaces where articles were made or prepared for sale. It provided for parity of conditions between and within industries (Hutchins and Harrison 1911: 183) but also extended the requirements to fence in machinery into workplaces where no children worked, thereby providing the first piece of general safety regulation. Finally, the Act introduced a significant piece of rationalising reform by requiring that all fatal accidents be reported and recorded, thereby giving rise to a fledgling statistical data set measuring the incidence of death at work (Bartrip and Fenn 1988). Of course, the limitations of fatal accident statistics rehearsed in Chapter 1 apply here given the underdeveloped systems of recording in place at the time, but despite these, the subsequent Chief Inspector's annual report recorded 363 deaths and 5319 accidents (BMJ 1879). The 1878 Act thus appeared to be a significant step towards establishing the Benthamite ideals of systematic oversight, consistency of application, and information-gathering as central to the regulatory process. It also began the process of converting the social phenomenon of death at work into a technical, aggregated category. This is important; one of the limitations of early factory legislation had been the inability of those involved to recognise the potential of intervention to bring about meaningful change. Hobsbawm argues that mid-19th-century employers had little understanding of management and the means by which it might be possible to improve productivity or standards (1964: 352; also Banks 2009: 133; Carson 1979: 47; Witt 1998: 1477). The existing orthodoxy was that the key to profitability lay in extracting the maximum working hours possible from workers in exchange for the minimum cost – a crude 'wage-fund' model of utilitarian instrumentalism that overlooked the roles of bad management and poor working methods in determining business performance (Hobsbawm 1964: Ch. 17; 1975: 217).

These limited ambitions extended to health and safety, where the potential for safety management generally went unrecognised. Legal '[m]easures were tried for the relief of the symptoms without much thought being given to the causes...' (Hutchins and Harrison 1911: 200). The tendency among the management and owners of industry was to attribute 'accidents' to employee carelessness, the intransigence of rogue foremen, and the unfortunate concurrence of local conditions and ill fate. It was only in the last part of the 19th century that a scientific understanding of health and safety began to be employed to identify the causes of workplace injury, a development prompted by advances in medical science and applied to issues hitherto regarded as 'social' problems, such as lead and phosphorous poisoning (Bartrip and Hartwell 1997: 51–59). A raft of legislation addressing the occupational health risks of the 'dangerous trades' followed, including the Factory Act 1891, which allowed the Home Secretary to certify industries as dangerous and to apply special rules to them, and the Factory and Workshop Act of 1895, which gave the Home Secretary the power to impose prohibitions on the employment of any class of person, extending health and safety coverage to all workers, including men, for the first time.

By 1901, the first Factory Act of the new century was aiming not only at a greater degree of specificity and coverage than before but also at the expansion of systems of reporting and oversight. The 1901 Act was notable because of its centralising administrative content; requirements of notification and reporting placed greater onus upon regulators and regulated to participate in procedures that managed the provision of a safe working environment. Local authorities were required to inspect and register workshops and pass on details of their inspection regime to the Secretary of State, who had oversight of national enforcement practices, and existing legal requirements were consolidated within an organised framework (Hutchins and Harrison 1911: 248; Mess 1926: 29). This broadened the scope of the legal controls in place, but did so by moving responsibilities for safety regulation away from the central Factory Inspectorate towards local authority control. Critics pointed out that this system of 'dual control', while expanding the machinery of inspection, also downgraded the quality of that regulation, placing it in the hands of authorities who were not predisposed to enforce it stringently (Hutchins and Harrison 1911: 242). As well as diversifying enforcement, subsequent Acts of Parliament continued to extend legal protections to a wider range of industries, workers, and workplaces. Children working outside the factory system were protected in 1903 and the employment of children was eventually curtailed by the compulsory school attendance mandated by the Education Act 1918. The regulation of workplace safety was enhanced via the Workman's Compensation Act of 1897, which provided for a minimum level of compensation for injured workers (or their relatives) without the need to prove negligence on the part of the employer, importantly because the courts had heavily circumscribed the ability of workers to secure compensation for injury under the tort of negligence (Banks 2009; Stein 2008). This new statutory scheme provided many workers with a means of redress which they previously lacked, and also had a positive impact upon both rates of injury and death (Bartrip and Fenn 1988). At the same time, however, it contributed to the distancing of these cases from the criminal law, categorising them as issues of private compensation rather than as public wrongs, reducing the likelihood of meaningful enforcement in cases of regulatory wrongdoing precisely *because* an alternative was available which would serve the instrumental goal of compensating the victim (Bartrip and Fenn 1988: 66).

Enforcement

Carson identifies the period following the 1833 Act as the point at which factory legislation began the process of 'conventionalisation', coming to be 'accepted as customary... only rarely subjected to criminal prosecution and... often not regarded as really constituting crimes at all' (1979: 38). The enforcement of the law played an important part in this process; by removing the issue of workplace safety from the sphere of criminal law, the Factory Inspectors signalled the acceptability of death and injury at work. Carson identifies three main components to this process: modes of inspection and enforcement that tolerated certain levels of violation and militated against prosecution; decision-making processes that based fault on notions of *mens rea* and so undermined the 'formal' offences; and the displacement of responsibility onto employees rather than employers (1979: 51–53). There has been much discussion about enforcement among the early safety inspectorates (Arthurs 1985; Bartrip and Fenn 1983; 1988; Bartrip and Hartwell 1997; Carson 1970; 1979; Field 1990; Peacock 1984; Tombs and Whyte 2007: 110), but a general consensus can be identified as to some core themes. Firstly, as discussed previously, prior to 1833 there was little in the way of meaningful enforcement action in relation to factory legislation. The establishment of the Factory Inspectorate in 1833 was an innovative administrative advance which made meaningful enforcement a possibility, but again the consensus is that this was not forthcoming. The frequency of prosecutions remained relatively low and would decline further as the century went on.

Despite some suggestions that prosecution practices at this time were successful (in terms of success rates: Peacock 1984), there is ample evidence that under-enforcement was the norm (Bartrip and Fenn 1983; Carson 1979). In part, this can be attributed to the lack of a clear vision of what the Inspectors' role should be, the under-resourcing of the Factory Inspectorate, and the derisory fines that followed conviction in cases that did proceed to court, which undermined the value of prosecution (Bartrip and Fenn 1983: 207–208). Critically, the inspectors themselves came quickly to regard their role as being one of advisor rather than enforcer; they held back from prosecution in order to avoid antagonising employers and sought to assist them in meeting legal requirements wherever possible (Thomas 1948: 76). Inspectors held ambivalent views about the moral culpability of the factory owners they investigated (Carson 1979: 48–49), and there were disagreements within the Inspectorate about the correct approach to take. During the 1870s, one of the two Factory Inspectors, Robert Baker, undertook prosecution vigorously and at twice the rate of the other Inspector, Alexander Redgrave, who refrained from prosecuting in all but the most egregious cases (Bartrip and Fenn 1983). After Redgrave became Chief Inspector in 1878, the compliance approach prevailed, establishing a precedent that has endured to the current day. On the one hand, this last-resort approach was born of the exigencies of the new regulatory system. There was much mistrust of the Factory Inspectorate, and employers were liable to regard interference in their private affairs as illegitimate. In the face of this opposition, and in the interests of implementing the Factory Acts efficiently and effectively (Bartrip and Fenn 1983: 218), Inspectors had to establish the validity of regulation in the eyes of the regulated; this necessitated refraining from using adversarial measures. Further, the Factory Inspectorate was so under-resourced that the rationing of prosecution was the most cost-effective way of regulating and ensuring that those resources were not concentrated in too small a number of cases.

On the other hand, ideological opposition to enforcement was also influential. As discussed previously, the newly appointed inspectors reported that, in practice, many employers accepted the need for the regulation of working conditions. This may have involved some recognition of the unfair competitive advantage available to unregulated employers, but Carson asserts that a key factor was the contribution such practices could make to the maintenance of a flexible and disciplined national workforce (1979: 44–45; Tombs and Whyte 2007: 112). Further, breaches of safety laws were not enforced with any rigour because to do so would criminalise a large number of employers; inspectors instead came to tolerate a certain level of illegality. Employers fought hard in opposition to the extension of criminalisation, lobbying Inspectors and politicians with the aim of restricting the law's application to their businesses. The result was the conventionalisation of Factory Act offences; the selectivity exercised in prosecuting applied a *de facto* requirement of *mens rea* to the safety offences by precluding prosecution where no intention or wilful disregard could be established. In this way, prosecution was marginalised as relevant only to the bad apples of industry, and the lack of *mens rea* terms within the offences undermined their perceived seriousness (Carson 1979: 52). Prosecutions under the Factory Acts were downgraded to the status of quasi-criminal 'formal offences', and the factory owners were protected from exposure to the moral weight of criminalisation.

The democratic constitutional state

So how can we explain these different themes – a pragmatic Inspectorate seeking to maximise the impact of minimal resources, but which also avoided widespread prosecution; a legal movement towards the granting of protective rights to workers, but which did not grant significant general protections; and a systematic regulatory system aiming to govern business activity more effectively? It is suggested that the answers can be found in the form of the 'democratic constitutional state' as described by Habermas (1988). The extension of political enfranchisement and civil participation, the establishment of trade unions and worker representation, and the expansion of the role of the state provide the socio-political backdrop to developments in the regulation of workplace safety. Laws were increasingly legitimated via the assent of those subject to them, a process which necessitated the establishment of systems of political participation. This accounts for the 'freedom-guaranteeing' character of legal rules (1988: 208) like the Factory Acts, which constitute progressive developments in the interests of the working classes, won via a prolonged process of political activism (Tombs and Whyte 2007: 116). As Hutchins and Harrison put it, '[a] Factory Act is not something "given away", like coals or blankets at Christmas time. It represents, rightly understood, the reasoned effort of the... community to raise its industrial and social life to a higher plane' (1911: 218). And yet, as we have seen, the substantive content of this protective provision was limited in practice because this democratic process occurs against the backdrop of a political 'structure of domination' (Habermas 1988: 208) which transposes the conflict between employee welfare and business interests from the lifeworld of public debate to the system-dominated spheres of money and power. The granting of progressive protections was curtailed (as documented by Marx 1887; Tombs and Whyte 2007), resulting in laws which mitigated the worst side effects of the factory system while also avoiding compromising the interests of employers. It was also a process of depoliticisation, moving the issue of worker's safety from the political arena to the administrative, where it could be conceptualised as a matter of practicality rather than ideology (Carson 1979: 46).

The central feature of working-class life during the 19th century was insecurity; workers did not know from one week to the next whether they would remain in employment, what they would earn, or whether injury would suddenly render them unable to work (Hobsbawm 1975: 220). Economic growth and industrial progress fed this insecurity, creating a flexible labour market where workers could be engaged or dismissed with ease, a surplus of additional labour to feed demand during boom periods, and workplaces where insecurities were realised via hazardous machinery. The granting of substantive rights was therefore a form of 'steering role', mitigating these insecurities in order to legitimate the economic system. Hence, the law was limited because it only provided protection to the level needed to fulfil this role. But the two functions of regulation, the progressive protection of workers and the self-preservation of capital, went hand-in-hand; in Polanyi's terms, 'if factory legislation and social laws were required to protect industrial man ... it was equally true that ... the organization of capitalistic production itself had to be sheltered from the devastating effects of a self-regulating market' (1944: 132). This was a double movement of two interconnected social organising principles, namely, free-market economic liberalism and welfarist social protectionism. There could be no legitimation of the market system without the granting of substantive protections to workers, but these protections were limited due to the restrictive influence of economic liberalism. This is the fundamental character of this process of legal reform, simultaneously progressive and restrictive, shaped by both economic power and social protectionism.

The other main innovation of this period was the systematisation of regulation via the creation of centralised inspectorates, formal reporting and recording processes, and the utilisation of statistics to monitor performance. This proceduralisation reflects the emergent rationalisation of society via systems of strategic control aimed at achieving instrumental outcomes such as the reduction of injury rates. At the end of the 19th century there was a movement towards the coordinated regulation of the causes of occupational injury and ill health. This can be taken as a sign of the increasingly legalised relationship between employer and employee, but it also reflects the law's role as a medium of instrumental control; by the turn of the century, safety regulation was becoming a coherent, rational system, offsetting harm and securing the continued operation of the factory system on terms that were acceptable to wider society at large (Habermas 1988: 213). At the same time, however, it was ceasing to be a moral or political issue and instead becoming one of technical infringement.

The third wave: Regulation and welfare

The third wave of workplace safety regulation emerged following the two World Wars during the first half of the 20th century. The widespread social reconstruction that followed those conflicts necessitated an increase in state intervention to exercise direct control over the conditions of social and economic life. Many of these interventions were progressive and democratic in nature, oriented towards ensuring the welfare of citizens and the poor. The Education Act of 1918 facilitated the expansion of a state-coordinated education system; suffrage was expanded to all adult males and women over 30 in 1918; and the fledgling National Insurance system began to provide old age pensions and relief for the unemployed and those incapacitated by ill health. Later, after the Second World War, the foundations of the modern welfare state were laid down, including the establishment of a National Health Service. The expansion of regulation as a mode of intervention was central to this shift, and health and safety at work was one area where regulation was utilised in pursuit of welfare-centred goals (Hobsbawm 1994: Ch. 10).

Four factors explain the emergence of this 'welfarist' wave of regulation. Firstly, there was some evidence of a political and social movement towards collectivism, centred around the desire to make adequate provision for those who suffered during the two World Wars ('a land fit for heroes', in the words of Lloyd George in 1918). Mess explicitly links the passing of the 1920s safety legislation to this post-war 'wave of humane feeling and high aspiration for the future' (1926: 33). Secondly, this collectivist tendency also reflected the pragmatic problem-solving tendencies of government; by taking on the role of provider in relation to healthcare, education, public utilities, railways, and so on, the state was able to address entrenched problems within the private market, such as poor standards, inconsistency, exploitative pricing, and a lack of safety (Braithwaite 2008: 15). The provider state model was influenced by collectivist ideas, but it was also a pragmatic means of centralising, and thus rationalising, provision. On a critical note, we can also see in this movement a divorcing of issues from their social contexts; state provision moved them from the politics of private interest into the politics of public welfare, thereby negating possible conflicts (Habermas 1973; Tucker 1995: 247).

The third explanation for this trend relates to the economic upheaval that Polanyi identifies as characterising the interwar years (1944: Chs. 17–20). The costs of war, rising unemployment, the stock market crash of 1929 and the subsequent depression, the abandonment of the gold standard, and the volatility of international markets all caused economic instability. State provision, particularly in areas of welfare, provided a means by which this volatility could be withstood without leading to wider social conflict. Relatedly, the fourth reason was concern over the rise of communism; the fear of revolution (as seen in Russia) prompted politicians to consider welfare state provision as a means of negating more radical demands from the working classes (Braithwaite 2008: 15; Hobsbawm 1987: 103). Together, these factors made governments receptive to the idea of the state as provider, building upon the pluralising tendencies of the democratic constitutional state (Habermas 1988: 208). Previously unconstrained markets were brought within the law's oversight, although this oversight was constrained by the need to manage the competing demands of capital and welfare.

Post-war regulation

The inter- and post-war periods saw only minor amendments made to existing health and safety provisions and no radical extensions of the law. The basic form of the factory 'code' had remained relatively unchanged since the 1870s, and it was the 1950s and 1960s that eventually saw the development of parallel codes to govern other forms of industry, such as the Mines and Quarries Act 1954, the Agriculture (Safety, Health and Welfare Provisions) Act 1956, and the Offices, Shops, and Railway Premises Act 1963. Further legislation was introduced to govern emergent industrial hazards, such as the Clean Air Act 1959 and the Nuclear Installations Acts of 1959 and 1965 (Drake and Wright

1983: 4). This culminated in the Factories Act 1961, which represented an attempt to bring together in one place general health and safety provisions and specific rules attaching to certain processes. The Robens Report of 1972 characterised the 1961 Act and its antecedents as examples of a 'practical, empirical approach' to reform which had produced high standards and comprehensive oversight (1972: para. 22), even as it criticised that approach for lacking consistency and conceptual coherence. Although the 1961 Act consolidated the existing legislation, it did not extend beyond factories, meaning that many other workplaces remained ungoverned. The legislation was also focused on the tangible working environment, with most of the Act's requirements relating to ventilation, machine guarding, and so on. This meant that, in practice, the defining regulatory questions became physical ones: Was the incident within the parameters of the 'factory'? Was it the result of a physical process within that workplace? (Drake and Wright 1983: 5; Robens 1972: para. 30). This seriously limited the factory code, placing issues of safety culture, policy, and system outside the scope of the law.

In all, the 185 sections of the 1961 Act provided a very detailed regulatory framework; the aim was to set out prescriptive requirements that would allow for the evaluation of safety standards in literal terms (Drake and Wright 1983: 4–6), but the problem with this approach was that the requirements constantly needed updating in order to keep them current. The legislative provisions were too inflexible to deal adequately with the pace of change in industry, and much legislation quickly became obsolete. This specificity created a degree of complexity which was mirrored in the enforcement structures. Prior to 1974 there were seven different health and safety inspectorates, based in five Government departments, enforcing nine Acts of Parliament and over 500 Statutory Instruments (Baldwin 1987: 132). The Inspectorate of Factories, part of the Department of Employment and Productivity, carried out the bulk of enforcement, with 600 inspectors responsible for overseeing around 380,000 premises and carrying out around 170,000 visits per year, levels that were insufficient to ensure that companies were aware of their legal obligations (Carson 1970: 388). The law also failed to make provision for workforce involvement, because the duties placed upon employers made health and safety provision a matter of discipline rather than of participatory effort (Dawson *et al.* 1988: 9); worker participation would become a core motif of the subsequent reforms.

The Robens Committee was appointed on 29th May 1970 to review the law governing health and safety at work. The Committee convened against the backdrop of an increase in accident rates between 1961 and 1970, which suggested that new workplace hazards had made the existing law obsolete (Robens 1972: paras. 17–21). The Factory Acts, it was argued, had ignored the underlying problems of health and safety, namely, attitudes and organisational systems within the workplace, and this, along with the complexity of the legislation, meant that there was simply 'too much law', much of which regulators could not enforce, and which had negative psychological effects:

> People are heavily conditioned to think of safety and health at work as . . . a matter of detailed rules imposed by external agencies . . . apathy is the greatest single contributing factor to accidents at work. This attitude will not be cured so long as people are encouraged to think that safety and health at work can be ensured by an ever-increasing army of inspectors.
>
> (Robens 1972: para. 28)

Technicality, prescriptiveness, complex language, and a focus on conditions rather than on processes and behaviours created a reliance on state regulation and removed issues of health and safety from the everyday experience and responsibility of workers. The new philosophy of health and safety would emphasise voluntariness rather than state intervention, providing a framework for self-regulation and shared responsibility (Baldwin 1987: 133; Robens 1972: para. 41). It would conceptualise obligations more broadly, demonstrating clearly who they applied to and how they would be regulated.

The HSWA 1974

The result was the Health and Safety at Work Act 1974 (HSWA), which placed duties onto employers and employees to comply with the law and to self-regulate. The practical standards to be enforced were not laid down in the formal legislation, but rather in a regularly updated system of subordinate instruments linked to the general duties. Gunningham and Johnstone refer to the problem of *form* that the HSWA addressed as one of 'regulatory overload', a phenomenon whereby the sheer volume and complexity of formal regulations undermine the effectiveness of the system by forcing duty-holders to focus too much on the laws they had to comply with rather than the risks and hazards they should be managing (1999: 30). The new Act pulled together most of the pre-existing measures within a legislative framework that was couched in terms of broad duty-based requirements, exemplified in section 2(1), which stated that 'It shall be the duty of every employer to ensure, so far as is reasonably practicable, the health, safety, and welfare at work of all his employees.' The Robens Report intended that this approach would make explicit the continuous legal and social duties incumbent upon all those involved in the workplace and encourage employers to think about safety less as a series of specific steps to be followed and more as an overall standard of operating behaviour (1972: para. 130). The generality of these duties was also intended to facilitate prosecution and to promote a conception of health and safety as a moral obligation (Hutter and Manning 1990: 112).

Two additional points are worth making about these duties; firstly, the *portmanteau* duties contained within the HSWA, particularly sections 2 and 3, dramatically broadened the coverage of health and safety protections to include every employee in every workplace, including previously unregulated places like hospitals and schools (Drake and Wright 1983: 70). The Act was also clear that the general duties included fulfilling voluntary industry standards and codes of practice (Baldwin 1987: 142) and incorporating safety systems and policies into the running of a company. The second point to note is that the Act was enabling rather than prescriptive; it specified that the duty must be fulfilled, but not *how*; this placed an onus upon companies to develop forms of provision to fit their own circumstances (Dawson *et al.* 1988: 14). This was a shift from 'specification' standards to 'performance' standards; from precise proscriptions relating to specific hazards, to general duties and open-ended obligations to reach levels of provision (Gunningham and Johnstone 1999: 24–25). Companies can fulfil these duties by showing they have taken all reasonably practicable steps to control the risks to health, safety and welfare that arise, with a form of due diligence defence available where a breach of the duty leads to harm, but reasonable steps had been taken to fulfil that duty. Reasonable practicability is defined in terms of the foreseeability of the risk in question and the appropriate balance between the risk and the cost of remedy: 'whether the time, trouble and expense of the precautions suggested are disproportionate to the risks involved'.[5]

These defences qualified the duties within the HSWA, ensuring that some fault was required on the part of the defendant before guilt could be established; liability was not being imposed in relation to the truly unforeseeable. Reasonable practicability mitigated the perceived unfairness of the strict liability standard (Wright 1997: 48–51) and was instrumental in legitimating the HSWA in the eyes of business (Lacey 2004: 161). That said, it may be argued that this dilutes those duties by introducing a utilitarian calculus into the question of safety protection, allowing an absolute obligation to be sidestepped where fulfilment would be detrimental to business competitiveness (Bain 1997; Pearce and Tombs 1990: 433). The HSWA indirectly framed the issue of safety management in instrumental terms by making it a matter of cost–benefit analysis, but this also made safety 'subordinate' to production; protection is only necessary insofar as profitability renders it practicable. It is not required because it is the right thing to do or reflective of any moral prerogative. The irony of this instrumentalism is that it facilitated deregulation in the 1980s and 1990s because, once safety is framed in cost–benefit terms, a recalculation of those costs and benefits can take place and this can be used to redefine the parameters of the duties that are imposed (Bain 1997; Beck and Woolfson 2000; Dawson *et al.* 1988; Tombs and Whyte 2010). Once the political and economic climate changed, the costs of safety provision were seen to be higher and the benefits less tangible, and so the definition of what was reasonably practicable changed. In this way, the definition of 'safety' could be shifted in a way that would be harder were it defined in terms of absolute duties (Dawson *et al.* 1988: 15).

The last point to make about the generalised duties contained within the HSWA is that they generalise issues of safety, emphasising the role of systems and culture in managing workplace safety. Focusing on these factors can mean that there is inconsistency in how duties are interpreted and applied (Hutter 1989; 1997: 77). It also means that risks to safety are internalised as normal features of the workplace, suggesting that 'the risks associated with increased efficiency and profitability can be responsibly managed and contained' (Silbey 2009: 343) and that we need not question the existence of that risk in the first place (Perrow 1984). Notions of 'safety culture' are a fundamental component of contemporary approaches to safety management, focusing on the attitudes, behaviours, and understandings of those within the workplace (Guldenmund 2000; Silbey 2009; Vaughan 1999; Zohar 1980). Such an understanding decentralises responsibility for safety, focusing on the actions of individuals, and masks the fundamental role played by the economic power of employers in determining exposure to risk (Gray 2006; 2009; Silbey 2009). The HSWA's emphasis on systems broadens the scope of inquiry into issues of management but also downplays the causes of risk and harm.

A voluntary regime

Many of the assumptions of the HSWA stemmed from the Robens Committee's commitment to the notion of voluntarism, the idea that health and safety reflected an 'identity of interests' between workers and employers, both of whom would benefit from better standards (1972: para. 66). It was felt that raising awareness among workers would lead to fewer accidents attributable to 'carelessness', and raising awareness among employers would allow them to improve their safety policies (Baldwin 1987; Genn 1993: 221; Hutter 1997: Ch. 2). To this end, the Robens approach was participatory, recommending the creation of consultative mechanisms to involve all parties in the fulfilment of the duties laid down by the HSWA. The regulator's management board (the Health and Safety Commission, or HSC) was tripartite and involved industry, trade unions, and government experts and policymakers (Hutter 1997: 24). These different constituencies had input via Industry and Subject Advisory Committees, and regulations emerged after a lengthy process of consultation. The question about this tripartite process was whether it was anything more than a rigorous consultative process; the desire for consensus meant that agreement took a long time to emerge, and tended to result in the maintenance of the *status quo* (Baldwin 1987: 139; 1995: 139; Dawson *et al.* 1988: 202; Hutter 1997: 24). The tripartite system was also not particularly representative, tending to be dominated by the powerful voices of the Confederation of Business Interests (CBI) and Trades Union Congress (TUC), and only discussing issues raised by HSC/E itself; having an 'input' into decision-making is not necessarily the same as having 'influence'.

The Act was explicitly concerned with the fostering of essentially voluntary commitments, and this has tended to mean the pursuit of self-regulation. HSE works towards empowering employers to take the initiative in determining what must be done to fulfil their duties, and then in monitoring compliance and taking action to address any breaches. This dictates a secondary role for the regulator, who becomes involved with the regulated either proactively, through a rolling programme of formal workplace inspections, which occur rarely and are as much about the Inspectors providing advice as about detecting violations of the law, or reactively, through investigation of a specific incident such as a fatality (Hawkins 2002; Hutter 1997). The rationale behind a self-regulatory approach is that it allows for more cost-effective regulation because the bulk of the costs are borne by the regulated rather than the regulator. Fixing standards in conjunction with the regulated means that they are more readily complied with than would be the case if they were imposed from above; self-regulation breeds commitment which, it is argued, is more productive and easier to maintain than an adversarial approach. The Robens Committee envisaged self-regulation as providing a more flexible system which would 'encourage industry to deal with more of its own problems, thereby enabling official regulation to be more effectively concentrated on serious problems where strict official regulation is appropriate' (1972: para. 148).

The extent to which this scheme constitutes self-regulation is debatable, since it is reliant upon the presence of an external framework of monitoring; as such it is perhaps best understood as a form of 'enforced self-regulation' (Ayres and Braithwaite 1992; Baldwin and Cave 1999: 129). In practice, there are gradations of self-regulation, with some employers being trusted to self-regulate almost entirely, while others require more stringent monitoring (Gunningham and Johnstone 1999; Hawkins 2002). There is an assumption that companies will pursue health and safety goals because it is the right thing to do; regulators are there to ensure that this commitment is channelled in the right directions via the cultivation of cooperative relationships (Almond 2006; Hawkins 1990; 2002; Hutter 1997). The main issue encountered by HSE has been how to balance voluntarism with the need for intervention. While commitment improves compliance, there is also evidence that some oversight is required to produce compliance with the law (Aalders and Wilthagen 1997; Gray and Scholz 1991; 1993; Gunningham and Johnstone 1999; Gunningham and Rees 1997; Ogus 1995), and the HSWA's emphasis upon self-regulation has been accused of underestimating the value of proactive enforcement (Gunningham and Johnstone 1999: 69–70; Hutter 1986; Pearce and Tombs 1990). Additionally, there are many different employer types, motivated by a range of factors such as knowledge of the law and economic and social considerations (Genn 1993: 221) and in possession of different levels of commitment to compliance (Baldwin 1995: 135; Gunningham and Johnstone 1999: Ch. 3; James 1992). Companies can also be less rational in their decision-making processes than is supposed, either because they act in irrational ways or because they possess a 'bounded rationality', meaning that cost–benefit calculations are made on the basis of incomplete information (Ayres and Braithwaite 1992; Gunningham and Rees 1997; Wells 2001). Self-regulation, it is argued, may be too contingent upon self-motivation to be viable in isolation.

The HSE and enforcement

The limitations of a purely self-regulatory system thus necessitate a degree of coordinated external oversight; HSE was created by s. 10 of the HSWA 1974 as a unified central inspectorate with powers to enforce the obligations imposed by that Act (Dawson *et al.* 1988: 11; Hutter and Manning 1990: 112). The intention was to address the fragmentation of enforcement that existed in the previous regulatory system (Robens 1972: para. 205). As of 2010, HSE employed some 3702 people, of whom 1342 were front-line inspectors (HSE 2010b). There has been a notable decrease in the size of the inspectorate; in 2003 there were 1638 inspectors, not far below the HSE's 1994 resource high-point; since then, rates of inspection and enforcement have declined. This regulatory framework incorporates both proactive and reactive strategies; proactive enforcement refers to a programme of formal inspections which can lead to the imposition of sanctions if violations of the law are detected. The scheme of proactive work is structured through the Inspections Rating System, a quantitative database that identifies 'risky' sites, based on time since last inspection, the latent hazards that the workplace contains, and inspector's assessments of those firms' performance (Wright 1997: 120). High-priority sites may be visited once a year or more, while lower priority sites are visited very rarely; recent figures suggest that, on average, HSE inspects each workplace once every 38 years (O'Neill 2010).

'Reactive' enforcement relates to investigations undertaken in response to reported incidents. Under the RIDDOR 1995 (Reporting of Injuries, Diseases and Dangerous Occurrence Regulations) scheme, all fatalities, major injuries, and injuries leading to three days or more absenteeism from work must be reported to HSE. HSE investigates all reported fatal incidents and a proportion of other major reported incidents according to seriousness, the employer's safety record, and whether it is a priority area. The majority of reported incidents are not investigated (Hawkins 2002; Hutter and Lloyd-Bostock 1990); less than 20% of major incidents result in an investigation (Tombs and Whyte 2007: 102). Following an investigation, HSE can choose to issue an improvement or prohibition notice or bring a prosecution. Improvement notices allow an inspector to compel a company found to be in contravention of a regulatory provision to take specific remedial actions to comply with the law. A prohibition notice declares that an activity should cease until further notice if an inspector believes there is an imminent risk of serious injury. The most serious measure open to HSE is a prosecution; inspectors are empowered under HSWA ss. 38–39 to conduct prosecutions in the Magistrates' court, and the decision to do so is made following consideration of the incident's seriousness, whether it is a priority area, and the record and demeanour of the offending company (Hawkins 2002: Chs. 10–11), as well as the terms of the Code for Crown Prosecutors.[6] Current HSE prosecution statistics were discussed in Chapter 1, and they indicate that administrative sanctions are utilised far more often than prosecution, and that while the use of administrative sanctions is increasing, the number of prosecutions brought is declining over time.

HSE tends to pursue formal enforcement action (particularly prosecution) relatively rarely because to do so disrupts the ongoing, cooperative regulatory relationships that the agency pursues; it is only used in the worst cases or when these relationships break down (Ayres and Braithwaite 1992; Scholz 1984). The preference for notices highlights the essentially instrumental nature of enforcement action, which is viewed as a means of promoting future compliance and the targeting of specific risks, and so addressing deficiencies that may result in future harm. This is reflected in the terms of HSE's Enforcement Policy Statement, which sets out a core concern with 'dealing with serious risks, securing compliance with health and safety law and preventing harm' (HSE 2009b: para. 4). Enforcement should serve future goals; it is not necessarily focused on securing redress for wrongdoing (although 'holding to account' is a subsidiary aim of the Enforcement Policy Statement). Even prosecution is envisaged as a method of achieving future public policy goals; as Hawkins puts it, a 'utilitarian... conception of prosecution in the occupational health and safety arena as a way of reducing the extent of death, injury, and disease in the workplace is... dominant' (2002: 4). The symbolic use of prosecution as a means of making a moral claim about the wrongfulness of causing or inflicting injury and death, or of excessive risk-taking, is secondary. HSE measures its performance in terms of securing lower rates of injury and higher standards of safety in aggregate terms, and enforcement action is only indirectly compatible with these goals.

Conclusion

The granting of autonomy to self-manage risks within the 'third wave' of safety regulation completed a shift away from the 19th-century conception of safety incidents as individual events that defied coordinated management towards a recognition of the capacity of systems to effectively control those risk events. In a sense, the HSWA extends the rights-giving tendencies of the late second-wave of regulation, where top-down regulatory oversight was imposed as a way of trying to guarantee the right to a safe workplace, but it also constitutionalised underlying social power relations via the imposition of broad duties that addressed workers' rights in the round (Tucker 1995: 245). The third wave of regulation grants rights of participation and seeks to facilitate 'internal' response systems to govern health and safety collaboratively within a workplace. It also addresses the 'external' responsibility system, with the establishment of a rationalised, formalised regulatory bureaucracy, and a pervasive safety framework (Tucker 1995: 248). This reflects the aspirational goals of the regulatory agenda as a means of securing social solidarity and freedom from domination (Black 2000; Braithwaite 2008; Feintuck 2004; Prosser 2006; Sunstein 1990). This freedom-giving function arises as a result of the need to mitigate the harmful consequences of economic activity; law pursues positive social outcomes by offsetting the consequences of the institutionalisation and domination of money and power within the market system (Habermas 1988: 213).

Yet, while regulation asserts itself against these forces of domination, it does not oppose them; regulation has always existed as a means of facilitating rather than challenging the operation of markets. Safety regulation is a 'steering mechanism', diverting conflicts over workplace death and injury into the political sphere and away from the market system, thereby mitigating potential crises and securing that system's long-term survival (Almond 2007; Carson 1979). As such, the rights-guaranteeing character of these welfare reforms is limited; regulation is a process of inducing progressive social change on terms that are constrained by the economic and bureaucratic system within which it occurs. The participatory rights and welfarist protections granted are thus bound up with issues of money and power, giving the law an instrumental character as a medium of social organisation, and this is the source of the problems that the law encounters. Tripartism, internal responsibility systems, safety cultures, broad duties, and the self-regulatory philosophy of Robens, all allow for the domination of issues of safety by bureaucratic and monetary considerations. The social value of health and safety is masked by the regulatory emphasis upon securing future compliance and improving aggregate safety standards, rather than communicating value judgements about the cases that arise.

Regulation has always been about the pursuit of welfarist reforms in pursuit of a broadly emancipatory, rights-giving, and progressive agenda. It has been part of a shift towards the granting of citizenship rights to an ever-widening sector of the population, and has, at times, reflected broader movements of social reform. But these aspirations have been counterbalanced by its increasingly strategic role as a means of fulfilling other goals, particularly those relating to the sustainability of existing economic systems. The HSWA 1974 remains the central piece of legislation regulating workplace safety in the UK and has fundamentally shaped regulatory practice, from legal requirements through to enforcement policies and consultative arrangements. But while it offers more comprehensive protections of workers' safety than the laws which preceded it, it also creates a more bureaucratic regulatory framework and encompasses the rationality and managerial logic of instrumentalism to a greater degree, and this renders it fragile to distortion by the interests of systems of money and power.

As Hawkins observes, regulatory bodies 'exist thanks to an instrumental view of law and its capacity to change things for the better' (2002: 4), but the benefits achieved since the 1800s, in terms of genuine improvements in safety, have come at the cost of an instrumental system of regulation which is increasingly driven by imperatives that are distant from the lives and interests of those whom it seeks to protect. The key dynamics that underpin this distancing relate to a putative move towards a new 'fourth wave' of regulation, centred on a more diversified and responsive form of oversight, in which a range of 'decentred' regulatory techniques are utilised to move the burden of regulating away from the state towards the regulated (Bartle and Vass 2007; Black 2005; 2007). The juridification that Habermas sees as occurring as an outcome of third-wave interventions creates an atomised and increasingly individualistic model of regulation that, in many ways, revives some of the key features of the contractual 'first wave' of regulation, in that the dynamics of the market and individualised calculations of self-interest come to the fore in engineering and motivating compliance with the law. This can be described as a 'neo-liberal' model of regulation (Gray 2009; Harcourt 2010), and it provides the primary context for the developments that have been sketched elsewhere in this book. The next chapter will consider the role of the criminal law in constructing, and responding to, this neo-liberal mode of regulation.

5
Criminalising Work-Related Death

As discussed, the last 30 years have seen a movement in many jurisdictions towards the criminalisation of corporate bodies that cause work-related deaths. This has been an area of some controversy, involving as it does a form of offending which does not fit easily into the criminal law's taxonomic system. This chapter will begin by elucidating the distinctions that are drawn between 'criminal' and 'regulatory' offences and explaining the consequences of this differentiation. The historical development of the movement towards 'corporate crime' will be examined in order to understand the fundamental ambiguity that has long characterised this area of law. As with Chapter 4, the primary focus will be on developments in the UK. What is the nature of the challenge that work-related deaths present to the state and society, and why has criminalisation been regarded as an appropriate response to this challenge? Contemporary trends towards the criminalisation of work-related deaths and arguments about the role that such law should play relative to other legal measures echo debates that have gone before, reflecting a fundamental distinction between the instrumental and symbolic functions of law. An understanding of these dynamics helps us to understand why criminalisation is increasingly sought in the current social and political climate and in the context of workplace death.

Differentiating crime and regulation

It has long been asserted that the system of criminal law offences has two constituent parts (Blackstone 1809; Gray 1995: 1374): the first deals with the control of conduct which is regarded as offending against a universal norm of behaviour via offences classed as *mala in se* or wrongs in themselves because of their inherent *a priori* moral quality (Ashworth

2000: 226; Blackstone 1809: 54; Brudner 1993; Husak 2008: 36; Ogus 1994: 79; Wells 2001: 7). The second involves the management of undesirable but not morally repugnant behaviour via offences that are classed as *mala prohibita*, wrongs because they are prohibited by law and defined as such by the authority of the Crown. The label of *mala in se* is applied to 'core crimes', such as murder, rape, and theft, which assert their normative status via the imposition of a *mens rea* requirement, while the category of *mala prohibita* offences includes those of strict liability, endangerment, risk-creation, and ancillary liability, which are often not classed as 'true' criminal offences, despite having the potential to result in criminal sanctions (Fletcher 1978; Husak 2008: 33–38). The former are usually defined in terms of 'agency' or individual choice, while the latter are usually defined in relation to a specific social welfare goal. Brudner argues that these values interrelate within the criminal law; while reference to public welfare is required to justify interfering with individual autonomy, basing criminal liability on welfare alone fails to recognise the actors involved as Kantian ends in themselves (1993: 52–53). Welfare-oriented criminalisation must be pursued through a system of law that prioritises respect for individual autonomy because 'happiness' goals are only rendered meaningful through the end-status of personality; this renders absolute liability offences unacceptable and suggests that regulatory offences should be differentiated from crimes. This differentiation underpins the European doctrine of *societas delinquere non potest* (Weigend 2008), and the crime–regulation divide is an accepted component of most national legal systems.

The problem with the *mala in se/mala prohibita* distinction is that any effort to define it in terms of content is doomed to failure by the sheer variety of criminal offences that exists, all of which prohibit some form of 'wrongdoing' in the name of 'public welfare' (Ashworth 2000; Norrie 2001: 83; Williams 1955). At the same time, 'regulatory' offences involve sometimes serious harms and are framed in terms of public welfare, both features that are said to make criminal laws distinctive. Ramsay argues that the development of agency-based notions of criminal fault goes hand-in-hand with the development of social-welfarist notions of citizenship that justify imposing regulatory burdens onto those social actors best placed to bear them (2006; also Ewald 2002; Lacey 2004). Regulatory offences are concerned with upholding agreed conditions of 'social' citizenship and the 'general enrichment of the concrete substance of civilised life'; criminal laws emphasise agency as the basis of the 'civil' citizenship rights of subjects, but both of these conditions form part of the same fundamental concept of 'political' citizenship

(Ramsay 2006: 49). Because they are elements of the same legal project, it is unhelpful to view regulatory offences as different from 'real' crimes; the emphasis on the fulfilment of social goods agreed via formal democratic politics gives regulatory law a moral component even where the precise terms of the offences do not invoke subjective moral judgement (Wells 2001: 70). In addition, the division between the two categories is historically and politically contingent and, for Norrie, reflects an 'ideology of triviality' (2001: 83–84) which marginalises particular forms of harm. Any distinction between these two classes of offence is one of political judgement and not of qualitative difference (Gray 1995: 1395).

Traditionally, systems of social regulation such as health and safety law have been seen as fitting into a category below the general criminal law in terms of status, in that they restrict activities which are not themselves illegal but which constitute the basis of an offence when performed inadequately. Since regulations are enforced via state-imposed sanctions, it may seem apt to categorise them as 'quasi-criminal', as they are subject to the procedural safeguards, standards of proof, and rights-protections that criminal proceedings involve.[1] As discussed in Chapter 2, regulatory health and safety laws are features of almost all national legal systems and are usually enforced by public bodies with the capacity to impose coercive punishments consistent with the notion of criminal law, which is itself not always a matter of hierarchical rule-enforcement (Gill 2002; Kagan 1984; Lacey 2004: 149). Despite this, the notion of regulation as *mala prohibita* is pervasive; the UK Government has drawn a distinction between 'serious offence[s] under the general criminal law' and 'offence[s] that might be characterised as regulatory' (Home Office 2005: para. 58). At the time, this seemed a startling admission, as it impliedly undermined existing safety laws (primarily the HSWA 1974). But it also constituted a reassertion of the traditional model of a two-tier criminal/regulatory system, wherein proceedings under the latter category are a matter of instrumental policy-delivery, rather than moral judgement. Subsequent Government reports (Hampton 2005; Law Commission 2010; Macrory 2006; Young 2010) upheld the notion that regulatory offences are one part of a wider toolbox of potential responses to offending and are not backed by the same moral compulsion as criminal law.

Part of the reason for this is that offending in the regulatory context is seen as a side effect of otherwise purposeful wealth-creating industrial activity which must be managed rather than prohibited (Baldwin *et al.* 1998: 3; Gill 2002; Hawkins and Thomas 1984). Wrongdoing is framed in terms of potential rather than actual harm (Husak 2008: 40;

Kagan 1984: 54), and as a matter of departure by degree from accepted practice (for example, pollutant discharge above a mandated level: Hawkins 1984: Ch. 2). In a capitalist society, the actions that safety regulators control are bound up with fundamental processes of economic organisation, and so regulation involves balancing competing social and political interests from economic and welfarist constituency groups (Almond 2007; Haines 2011; Hawkins 1984). These considerations ensure that breaches of regulatory law are not normally viewed as 'unequivocally' wrong; they are open to contestation, and while they may be recognised as breaches of the law, they are not universally condemned in the same way as crimes (Almond 2008; Almond and Colover 2010). Of course, this perception does not justify the distinction; rather, it points to the existence of a social truth explicable via reference to the historical and political contexts that have shaped current practices (Carson 1979; Norrie 2001).

The practical results of this conception of regulatory offending as *mala prohibita* have been twofold. Firstly, the proliferation of regulatory offences during the last 100 years has signalled the adoption by government of responsibility for the mitigation of risks associated with the economic system (Braithwaite 2008; Majone 1997). The development of this 'regulatory state' can be related to the emergence of concepts of social citizenship (Ramsay 2006), a new politics of solidarity (Ewald 2002), and greater political and social participation (Tucker 1995). What is crucial is the corresponding determination that regulatory law is a suitable tool to use in pursuit of these goals: a process linked to both a legitimatory popular concern about the risks being controlled and the recognition that this control process would not challenge existing power relations (Lacey 2004: 161; Norrie 2001; Snider 1991). This distinction between signalling that a risk is being addressed via law, and actually utilising that law to effect fundamental change, can be significant; but although regulatory criminal offences are not necessarily utilised widely or recognised as criminal law, they remain a central feature of regulatory lawmaking and a preferred tool of government (Baldwin 2004; Husak 2008; Law Commission 2010).

The second main outcome has been the 'deflationary' effect that this use of criminal law as a regulatory tool has had in terms of the social and legal perception of the offences involved. By pursuing enforcement practices that utilise discretion to ration the use of prosecution (Hawkins 1984; 2002; Lloyd-Bostock 1992; Mascini and Houtman 2011) and prosecuting only in cases of the sort of moral wrongdoing normally associated with *mala in se* offending, regulators employ what Brudner calls 'administrative leniencies' to differentiate between offenders and respect their individual autonomy (1993: 53). This reluctance to utilise regulatory offences feeds the perception that they are not matters of 'real crime' and downgrades the regulatory branch of the criminal law further. Regulatory enforcement is therefore envisaged as possessing sufficient power to mean that it must be used sparingly (Hampton 2005; Hawkins 2002; Macrory 2006), but at the same time, as a matter of 'mere regulation' which does not connote the same degree of wrongdoing as a criminal prosecution. As a result, regulatory offences are ambiguous in nature, in that '[a]s well as being key institutions for moral denunciation, they epitomise systems of rules... that have been profoundly shaped and constrained by the interests of capital' (Haines and Sutton 2007: 22). This duality of status places them in a unique position, one which reflects a wider ambiguity surrounding the role of systems of regulation within modern society. The remainder of this chapter will explore the ways in which this ambiguity has impacted the form of the criminal law in terms of the extension of this 'institution for moral denunciation' into the regulatory context.

Developing an ambiguous 'corporate criminal law'

As Chapter 4 discussed, the state regulation of commercial activity has a long history; the application of criminal law to corporations is a more recent initiative. Since the origins of criminal liability related to religious notions of moral culpability, it followed that a corporation, not possessing a transcendental conscience, could not bear the kind of moral responsibility that criminal fault was predicated upon (Bernard 1984: 4–5). But once it was determined that corporations could undertake business ventures in their own right, it then became possible to conceive of them as owning property and acting as a 'master' for the purposes of employment and, resultantly, vicarious liability (Wells 2001: 88). The civil liability of corporate bodies emerged first, with the courts holding corporate bodies liable for the wrongful actions of their servants in the same way as human masters. Although wide-ranging, these liabilities did not extend to the criminal law due to the law's assumption that corporations were incapable of the kind of 'acts of understanding' that underpin the capacity to commit crime (Bernard 1984; Wells 2001: 89, citing the 'Case of Sutton's Hospital' of 1612). Baron Manwood's dictum in the 1688 case of 'Tipling v Pexall' that corporations 'have no soul to be damned and no body to be kicked'[2] encapsulated the essence of the law for over 300 years.

Change came because of the municipal and public obligations that emerged alongside the process of industrialisation during the 18th and early 19th centuries. The governance of urban public spaces required that local authorities and corporations assume responsibility for the construction and maintenance of the utility and transport infrastructure, and the specific duties imposed in these circumstances provided a basis for criminal liability where they were breached. Public authorities had held these duties for some time (Bernard 1984: 8; Wells 2001: 88), and it seemed a small step to extend this to corporate bodies. 'R v Birmingham and Gloucester Railway Co.'[3] held that it was possible for an indictment to stand against a company for an omission in relation to a statutory duty, in that case a duty to construct arches over its railway line. The fact that this case concerned an omission meant that it bypassed the problem of finding an individual responsible for an illegal act, although the subsequent case of 'R v Great North of England Railway Co.'[4] held that the same principle applied to positive acts. This case also held that there was a distinction between offences of immorality, which a corporation could not commit, and those of breaching a specific statutory duty, which it could (*per* Lord Denman CJ at p. 327). The real importance of these decisions was not that they extended the limits of corporate criminal liability to include misfeasance as well as nonfeasance but that they did so in a way that limited this extension; corporations can commit crimes by breaching the duties that business dealings and statute law impose upon them, but they cannot commit offences involving broader moral wrongdoing (Bernard 1984: 8). In a sense, this established a utilitarian form of liability, in that corporate offending was confined to the objectives that such legal obligations are created in order to pursue. It was not a matter of upholding any conception of moral right and wrong; indeed, such notions were explicitly ruled out in relation to corporations. Criminal law was part of the regulatory framework, not vice versa.

Classifying the Factory Acts

As the previous chapter discussed, the Factory Acts of the 19th century introduced new offences that sought to impose liability where an employer was in breach of a specified obligation as to working hours and conditions. After the Acts of 1833 and 1844, these obligations also began to include conditions relating to specific safety hazards, breaches of which rendered the employer liable to a fine. These laws are not solely side effects of private commerce; the law was beginning to protect the private interests of individuals. When it came to the enforcement of these offences, the relationship between the form of the law and its underlying purpose became problematic. Corporate criminal liability was predicated on the idea that breaches of the law were matters of merely technical fault, but the purpose behind the legislation was increasingly imbued with moral character. Reformers had framed these laws in rights-based terms, similar to those adopted by anti-slavery campaigners (Hutchins and Harrison 1911: 33; Mess 1926: 3; Thomas 1948: 28; Ward 1962: 30). But this moralising sentiment was counterbalanced by an interest in ensuring that the new offences served the interests of business by maintaining of a healthy workforce and marginalising rogue employers while at the same time avoiding curtailing free enterprise (Carson 1979: 44–45; Haines and Sutton 2007: 25; Norrie 2001: 84). The question thus became one of how far the law could, and should, reflect this sense of moral wrongdoing.

For commentators such as Kit Carson (1979), the key issue was whether the offences under the Factory Acts should be interpreted as requiring that culpable advertence be present on the part of an offending employer. The Factories Acts initially imposed *mens rea* requirements as components of the offences that were created, but the 1844 Act removed references to wilfulness and intentionality from the relevant offences (1979: 53–54). The enforcing inspectors had found that their ability to secure convictions was undermined by this requirement; it was extremely difficult to prove that a factory owner possessed the requisite knowledge of wrongdoing, and this meant that a sometimes partisan judiciary and jury could avoid convicting 'one of their own' by disputing the wilfulness of the breach (1979: 53; also Norrie 2001: 86). The result was the creation of strict liability offences, which based fault simply on the presence of a breach of the law, subject to a due diligence defence. This was intended to simplify the requirements incumbent upon prosecutors and reduce the capacity of the accused to sidestep liability by pleading ignorance or worker-blaming. But the problem with strict liability offences is that they are 'strict' in name only; they lack the severity that their name implies because, by omitting the ingredients that establish moral fault, they are reduced to the status of procedural infringements very different from ordinary crimes (Carson 1979: 54).

The paradox here is that Factory Inspectors were pressing for the removal of formal *mens rea* requirements at the same time as they were instituting 'informal' ones via their enforcement practices; prosecution under the strict liability offences occurred only where there was felt to be a significant level of moral wrongdoing that might suggest *mens rea*, such as where employers deliberately flouted the law in such a way as to mark themselves out as a bad apple (Carson 1979: 53; Norrie 2001: 85; Tombs and Whyte 2007: 114). In doing so, they avoided having to prove that moral fault in court, and health and safety inspectors continue to factor perceived culpability into prosecution decision-making (Hawkins 2002). The primary effect of this decision was the entrenchment of a pattern of 'under-enforcement' which had arisen as a result of political opposition and the under-resourcing of the Inspectorate. Being unable to prosecute widely, and being often unsuccessful when they did, the regulators shifted to an enforcement model that presented this inability to enforce as a virtue; the *mere fact* of prosecution was used to signify moral fault, and so a last-resort strategy was necessary in order to preserve the law's gravity. This was so despite the fact that these offences could not be relied upon to impart the message that Inspectors sought. It was hoped that the restrictive use of prosecution would be a case of 'less is more', providing an ersatz means of communicating a moral message, but it only succeeded in establishing that, sometimes, less is less.

An inherent ambiguity attaches to health and safety offences, and it results largely from this contradictory approach to enforcement. Safety laws do not have the social status associated with criminal law (Almond 2008; Almond and Colover 2010), but they are enforced 'as if they do'; their perceived status is broadly commensurate with that of an administrative penalty, but they are not enforced with the commitment to generality of application that this implies. These offences are important in signalling that control is being exercised over business activity, but at the same time, they are often ineffective in actually exercising this control. For Carson, this ambiguity was a matter of 'conventionalisation', in that activities were not only proscribed by law but also widely resorted to without punishment, in a self-reinforcing cycle: 'the crime remains conventional because it is only infrequently prosecuted, and is infrequently prosecuted because it is conventional' (Carson 1979: 55). They were conceptually and practically differentiated from 'real' crimes, and this formed the basis of a perceived distinction that has endured.

Determining corporate fault

While systems of safety regulation were introducing new categories of strict liability offence, the traditional presumption against corporate *mens rea* still excluded companies from the mainstream criminal law. These restrictions were not challenged until the 20th century, when a wider range of statutory offences began to be applied to corporate defendants. 'Mousell v London and North Western Railway'[5] involved a statutory offence committed by the manager of the defendant company (giving a false account with the intention to avoid paying tolls) which required that *mens rea* be proven (Bernard 1984: 10; Wells 2001: 90). In the case, vicarious corporate liability for the *mens rea* offence was viewed as simply reflecting the purpose of the statute being enforced, in line with precedent; there was no principled extension of the law. Subsequently, 'R v Cory Bros'[6] saw a corporate landowner indicted for manslaughter following a death involving an electrified fence; the indictment was dismissed on the basis that a corporation could not commit an offence against the person requiring advertence or foresight (Wells 2001: 92). As a common-law crime, manslaughter fell outside the scope of the established precedent that corporate liability could arise in relation to statutory offences.

Corporate liability for *mens rea* offences was finally recognised in English law in 1944, when three cases ('DPP v Kent and Sussex Contractors, R v ICR Haulage', and 'Moore v Bresler')[7] established the 'identification' model of liability, so called because it views the *mens rea* of the company as identifiable via that of senior officers. These cases applied this approach to offences involving, respectively, knowingly making false statements, conspiring to commit fraud, and making false use of documents. Rather than following the vicarious liability approach, which frames corporate liability in terms of responsibility for the acts of servants, and so is essentially 'factual' in nature (the company is responsible due to the 'fact' of its relationship with the individual), the identification doctrine sees the corporation as acting in its own right and is more 'normative' in nature (the company is responsible due to the 'quality' of its relationship with the individual). Under this model, the corporation commits the offence itself, via the actions of the senior manager or director who represents it; this person is acting *as* the company, and it is acting *through* him. The case of 'Bolton v Graham' saw Lord Denning use the analogy of a human body in order to explain this relationship: 'It [the corporation] has a brain and nerve centre which controls what it does. It also has hands which hold the tools and act in accordance with directions from the centre.'[8] In these cases, there is an explicit reframing of corporate responsibility in terms of things done by the individuals who 'act or speak or think for it' ('R v ICR Haulage', *per* Viscount Caldecote at p. 155); there is a 'direct transfer' of *mens rea* from the individual to the company (Norrie 2001: 93). Liability for both statutory and common-law offences of all kinds could be attributed to a corporate body in this way. Additionally, in 'Moore v Bresler', the criminal acts were committed 'to the detriment of' the convicted company, meaning that there is no requirement that the offence be committed for the benefit of the corporation.

Subsequent decisions clarified both the terms on which such liability may arise and the rationale behind this test. The landmark case was that of 'Tesco Supermarkets Ltd. v Nattrass',[9] concerning a breach of the Trades Description Act 1968, a public welfare offence. The defendant company had advertised goods for sale at a price lower than that actually being charged due to an oversight by a store manager. It was not necessary under the offence to prove *mens rea*, but it was a defence under s. 24(1) of that Act to prove that the offence was 'due to the act or default of another person ... beyond his [the company's] control' and that the company 'took all reasonable precautions and exercised all due diligence to avoid the commission of such an offence by himself or any person under his control'. The issue was whether the precautions to be considered should include those exercised by the store manager. The company operated hundreds of stores in the UK and had in place a supervision and training scheme, amounting to a reasonable level of diligence, but if the store manager was acting 'as' the company then the precautions he took against committing an offence 'by himself' must necessarily be insufficient. It was held that the manager was 'another person' for the purposes of the Act, and so his lack of due diligence was not attributable to the company. The defence was intended to mitigate an otherwise absolute offence and introduce a 'rational and moral justification' (*per* Lord Diplock at p. 195) into a policy of consumer protection. The store manager was too junior to represent the 'controlling mind' of the company.

This decision informs criticism of the identification doctrine, as the parameters of the 'controlling mind' were drawn so narrowly that almost no-one outside of a handful of senior directors could ever represent the company in this sense (Clarkson 1996; 2008; Gobert 2008; Sullivan 2001; Wells 2001). Lord Reid approved of Lord Denning's dictum in 'Bolton v Graham' (at p. 172), stating that the 'board of directors, the managing director and perhaps other senior officers' were capable of acting as the company, and Lord Diplock referred to a *de minimis* threshold of corporate officials with authority over strategic corporate management. While this provides for a degree of doctrinal certainty, it also severely restricts the capacity of the law to hold corporate bodies liable for criminal offences. The requirement that a senior manager or director must provide the *mens rea* for an offence, even though the acts or omissions involved are likely to occur at the operational level, creates evidential problems; how can a connection be made between a director in head office and a dangerous working practice on a distant building site? It is often difficult to show that the 'brain' knew what the 'hands' were doing and, while a failure of supervision might form the basis of an offence, this reframes corporate fault in inchoate terms, in that liability relates to some incipient factor and not to the harm done. This is important in relation to consequentialist criminal offences (such as manslaughter), where the directing mind must have personally displayed the gross negligence required in relation to a risk of death or injury,[10] and where it can be difficult to show that failures of oversight give rise to culpably negligent consequences.

In addition, there is often no clear-cut distinction between the 'brain' and 'hands' of a corporation; just as some human behaviour can easily be classed as conscious (such as writing a book) and some as entirely non-conscious (such as blinking or sneezing), much behaviour lies somewhere between the two (such as driving a car), with conscious decisions being made but also moderated, enacted, and instinctively *done* without conscious review (Bargh 1997). Similarly, business action cannot be reduced to a simple dichotomy between strategic decision-making at board-level (choosing to invest in company X) and involuntary action at operational level (employee X filling in a form incorrectly); most business activity involves enacting choices at multiple levels (devising a safety system and then implementing it in practice). The identification doctrine is predicated on a restrictive view of corporate decision-making that fails to recognise how far corporate action is the outcome of these interactions. Subsequent cases mitigated this hierarchical model, recognising that the rationale of some offences requires that 'the company' act through a low-level employee; a shop worker who provides age-restricted items to an underage child is the only person who acts 'as' the company for this purpose, and it would defeat the intention of the offence if liability could be avoided wherever the directors of a company did not personally approve an illegal sale.[11] Relatedly, it was determined that lower-level managers with responsibility for particular areas of corporate activity, for example, a regional investment manager responsible for share purchases, could act 'as' the company in relation to the activities they held responsibility for.[12] This made the identification doctrine more applicable to the reality of contemporary business practice, in that empowered employees with front-line responsibility could thus be regarded as acting on behalf of the company (Wells 2001: 104). But the identification doctrine remains a restrictive model which generally circumscribes, rather than facilitates, corporate accountability (Clarkson 2005; 2008; Wells 2001).

Although the cases identified here involve technical, 'quasi'-regulatory public welfare offences, the emergence of the identification doctrine was connected with the broadening of this liability into new areas which were more obviously central to the criminal law. The most important example of this for current purposes is that of manslaughter, a homicide offence involving unintentional but culpable killing. The unreported 1965 case of 'R v Northern Strip Mining Construction Co.' saw the first prosecution of a company for this offence, following the death of a workman when a railway bridge collapsed during demolition (Slapper 1993: 423). The identification doctrine was applied and, even though the company was acquitted on the basis that the managing director was not himself reckless, the possibility of such an offence was confirmed (Slapper 1993: 424). Despite this, it would be many years before this precedent was followed; establishing the means to prosecute did not bring a change in practice. There are several reasons for this emergence of corporate criminal 'fault'; corporations have come to play an increasingly prominent role in public and private life, and they have the capacity to inflict serious and widespread physical and economic harm. A better scientific understanding of issues of causation and the technological nature of risk has given rise to a greater social awareness of those harms as something other than inevitable or 'normal' events. This knowledge, coupled with the growth of a more democratic and interventionist state, necessitated the development of systems of law that were capable of signalling political control over social threats (Habermas 1988). Criminal law, a system that is communicative of symbolic values, fulfils this role. This account regards the emergence of criminal liability as a progressive development through which issues of public concern were addressed, but the problem with this is that these concerns were *not* being addressed in fact; prosecutions were not brought and change was not achieved.

As such, we must consider the concept of political risk in this context. Political risk is a form of challenge to the elected representatives of a democratic society, who undertake to ensure the security and wellbeing of the citizenry (Haines 2011: Ch. 3). When a serious risk event demonstrates the failure of political actors to exert effective control over a threat to this security, their credibility is damaged. This is a process of 'legitimation'; conflicts in the economic and political systems must be mitigated and displaced by actions (like law reform) that reassert the capacity of the state to guarantee the satisfaction of general social interests (Habermas 1976). And yet it is hard to identify the political risks that the state was facing when corporate criminal liability emerged;

apart from a creeping awareness of corporate power, there are few clear pressure points that might have triggered this response. An alternative approach to this issue of legitimacy is provided by Nicola Lacey (2001; 2004). Notions of subjective fault and *mens rea* only really emerged in English law in the 20th century; before then, the criminal law followed something approaching a character responsibility model which based liability on the external evaluation of a defendant's character (2001: 361). Issues of agency and subjectivity only became central to the criminal law by the 1950s because 'as the terrain of criminal law expanded and its social functions diversified... its normative foundations, which had been adequate... [came] under increasing strain' (2001: 362). The values that underpinned criminal liability were in need of legitimation as a result of its application in contexts where assumptions about bad character and manifest criminality did not apply. Criminal norms had to be restated in order to ensure their continued application within a changing society; criminalisation must accord with prevailing social norms if the law is to command public support (Lacey 2004: 149–150). The concept of subjective moral responsibility was developed in order to achieve this by moving the emphasis from 'character' to 'capacity'; the justifications for liability are thus restated in universal terms relating to the defendant's ability to control criminal outcomes, not to inchoate issues of disposition.

On this reading, the development of a system of corporate *mens rea* can be seen as an effort to legitimate the wider system of corporate legal responsibility. If regulatory offences emerged as a way of enforcing standards of care across dangerous social contexts, then subjective liability emerged in order to restate the normative reasons for imposing these restrictions, particularly onto those who appear to lack a criminal disposition (Lacey 2001: 365). The strict liability approach to corporate responsibility adopts a functional, 'balance-sheet' view of the corporation as an accumulation of duties owed and owing, as established via contractual agreement, statutory obligation, and mutual undertaking. Liability is associated with these obligations, arising where they are breached, and is vicariously determined via the contractual relationships that dictate who is an employee of the corporation and what duties they owe it. As such, it is a 'factual' account of responsibility. The identification doctrine, on the other hand, is concerned with issues of agency: of acts done and choices made. It is more morally informed, investing the decisions made about guilt with an explicit account of normative character. Criminal liability is invoked to justify the control of corporate conduct as a whole; it advertises the fact that (in principle) corporate actors are subject to the same normative evaluation as other defendants. As we have seen, this was more symbolic than functional; there was not necessarily a pressure on the state to show it was fulfilling promises made about controlling risks. But a shift in social debates about the relationship between state and corporate power would ensure that this was no longer the case.

The emergence of a corporate crime discourse

The law relating to corporate criminal liability faced a new critical challenge in the 1980s, when the contemporary political context conspired with a series of events and incidents to present a new set of political risks to government. The 1970s had seen the development of a 'third wave' of regulation (Tucker 1995), which centred on a consensual, participatory mode of governance, as typified by the UK's Robens Report (1972) and Health and Safety at Work Act 1974. While this is often held up as a definitive example of corporatist policy (Hutter 1997), it was not without its limitations. Perhaps the most fundamental of these is the fact that the UK does not have the same social and political context or traditions of union membership and safety representation, as the Scandinavian nations on which this approach was modelled (Frick and Walters 1998; Walters 1995; 1996). Strong trade union involvement in the regulation of safety can play a fundamental role in improving standards (James and Walters 2002), but the UK has not seen the same degree of implementation as mainland Europe (Tombs and Whyte 2007: 50). Certainly by the 1970s, the UK had a much more entrenched history of adversarial industrial relations than many contemporary European jurisdictions, and this meant that Robens' recommendations were never fully implemented.

The end of consensus?

These trends were exacerbated in the following decade, when the Conservative Thatcher governments pursued an avowedly non-corporatist, anti-union industrial relations policy, weakening the political influence of organised labour (Gamble 1994). A deregulatory, pro-business agenda of neo-liberal reform was pursued, which involved the removal of governmental controls that constituted 'burdens on business'; regulation (including health and safety law) was cast as a matter of 'red tape' (Bain 1997: 179; Hawkins 2002: 118; Hutter 1997: 45; Hutter and Manning 1990: 128; Tombs and Whyte 2007: 158), a Deregulation Task Force was instituted, funding for regulators was cut, new legal provisions were vetted to limit their economic impact, and regulations were subject to repeal (Bain 1997). This has been identified by critical scholars as the start of an era of neo-liberal or market-based regulation, whereby externally imposed restrictions are removed and it is the decisions of private actors that govern the distribution of risks and costs associated with safety (Bain 1997; Bittle and Snider 2006; Gray 2006; 2009; Snider 1991; Tombs and Whyte 2010). This leads to the decentring and privatising of regulation, the responsibilisation of individual workers and risk-bearing actors, and the pursuit of a libertarian, small-state agenda.

Other scholars see this reordering as a fundamental 'change' in the nature of regulation, rather than simply as a process of deregulation. For while regulatory policy has moved away from notions of top-down, state-led command-and-control, the net 'amount' of regulation has not reduced; decentralised, voluntary, supranational, and market-based modes of regulation have proliferated within a 'meta-regulatory' regime (Black 2007; Braithwaite 2008; Levi-Faur 2005; Morgan 2003; Parker 2002). On this reading, regulation has become a matter of achieving maximum effect for minimum cost ('better' or 'good' regulation: Bartle and Vass 2007; Dodds 2006). This is pursued through a wide range of regulatory strategies, including licensing/auditing regimes, the risk-based application of resources (Baldwin and Black 2008; Black 2005; Hampton 2005), and the delegation of responsibility to industry associations, voluntary groups, and regulated companies, via a form of 'polycentric' regulatory 'subsidiarity' which emphasises the shifting of regulatory responsibility away from the state (Bartle and Vass 2007; Black 2007). On this approach, businesses are best placed to effect change, and so the state's role becomes one of coordinating self-generated efforts at compliance. This necessitates a reduction in the role of the state and the careful management of measures (like enforcement) which disrupt this polycentricity (Hampton 2005; Macrory 2006).

This remodelling of the regulatory environment brought an end to any political consensus over regulation that might have existed before. The economic reforms pursued by the Thatcher governments were controversial, and the privatisation of nationalised industries and the curtailment of trade union power proved divisive and contributed to the image (adopted with differing nuances by supporters and opponents of Thatcher) of the government as having a business-first agenda. Regulatory reforms came to be identified with this economic agenda and were subject to the same opposition. Regulatory agencies were constrained via funding cuts and the withdrawal of the political mandate to act, leading to reductions in rates of inspection and enforcement action, and an increase in rates of work-related injury and death (James 1992). Hawkins observed that a 'perceived governmental hostility [produced] a sense of vulnerability in [HSE], since it was...engaged in regulatory restraint in ways that had powerful implications for the conduct of business, operating as it did in a world suffused with high levels of ideological commitment to laissez-faire values' (2002: 117). This fraught political context provided the backdrop to a series of very serious work-related death cases in the mid- to late-1980s (as discussed in Chapter 1). Events can be a powerful catalyst for legal change (Gobert 2005; Hutter and Lloyd-Bostock 1990; Wells 1988), particularly where they tap into wider concerns. The loss of life at Zeebrugge, Piper Alpha, and elsewhere fitted into a narrative about excess, exploitation, and the profit-first mentality of the contemporary political/economic elite. It seemed that these events were a direct outcome of the deregulatory ethos of the time.

Accordingly, this period saw the emergence of a clearer conception that there might be a role for the criminal law to play in protecting individuals from the destructive potential of corporations. While trade unions, pressure groups, and commentators all played a part in this process of critical challenge (Gobert 2005; Tombs and Whyte 2007; Wells 2001), the fundamental impetus came from a broader recognition of the risks of social life, and the tenuousness of the systems of control that mitigate them. This is often described via a 'risk society' perspective (Bauman 2000; Beck 1992; Garland 2001; Giddens 1991), under which it is argued that changes in late-20th-century society, such as globalisation, an increasingly flexible economy and employment market, the pluralisation of culture, and the breakdown of traditional structures of family, community and state, have created a society which, although freer, is also more unpredictable than ever before. New technology creates 'new parameters of risk and danger as well as offering beneficent possibilities for humankind' (Giddens 1991: 28), and these risks are knowable via the medium of professional expertise. Engagement in prosocial activities such as employment and travel therefore becomes a matter of conscious risk-taking, as internal and external hazards are increasingly identified. In a time of social upheaval, events such as work-related deaths render these risks knowable and salient (Almond 2008; Almond and Colover 2010; Hutter and Lloyd-Bostock 1990; Wells 2001) and invest them with emotional weight. Following Mary Douglas (1992; Douglas and Wildavsky 1982), Haines *et al.* argue that risks are identified according to the threat they pose to the values and boundaries of the socio-cultural order (2007: 440), and deemed significant on the basis of the negative emotions and censure that breaches of these boundaries provoke. These socio-cultural risks encapsulate the notion of public concern that is often cited as justifying reform of the law.

Certainly, much of the criticism levelled at health and safety regulation has centred on its inability to respond to these socio-cultural concerns; as discussed, regulators such as HSE were constrained from utilising enforcement action widely and unable to secure desired outcomes when they did. Rates of prosecution have always been low and were further depressed during the 1980s and 1990s (Pearce and Tombs 1990; Slapper 1993; 1999; Tombs and Whyte 2007). This ties back to the inability of health and safety law to reinforce the socio-cultural boundaries of accepted conduct; these offences simply lacked the capacity to fulfil the communicative role required. This was so despite increases in the capacity and expertise of public and private actors engaged in what Haines *et al.* (2007: 439) term 'actuarial' risk management, referring to the scientific drive towards the measurement of risk, which is then used to inform regulatory policies. But evidence-led risk regimes tend to possess an instrumental rationality but not a communicative capacity, and so are unsuited for the purpose of linking legal controls to underlying social values. When this connection is lacking, the regulatory system becomes increasingly fragile, unable to justify its own existence, and vulnerable to 'regulatory degradation' (Tombs and Whyte 2010).

Revolution postponed: The battle for criminalisation

So it was at the moment when public concerns about the risks inherent in business practices were beginning to exercise increasing influence that the capacity of the regulatory bodies to respond to those concerns was being most heavily restricted. Regulatory law found itself increasingly unable to fulfil its public interest functions due to the political and economic circumstances in which it operated. In Habermasian terms (1987; 1988), the regulatory sphere was becoming dominated by the influences of systems of money and power; the business lobby was increasingly influencing the direction taken by government in setting policy (Bain 1997: 185–186; Gobert 2005: 7–14), and the ideological concerns of the government influenced regulatory practices via the control of resources (Hawkins 2002: 117). The logic of regulation accordingly became more explicitly concerned with issues of efficiency, economic rationality, and quantifiable impact. Regulation became a matter of achieving the maximum benefit (in terms of improved performance across measurable outcomes) at the minimum cost to business, as reflected in the emergence of the 'better regulation' agenda and regulatory impact assessment (Bain 1997; Helm 2006; Tombs and Whyte

2010). Health and safety regulation became a means of settling the negotiable individual interests of worker, employer, government, and public, rather than a matter of upholding a universal interest in safe workplaces that respect the welfare of all.

This shift prompted the move towards the use of criminal law as a regulatory tool. For while regulation is instrumental, a means of achieving policy goals and balancing competing interests, criminal prosecution occurs not because it is efficient or aids in the achievement of some external goal (such as the prevention of harm), but because it is morally 'deserved' (Ashworth 2000: 249–250; Lacey 2001). Criminal law exists to penalise substantial wrongdoing, and this should be pursued irrespective of the economic and political consequences; it should be 'context-transcending' in nature. In the context of a field like workplace health and safety, what was sought was a statement about the values fundamental to society that rendered safety risks morally unacceptable. The growing dissatisfaction with regulatory enforcement at this time reflected, therefore, a desire for normative adjudication, for the law to state what is right and wrong, and this can be glimpsed in both the arguments made by victims' organisations and trade unions (Gobert 2005: 20–25). Wells frames this shift in terms of the need to 'demonstrate a commitment...to the symbolic message which is carried by the criminal law' (1988: 801). This search for moral adjudication also underpins the attempts made during this period to utilise the criminal law as a means of responding to work-related deaths.

Three cases demonstrate the nature of this struggle for corporate criminalisation. Firstly, the sinking of the Herald of Free Enterprise in 1987 (discussed in Chapter 1), which caused the deaths of 193 people, is now regarded as a watershed moment in terms of this issue (Gobert 2005: 11; Slapper 1993; Tombs and Whyte 2007: 18; Wells 1988; 2001). While the 'theoretical' notion of corporate homicide was not new, the idea of prosecuting for corporate manslaughter was so unfamiliar that 'as a matter of social construction of crime it was almost unthinkable' (Wells 1988: 789). The Herald sinking was a visible indicator of the risks inherent in contemporary society and the failures of the law to control them. The Sheen Report (Department of Transport 1987), the official investigation into the disaster, highlighted systemic failures of accountability and control within the offending company, meaning that the disaster had causes of a sort that the corporation *ought* to be accountable for. The fact that this accountability was not forthcoming prompted the jury sitting in the inquest hearings that followed the disaster to ignore the coroner's directions that corporate criminal liability could not exist in the absence of a case against a senior individual and return verdicts of unlawful killing in relation to those deaths (Wells 1988: 789; 2001: 108). This 'mutiny' seemed indicative of a shift in social perceptions which was sufficient to prompt the Director of Public Prosecutions to launch an investigation with an eye on a potential manslaughter charge (no criminal investigation had taken place prior to the inquest).

The resultant trial[13] foundered due to the restrictions imposed by the identification doctrine. Reckless manslaughter, the offence charged, was held to require that a person should not be guilty in the absence of blameworthiness which could only be provided via the acts and choices of a culpable individual (Wells 2001: 113). The effect of this reading of the law was that the systems, policies, and procedures of the body corporate were placed outside the reach of the criminal law. Crucially, what the case highlighted was a desire for the moral judgement that criminal proceedings are meant to achieve; while Sheen had settled issues of factual causation, and regulation had the potential to achieve behavioural change, neither of these was sufficient to provide the evaluation of 'moral' culpability desired by the public and the inquest jury. The law was found wanting in its ability to express a judgement about the normative position of the offending company. The fact that criminal accountability was blocked on technical grounds rather than on the basis of any substantive judgement about fault accentuated this sense of deficit, and subsequent decisions added to this awareness of the criminal law's limitations as a forum for moral adjudication.

The Southall rail crash of 1997, in which seven people died when a freight train collided with a passenger train that had run through a red light on its way into Paddington station, led to a manslaughter prosecution being brought against Great Western Trains, the operator of the passenger train.[14] Responsibility for the crash was attributed to the company's failure to train staff adequately, to provide working precautionary safety equipment, and to operate an adequate safety system. The issue was whether the company could be convicted as a result without resort to the identification doctrine (Wells 2001: 112–113). The Attorney-General referred the case to the Court of Appeal,[15] who confirmed that while a defendant could be convicted of gross negligence manslaughter in the absence of evidence as to their state of mind, a non-human defendant could not be convicted of manslaughter in the absence of evidence as to the guilt of a specific individual. The identification doctrine required that gross negligence must be attributable to an individual because there is an implied requirement that a higher degree of blameworthiness must be present for a criminal offence than might apply in a civil negligence context. In doing so, the court drew a distinction between criminal liability, as a matter of individual moral culpability, and regulatory liability, which does not have this quality. For an offence like manslaughter, liability based purely on conduct would be inappropriate because the seriousness of the offence meant that the overarching criminal law norm of advertent moral culpability, expressed via *mens rea*, must be adhered to (despite gross negligence being conduct-based: Wells 2001: 113). The defendants were fined a record £1.5m for a breach of s. 3(1) of the Health and Safety at Work Act 1974 but avoided liability for manslaughter, and so any fundamental change of the law was once again postponed.

So when faced with a growing social expectation that corporate responsibility ought to lead to legal accountability, the courts fell back onto the distinction between *mala in se* and *mala prohibita* that had characterised the law for so long. A corporate defendant cannot bear criminal responsibility, with all of its associated moral significance, because the basis of criminal liability is individual blameworthiness expressed in terms of *mens rea* (Norrie 2001: 104). Corporate liability has been restricted to the sphere of instrumental law, where enforcement is used in order to achieve policy goals which reflect accommodations reached over competing economic and welfarist concerns (Almond 2007; Hawkins 2002). Traditional approaches to *mens rea* ensure that these debates are steered away from the political arena and treated as matters of morally neutral problem-solving, rather than as issues of fundamental right and wrong. In Alan Norrie's words, the identification doctrine's 'lack of realism, tied to the individualism of mens rea . . . maintains the appearance of a narrow, "apolitical", technical doctrine of the law removed from political judgement about the nature of fault in a social world dominated by economic calculation' (2001: 99). There may be an increasing demand for a form of moral arbitration over the status of work-related deaths, but the criminal law would not yet play a role in that process.

From crime to regulation, from regulation to crime

In 1994, a successful corporate manslaughter prosecution was finally brought, against an outdoor education provider (OLL Ltd.) following the drowning of four schoolchildren on a canoeing expedition across Lyme Bay, Dorset.[16] This case succeeded primarily because it involved a very small organisation with only a couple of employees, meaning that the managing director, Peter Kite, essentially *was* OLL Ltd. The fact that he was involved in both managerial decisions and day-to-day operations meant that there was no difficulty in showing that he, as the directing mind, had the knowledge required to make the company guilty. Despite this, the case did not really test the parameters of the law, and appeared to be an extraordinary response to the facts of that particular case. The identities of the victims involved (four children), and the significance of the issues of trust involved in sending children on a school trip, made the case suitable for extraordinary treatment in order to address specific public and media concerns (Almond 2008; Almond and Colover 2010). The abnormality of this response is emphasised by the fact that the subsequent decade saw only four more such prosecutions, all against similarly small-scale companies.[17] This slow pace of development prompted criticism from those who saw these cases as exceptions which proved that the law in its current form *could not* meaningfully address corporate criminality (Clarkson 1996; Wells 2001). But in 1994, the same year as the OLL conviction, the Law Commission first tabled the idea of a corporate manslaughter offence, setting into motion the reform process outlined in Chapter 1. Subsequent Law Commission proposals were published in 1996, followed by government consultation in 2000 and proposals in 2005; reform of the law would follow in 2007. It is important to try and understand why it was that work-related deaths seemed a problem in need of solving via a new offence.

Work-related deaths as a political challenge

As discussed previously, the political climate of the 1980s and 1990s was broadly neo-liberal (Harvey 2005). Within this framework, regulation was perceived as a potential obstruction to the functioning of the economy. But more regulation was created during this period than at any time before, because systems of arms-length co-regulation were being used to replace direct governmental oversight (Braithwaite 2008; Majone 1997). This wave of regulation was avowedly instrumental in nature, concerned essentially with the coordination of the market system (reflected in the market failure model of regulatory intervention: Baldwin and Cave 1999; Ogus 1994). At the same time, however, there was a movement towards expressive reform in the shape of the corporate manslaughter offence; this appears to have no underlying 'market failure' rationale (although a Regulatory Impact Assessment was carried out: Home Office 2006), so the reasons for its introduction must lie elsewhere (Prosser 2011: Ch. 5). Gobert argues that the reform process had a 'life of its own' prompted by the influence of catastrophic events that put pressure on political actors and the government to 'be seen as promoting the "public good"' (2005: 21; also Haines and Hall 2004). In particular, the 1997 Labour government had made it a manifesto pledge to introduce legislation of this sort and faced a particular internal pressure to do so due to their links with the trade union movement. External events and the need to satisfy electoral constituencies meant that even a government with a pro-business agenda and commitment to neo-liberal principles would still have to show some responsiveness to requests for legal control of business behaviour.

This brings us back to the notion of political risk, a form of challenge to the elected representatives of a democratic society who undertake to ensure the security and wellbeing of the citizenry (Haines 2011; Haines *et al.* 2007: 441). When a serious event demonstrates the failure of political actors to exert effective control over a threat to this security, the credibility of those actors is damaged. This notion of political risk draws on Habermas' (1976) notion of legitimation crisis. Governments must strike a balance between ensuring the effective functioning of the economic system and maintaining the social infrastructure needed to mitigate the side effects of that system. When the state is unable to do this, opposition to its steering role becomes prevalent, and its legitimacy is lost. So political risks arise when circumstances suggest that political actors are not able to protect against the dangers inherent in modern society, and political risk management becomes a matter of 'keeping the economy going and make people feel safe' (Haines 2011). Work-related deaths play a significant role in terms of political risk as they signal the existence of insecurities within modern social life which prompt public demands for control (Almond 2007; Haines and Hall 2004).

The normative impact of political risk is closely related to the emotional impact of socio-cultural risk. As Hutter and Lloyd-Bostock observe, '[t]he power of accidents to command attention and arouse emotion in turn has social consequences. Accidents create expectations and demands for action. Not only must some response be made; it must be seen to be made' (1990: 410). As such, major disasters bring into question the status of government and regulators as the guardians of public security. In order to ward off perceptions of ineffectiveness, political actors must demonstrate a meaningful response; states reform their health and safety laws 'when forced to do so by [a] public crisis' (Snider 1991: 216) of the sort that can be prompted by work-related deaths. These events can highlight that a government which prioritises the economic system has created a climate in which risk-taking is encouraged to the detriment of other interests. This was an argument made in the aftermath of many fatal safety incidents in Britain during the 1980s and early 1990s, where the free-market liberalism and privatisation programmes of the Thatcher governments were identified as key contextual antecedents of, among others, the Herald of Free Enterprise sinking and the Piper Alpha oil rig explosion (Pearce and Tombs 1991: 420; Slapper 1999; Wells 2001; Woolfson *et al.* 1996) and accounts to some extent for subsequent public demands for more effective regulation.

One of the most distinctive features of this political risk is the degree to which it runs contrary to the political climate of the time. The corporate manslaughter offence appears to be a derivation from a wider policy of 'regulatory degradation' (Tombs and Whyte 2010; also Bain 1997; Beck and Woolfson 2000). While the period during which the manslaughter reforms occurred also saw increases in the top-end fines imposed onto companies convicted of health and safety offences,[18] all other available indices during this period (frequency of inspection, enforcement, and prosecution; regulator: regulated company ratios; levels of funding given to regulators) indicated that safety was declining in priority (James and Walters 1992; Tombs and Whyte 2007). These trends have proved consistent and continue up to the current day, exacerbated in particular by the financial crisis of 2008. If anything, the attitude of governmental indifference that existed prior to the crisis has been increasingly replaced by one of open hostility, with the Prime Minister, David Cameron, referring to a 'health and safety culture' that has infected public life (Almond 2009b: 368), created a 'blanket of bureaucracy, suspicion and fear',[19] and even been partly responsible for the riots in London in August 2011.[20] Media and political rhetoric about health and safety has long been deeply hostile (Almond 2009b), and in 2010 combined in the form of the Young Review, a set of proposals drafted for the Cabinet Office, which sought to address the 'low standing' of health and safety law (Young 2010). This was a less charitable document than its terms of reference suggested, as it characterised health and safety regulation as a mass of absurdity and red tape. Reforms of the law (including many focusing on reducing regulatory burdens) were tabled to follow throughout 2012 and beyond, and the Löfstedt Review (2011a) of health and safety regulation constituted the first part of this process.

The manslaughter reforms constitute an exception to the general approach taken throughout this period, but this is very much the point of a measure of this sort, according to the notion of political risk (Almond 2007; Haines 2011). When economic considerations come to the fore, as they tend to within a neo-liberal capitalist system, it becomes necessary to counter the perception that the current balance of policy is beneficial to the interests of capital but not to those of the public (Habermas 1976). Reforms such as the introduction of the corporate manslaughter offence arise in order to mitigate the structural tensions that can be exacerbated by the general direction of policy in this area. This underpins arguments that the reform process is a kind of window-dressing, a symbolic measure designed to pacify opposition rather than effect substantive change (Haines and Hall 2004; Hall and Johnstone 2005). As Gobert points out, the manslaughter reforms encountered concerted opposition from the business lobby, leading to a watering-down of the proposals and procrastination on the part of the government (2005: 7–20). This neo-liberal resistance to reform is indicative of the new offence's role as a counterweight to the interests of the systems of money and power that regulation is so often constrained to avoid compromising.

Legislative reform as a solution

One final point to note is the alacrity with which criminalisation was pursued as a way of addressing these legitimatory concerns. 'Overcriminalisation', or the proliferation of criminal law, is a well-documented feature of contemporary society (Ashworth 2000; Husak 2008; Simon 2007); the corporate manslaughter offence is one of more than 3000 criminal offences created in the UK between 1997 and 2010 (Law Commission 2010: 1.17). This trend can be attributed to many factors, some of which, like the insecurity associated with the 'risk society', have been discussed already; certainly, an increasingly populist and punitive intolerance of crime has played a significant part in this expansion. But, as the Law Commission identified (2010), much of this expansion has occurred into areas that conform to the notion of *mala prohibita*. Criminal law is increasingly used as a means of responding to administrative rule violations and as a tool of social policy-making rather than just as a means for the condemnation of fundamental wrongdoing. In particular, the emergence of 'managerial' and 'actuarial' trends within the criminal justice system, involving an emphasis on using performance indicators and targeted enforcement to manage categories of offender (Bottoms 1995; Feeley and Simon 1992; 1994) has been identified as running alongside a 'punitive turn' in policy and debate (Garland 2001: 16–19).

What is distinctive about this development is the degree to which the criminal law is perceived as fulfilling a problem-solving role, as a tool of wider policy-delivery in areas of social welfare, public ordering, the workplace, and so on (Ashworth 2000; Husak 2008; Simon 2007). The expressive function of the criminal law is distinctive, centring on the ability to demarcate forms of conduct as morally unacceptable and constitutes a mechanism for hierarchical standard-setting, or the establishment and imposition of expected norms of conduct (Ashworth 2000; Lacey 2004: 163). The Law Commission has critiqued the resultant tendency for criminal law to be utilised by public law-makers instrumentally, as a means of exercising control over undesirable conduct, and for this to result in large numbers of very specific, poorly defined, and often underused, criminal offences (2010: 1.22). These considerations also help to explain the emergence of the new corporate manslaughter offence. If criminalisation is the *de facto* response to any shortcoming in the existing legal structure, then the invocation of criminal law to address the shortcomings of health and safety regulation should come as no surprise. Indeed, most of the 'overcriminalising' laws identified by the Law Commission relate to the control of business conduct, making the introduction of the new offence consistent with practices elsewhere.

The appeal of the criminal law

To summarise, the recent history of criminalisation in the health and safety sphere has shown that the development of regulation outlined in Chapter 4 has been accompanied by a search for a system of moral adjudication to make sense of work-related deaths. Criminal law is distinctive because it contains a moral component, as well as disincentivising conduct in pursuit of policy goals, it involves a form of calling to account that invokes disapproval and condemnation relating to the good reasons identified not to engage in the conduct in question (Duff 2001; Tadros 2005). This moral indignation relates to a recognition that the defendant has shown an improper disregard towards the interests of another (Tadros 2005: 88), or has in some way exercised domination over their interests and will (Braithwaite and Pettit 1990), or has violated a deep-rooted *a priori* set of community values (Duff 2001: 59). It is submitted that this quality, the ability to exercise moral judgement, explains the persistence of demands for criminalisation in the area of health and safety law, because it is something that regulatory law is unable to provide. From the 19th century onwards, this body of law has been rendered increasingly instrumental in character, and the efforts made to apply criminal law within this context reflect a public awareness of its shortcomings. The criminal law is able to perform hierarchical standard-setting functions because it is underpinned by a bedrock of social support for its operation, which stems from a 'resonance... between the substantive norms of criminal law and prevailing social norms' (Lacey 2004: 149–150). Without this, the limited capacity of law enforcers would be insufficient to secure widespread compliance with the law.

Criminal law is legitimated by the belief in its rightness which results from its connection to community understandings of right and wrong. For regulatory law, however, a '[l]ack of articulation with community-based control will…place limits on the effectiveness with which…hierarchically imposed regulatory objectives can be pursued' (Lacey 2004: 149); the absence of belief in rightness, stemming from an inability to demonstrate a foundation in underlying social values, undermines the capacity of regulators to secure compliance with the law. Because it is couched in what Duff terms 'content-independent' reasons for complying (2001: 56), regulation fails to address citizens as members of a normative political community and frame itself as a matter of 'public wrongs'. Andrew Ashworth, in a perceptive critique of responsive regulatory strategies, argues that criminal law is distinctive because it is a form of 'public' law, and so should exist 'above politics' where discretion and competing private interests do not intercede (2000: 245). Criminal prosecution occurs because it is deserved. If a fundamental value is being protected, enforcement cannot be subject to external considerations such as the likelihood of future compliance and the degree to which the defendant cooperates with enforcers (2000: 248). These may be relevant factors for mitigation in sentencing, and the realities of criminal law enforcement mean that issues of discretion and compliance-seeking do play a role there (Gill 2002; Kagan 1984), but they do not affect the nature of the wrong done; criminal law practices acknowledge the wrong done while discretion is exercised in relation to it, while regulatory law uses these factors 'as the basis of' decisions about the nature of the wrong done.

While this sort of targeting of enforcement action is desirable within a regulatory context, at least in terms of maximising instrumental impact, it 'particularises' the application of the law according to the defendant in hand, rendering it even less likely that it can be accepted as a legitimate forum for consideration of fundamental rights and wrongs. Regulatory law, by introducing *ex post* factors relating to the identity of the defendant into the adjudication process, opens the door for policy-oriented consideration of the desirability of enforcement, which is open to distortion as a result of the competing interests under consideration. It is thus unable to convincingly provide a forum for deliberation over the 'nature of fault in a social world dominated by economic calculation' of the type sought by Norrie (2001: 99). The desire for this sort of forum has driven calls for corporate liability over the last 25 years and lies at the root of the corporate manslaughter reforms; the symbolic status of criminal law, as a social institution, offers something that regulation cannot, namely, a means of evaluating corporate conduct and the existing settlement of interests (economic and welfarist) by reference to a deeper set of community norms.

6
The Purpose of Corporate Homicide Liability

The preceding two chapters have shown how systems of regulatory law that govern health and safety emerged as part of a broadly emancipatory rights-giving process, but were constrained from the start by the needs of the economic and political systems. This led to the emergence of a regulatory system that is instrumental in outlook, able to implement policy choices in pursuit of defined goals, but unable to demonstrate its own normative purpose because it has become disengaged from the social values that justify action in the public interest. This deficit has underpinned subsequent attempts to invoke the criminal law as a means of responding to work-related deaths. Criminal law offers a potential forum for moral adjudication, as it is notionally concerned with censuring conduct that is wrongful according to shared values; criminalisation is an attempt to restate the moral 'reasons for' regulating and has come to the fore at exactly the time when the broader political climate has turned against regulation. This chapter will explore the role and purpose of the new offence, in a practical and conceptual sense. The criminal law can play a role in re-establishing the reputation of health and safety regulation; this chapter will argue that this role can be understood in terms of a reframing of public debates in such a way as to allow for consideration of the balance between welfarist and economic considerations. Criminalisation has the capacity to validate regulation by providing a forum for moral accountability that enhances the legitimacy of the regulatory project.

The normative gap within health and safety regulation

The political and ideological context of health and safety regulation has been discussed in the preceding chapter. A contemporary climate of neo-liberalism has rendered health and safety law vulnerable to a governmental hostility towards regulatory red tape and perceived burdens on business. This has been expressed via the setting of overarching policy priorities and the withdrawal of funding and the political license to act (Almond 2007; Bain 1997; Baldwin 1987; Tombs and Whyte 2010). The extent of this hostility has varied from time to time, according to the prevailing political climate (Beck and Woolfson 2000; Hawkins 2002), but the broad trend has been towards a reduction in the inspection and enforcement capacity of state regulators, and towards a more restrictive conception of the degree to which they should intervene to impose enforceable requirements upon companies. There are many ways of conceptualising this shift; as a process of deregulation underpinned by a political commitment to safeguarding market interests (Pearce and Tombs 1990; Snider 1991; Slapper 1999; Tombs and Whyte 2007; 2010) or as part of a neo-liberal strategy of responsibilising actors outside government as part of a shift towards a 'regulatory state' (Braithwaite 2008; Gray 2009; Levi-Faur 2005; Majone 1997), or as the pursuit of the most effective regulatory strategies, which happen to be those that are risk-based and emphasise non-adversarial approaches (Ayres and Braithwaite 1992; Baldwin and Black 2008; 2010; Black 2005; Gunningham and Grabosky 1998).

The likelihood is that elements of all of these approaches are true; that cooperative approaches do offer a degree of instrumental effect that renders them a valid policy choice, but that their implementation is constrained by system imperatives of money and power, and that the overarching approach has been more about re-regulating in a governance mode rather than purely deregulating. These trends can be seen in the history of safety regulation; there have always been those who opposed it as an unjustifiable interference in the free operation of the market, including many whom the law was designed to protect (Gaskell 1936; Thomas 1948; Ward 1962). During the 19th-century, many workers regarded with suspicion and hostility the protections put in place by the early reformers because of the potential loss of earnings that they heralded. And this hostility, expressed on both economic and cultural levels, has endured throughout the subsequent history of health and safety regulation. It was not until the regulatory project was aligned with the interests of organised labour that much of this worker hostility was diffused, but health and safety then became a disputed political issue within the wider industrial relations context.

While the 19th-century resistance to regulation centred primarily on its economic consequences for workers, and the 20th-century resistance focused on workplace politics and industrial relations, contemporary resistance has been more 'social' in nature. The public sphere has seen the most significant expressions of hostility towards regulation (Almond 2009b), centring on its wider cultural impact. Hawkins identified the vulnerability of regulatory systems to negative public perceptions, particularly to 'rather punitive' public expectations about HSE's policing functions (2002: 212). Regulatory agencies are particularly responsive to perceived public attitudes and the need to be seen to be doing something in response to major incidents such as work-related deaths (Almond 2007; Gilboy 1995; Hawkins 2002; Hutter 1997). Safety regulators must establish their organisational legitimacy by demonstrating that they act in the public interest (Almond 2007: 298). This process is also dialectical; Hawkins observes that by 'enforcing laws within a familiar moral framework, regulators are cementing public beliefs, values, and attitudes about lawbreaking, and about what is right and proper' (2002: 243). The difficulty faced by health and safety regulators is that enforcement practices do not demonstrate their alignment with this moral framework; scarce prosecutions, low fines, and offences that are regarded as merely technical (Tombs and Whyte 2007; 2010) all undermine the ability of regulators to express their normative credentials. The political constraints associated with a neo-liberal paradigm further limit regulators' capacity to act and downgrade the public standing of health and safety law.

The influence of the public sphere

The defining feature of the contextual challenge that health and safety regulators have faced in this period has not necessarily been the institutional relationship between the regulator and central government, although this has of course been significant. Rather, it is the nature of the broader normative discourses that surround health and safety regulation more generally that have wielded the greatest influence over the direction of policy and regulatory practice. In general terms, public attitudes towards risk events such as crime are usually categorised in terms of an increasing punitiveness and support for exclusionary policies aimed at offending populations (Bottoms 1995; Garland 2001; Green 2009; King and Maruna 2009; Lacey 2008; Pratt 2000; Roberts and Hough 2005; Simon 2007). But public attitudes are more subtle and complex than this account might suggest (Green 2006; Hutton 2005; Matthews 2005; Roberts and Hough 2005); in any case, there is little evidence to suggest that the same dynamics of punitiveness extend to the regulatory sphere, not least because of the different political climate surrounding this issue (Almond 2008; 2011; Braithwaite 2003; Wells 2001). There is also little evidence to support Baldwin's suggestion that a new culture of 'regulatory punitiveness' has emerged as an outcome of 'emergent public appetites for blame' (2004: 382), despite the introduction of the corporate manslaughter offence and the passing of the Health and Safety (Offences) Act 2008, which increased the range of penalties available following a breach of a regulatory offence. Most obviously, the lack of enforcement capacity outlined elsewhere suggests that there has been no punitive turn.

In broader terms, public attitudes towards health and safety regulation are relatively mixed, with evidence of support for intervention in some contexts (relating to serious risks) but not in others (Hood *et al.* 2001: 94–97), and relatively little agreement about the value of regulation. Public hostilities towards regulatory law reflect its long-standing ambiguity of status; Livingstone and Lunt (2007: 61) found that recognition of the protective public goods associated with regulation is offset by a deep-seated resentment of restrictions on the free market. Health and safety regulation in particular demonstrates the lukewarm nature of attitudes towards regulation. While high-profile breaches of the law resulting in serious harms are capable of prompting significant public concern (Almond 2008; Almond and Colover 2010), it is rare that a safety offence garners significant attention. When health and safety does impinge upon the public consciousness, there is evidence that regulators are viewed in broadly favourable terms, at least in terms of their normative alignment; Walls *et al.* found that HSE has a positive public trust profile and is perceived as altruistic in outlook (2004: 139), although few people have a clear understanding of its activities. This perceived alignment is fragile, though, and an association with an issue that provokes disquiet, such as the state of the UK's privatised railway system, can transfer into negative assessments of the regulator responsible for governing that area (2004: 146). Regulation is concerned with the control of risk and is therefore expected to show that it can control risks effectively. A major work-related disaster has the potential to highlight the ineffectiveness of a regulator, and a failing regulator may face a political review, a public backlash, and a reduction in the cooperation they receive from stakeholders. To this end, the maintenance of a broadly supportive public profile is important.

The role of 'regulatory myths'

By contrast, prevailing media discourses portray health and safety regulation as a matter of 'red tape' and unreasonable bureaucratic interference in economic and social activities (Almond 2009b; Livingstone and Lunt 2007). Such stories are a common staple of news media coverage, at least in the UK, and are a sufficiently distinctive feature of the regulatory landscape as to merit analysis. These stories outline situations where regulators are interpreted as having been overly zealous or heavy-handed in applying or enforcing legal requirements. Common examples include children being banned from playing conkers in the school playground unless wearing safety goggles because of fears that they may be injured, the banning of floral hanging baskets from town centres as they could fall and injure passers-by, children being banned from competing in school sports days, the banning of charity cake sales, and many more (Almond 2009b: 354–356). Regulators are portrayed as faceless bureaucrats who interfere in cherished areas of social life in increasingly obtrusive ways, and the law is presented as a system that damages cherished values of self-reliance, as is the case with 'tort tales', widely cited stories about legal compensation claims (Haltom and McCann 2004; Williams 2006), which are also part of a public backlash against the 'nanny state'. What makes these stories important is the fact that they are widely recognised, commonly retold, and accepted as true despite being essentially false. Despite this, they exercise significant influence, shaping the agenda of health and safety reform, as evidenced by the Government's Young Review of 2010, which sought to address the 'low public standing' of health and safety resulting from these stories (while at the same time attaching a degree of credence to these 'misrepresentations').

The HSE has attempted to counter the negative coverage that these stories generate via both publicity campaigns and policy steps like the publication of 'Principles of Sensible Risk Management' to encourage a 'focus on reducing real risks' and the prevention of activities that 'scare people by exaggerating or publicising trivial risks'.[1] Despite these efforts, the stories persist, undermining the regulatory project and downgrading the perceived value of health and safety laws. For example, Walls *et al.* found that evaluations of HSE were negatively affected by the perceived issue of over-regulation and the 'funny little regulations' that the agency implemented (2004: 141). Similarly, Almond and Colover (2012) found that stories of this sort were instrumental in affecting public evaluations of the regulatory project as a whole. What is distinctive about this contemporary regulatory scepticism is the degree to which it has resurfaced in tandem with a neo-liberal reimagining of the role of regulation generally. Regulatory myth stories constitute vignettes that depict a 'clash between modern conditions and some aspect of a traditional life-style'

(Brunvand 1981: 189), and imbue the pre-legal society invoked with an idealised moral character centred on values of self-reliance as opposed to the legal management of individuals' lives. They champion tradition as a means of returning 'to sources of moral fixity in day-to-day life, in contrast to the "always revisable" outlook of modern progressivism' (Giddens 1991: 207).

These two key values, self-reliance and traditionality, along with an explicit hostility to state intervention in the economic sphere, demonstrate that regulatory myths gain currency because they fit into an existing political discourse that seeks to delegitimate elements of the regulatory state (Almond 2009b: 369). Within a neo-liberal regulatory paradigm, the imposition of external constraints on behaviour is replaced by arms-length government and a reliance on market forces to determine the appropriate balance of risk and reward (Gray 2009; Silbey 2009). As such, it is not for the state, or the discredited 'platonic guardians' (Loader 2006) of the regulatory system, to attempt to control risk through law; self-regulation and responsibilisation provide a preferable basis for the management of risk. The political agenda embedded within regulatory myth stories attacks not only the substantive outcomes of regulation but also its 'procedural' validity and the 'right' of regulators to interfere (Almond 2009b). In Habermasian terms, the legal basis on which the regulator acts constitutes an 'internal' source of validation and allows for justification of regulation without any reference to 'external' validations, in the form of substantive values (Habermas 1988; 1992). When the right of regulators to regulate is called into question, this lays bare the absence of 'external' sources of validation that demonstrate the normative justifications for the regulatory project (Habermas 1992: 33). In this way, regulatory myths and other popular challenges to health and safety regulation exacerbate the communicative deficit inherent in systems of regulation.

The 'crippled epistemology' of public dialogue about safety

Health and safety regulation is an area where the public typically express strong views but have fairly minimal knowledge and experience, and their views are shaped by media reporting (Almond 2008; Walls *et al.* 2004). Work-related fatality cases do not normally receive mainstream media coverage and so the public are unable to engage with them in an informed way. While major public disasters can prompt high levels of concern, this does not translate into a sustained engagement with the issue, except in the form of the negative media commentary outlined above. This lack of knowledge is, in part, an outcome of the disengagement of these issues from public debate; the low public profile of health and safety law, the technical and juridified nature of regulation, and the reliance on expert risk assessments, all distance health and safety regulation from the public, resulting in a 'crippled epistemology' within public attitudes. This term was coined in relation to political extremism (Hardin 2002); it signifies that attitudes and evaluations are based on a fundamentally deficient knowledge basis and so tend towards the extreme. In applying the idea to rumours and conspiracy theories, Sunstein and Vermeule describe this as when people 'know very few things, and what they do know is wrong' (2009: 228). In the absence of credible information, individuals become reliant upon marginal and inaccurate material, fundamentally distorting understandings. In addition, the cognitive tendency to accept information that fits with existing worldviews means that deficient sources (like regulatory myths) exert a significant pull over attitudes (Klayman and Ha 1987).

It is suggested that this position characterises the public debate about occupational health and safety, at least in the UK. Health and safety is an obscure field, and much of this obscurity is an outcome of the instrumentalism of the regulatory system. At the same time, it is also a marginalised issue, in that it receives much less political and media attention than other issues like crime (Ericson 1991; Wells 2001) and a significantly lower degree of prioritisation in terms of resource allocations, structural capacity, and political mandate to act. At the same time, there are concerns over the degree to which particular interests shape the outcomes that this system achieves, and indications that the failure of the regulatory system to allow for moral adjudication over these outcomes might be eroding the standing of that system (Almond and Colover 2012). And crucially, it does not provide significant opportunities for meaningful communication about these issues between regulator and regulated in a 'regulatory conversation' (Black 2002). The outcome of these developments has been a 'poor-quality' public dialogue about health and safety regulation, characterised by misapprehension, scepticism, a lack of knowledge, and explicit hostility. There is no fundamental discussion of the 'reasons for' regulating or the priorities that guide regulatory endeavour. The outcome is a shallow dialogue, where fundamental debates about the value of regulation are ignored.

This extends into the political sphere as well as the public sphere. A good example of this is provided by the willingness of political leaders like David Cameron to endorse regulatory myths for political gain.[2] Similarly, the Young Review (2010) featured both an appraisal of policy and an uncritical acceptance of many hotly disputed, or plainly incorrect, assumptions about health and safety regulation. Political rhetoric, echoed in many media sources following the Young Review's publications, focused on the prospect of a 'bonfire of regulations', a smashing of the 'health and safety culture' and a scrapping of red tape. The Löfstedt review of health and safety, commissioned subsequent to this, was technical in its terms of reference but still gives coverage to the issue of safety regulation leading to 'unreasonable outcomes, or to inappropriate litigation' (2011a: question 6). Together this constitutes the greatest contemporary challenge to health and safety regulation, neither the demand that regulators demonstrate value-for-money nor the reduction of regulatory resources, but the erosion of its moral standing. The normative gap in regulation is the one between the progressive, emancipatory, justice-based aspirations of regulation, and the social standing that it currently endures. As argued previously, the origins of this normative gap lie in the disengagement of the regulatory project from its basis in the sphere of shared social meaning. The first goal for the corporate manslaughter offence, as a legal phenomenon, is to begin to address this gap; but how might this be achieved?

Understanding 'true' public attitudes towards work-related death

A better understanding of the role that an offence of this sort might play can be obtained if we possess a clearer conception of true public attitudes towards the law in this area. The distinction between apparent and true attitudes is drawn by writers such as Green (2006), who documents the pitfalls associated with engaging with public 'opinions' rather than public 'judgements'; the former are surface-level and reflexive, while the latter are more considered and reflective. While the former tend to be elicited in response to opinion poll-style questions gathering 'top-of-the-head' expressions of preference, the latter emerge only as a result of deliberative decision-making (2006: 133). The danger is that a policy based on public opinion is liable to distortion and extremism, the features of a crippled epistemology, because it does not reflect any deeper consideration of the issues in hand. When policymakers respond to this version of public opinion, the result tends to be that unprincipled decisions are made; this problem underpins many of the tendencies towards punitiveness found in contemporary accounts of the politics of law and order. By providing opportunities for deliberative engagement with the issues in hand, it is possible to obtain an appreciation of informed public preferences that provides a more secure basis for policy-making (Green

2006; Hutton 2005; Roberts and Hough 2005). An understanding of 'true' public attitudes can also be part of a democratising movement which increases the legitimacy of the law by ensuring that it rests upon a basis of public commitment (Tyler and Darley 2000) and accords with 'fair labelling' principles (Warr 1989).

This is particularly true in relation to health and safety regulation where, as we have seen, a poor-quality public debate has emerged in recent years, dominated by misleading information and constrained by an essential difficulty in understanding what regulatory law actually *does*. As Walls *et al.* showed (2004), the defining feature of public attitudes in this area is a lack of knowledge. This stems from the inability of regulatory law to demonstrate the 'reasons for' its existence because of the nature of those laws, the ways in which they are enforced, and the meanings that they communicate. Regulatory law is about effecting instrumental change; the criminal law is invoked as a way of imbuing the decisions made with additional meaning. But what is this meaning? What can members of the public take from the criminal law that they cannot from regulatory law? Empirical research has been undertaken to answer some of these questions by investigating public evaluations of work-related deaths and the laws that govern them (Almond 2008; Almond and Colover 2010; 2012). Via semi-structured interviews, members of the public were asked to discuss case 'vignettes', summaries of real work-related deaths drawn from court reports, transcripts, and official investigation reports. This 'deliberative' methodology provided participants with a greater degree of information and opportunity for reflection than other survey methods (Green 2006; Hutton 2005). The cases that were discussed included major disasters and individual deaths, cases that resulted in manslaughter convictions and cases dealt with under the HSWA 1974, and those involving large and small corporate defendants.

The main findings to emerge from this investigation were: firstly, that work-related deaths were regarded as 'serious' incidents and all respondents attached a great deal of importance to them as harmful social events (Almond 2008: 459). The cases perceived to be most serious were large-scale disasters or those involving vulnerable victims and the least serious tended to be those where the circumstances were significantly removed from the frame of reference of the respondents (for example, a death in the chemical industry as opposed to one on public transport). In addition, where there was an element of powerlessness on the part of the victim, the case was seen as more serious (Almond and Colover 2010: 8). Conversely, where the victims were in some sense seen as partially responsible for their own death (for instance, by not using safety equipment), this was reduced. Secondly, while the manslaughter offence was supported as a means of responding to the most serious cases discussed, the sanctioning preferences most commonly expressed by respondents were for the prosecution and fining of corporate bodies involved under health and safety law. When the criminal law was invoked, it tended to be in relation to the liability of individual directors rather than the company *per se* (2010: 8–9). In general terms, this reflected the difficulty that participants had in separating corporate responsibility from issues of individual *mens rea* (2010: 11–12). Thirdly, although strong preferences for punishment were expressed, these tended to be underpinned by apparently rational and reasoned decision-making processes, rather than the kind of emotive and unconsidered reactions that accounts of the 'punitive public' might suggest (2010: 9–10; Almond 2008: 462–463). Public attitudes tend to be motivated by a desire to bring about positive and preventative change rather than a desire for retribution.

While these findings undermine the notion of public support for the criminalisation of corporate conduct as a matter of simple punitiveness, the key points to emerge relate to the perceived value of criminal law in this context (Almond and Colover 2012). Participants viewed the purpose of the legal process as one of holding to account in a moral sense, seeking to emphasise the wrongfulness involved in serious cases as well as securing improvements in future conduct (Almond and Colover 2010: 14). While regulatory laws were seen as 'only a health and safety thing' (2010: 11), criminal law was invoked as a means of providing a more definitive evaluation of the nature and quality of the acts involved; it possesses a moral core and involves determinations of responsibility that allow for meaningful arbitration. The decisions made when participants weighed up the cases were essentially moral in nature, highlighting perceived motive and character, and other factors such as perceived ruthlessness, arrogance, and greed, as important in informing decisions about responsibility (Almond 2008: 463–464). Regulation and enforcement are activities that are perceived in communicative terms and are *in fact* related to a broader set of values by the public (Almond and Colover 2012).

But support for the general idea of health and safety regulation is offset by dissatisfaction with its deterrent capacity and moral ambiguity. There is a public desire for health and safety regulation to play a role but also an awareness that it does not actually succeed in doing so in practice. Relatedly, there was significant evidence of a lack of familiarity with health and safety regulation and the manslaughter offence on the part of participants. It was clear that the concepts involved were unfamiliar and that participants lacked a clear set of reference points to guide decision-making in this area; many struggled with the notion of a corporate body being described as criminal in its own right (Almond and Colover 2010: 11). Set against this, however, was the tendency for participants to view it as appropriate for corporate actors to be the focus of sanctioning; it was just that they grounded corporate blameworthiness via reference to individual culpability. There was no evidence of a widespread appreciation of the fact that corporations could constitute legal actors in their own right in this sense, underlining once again the distancing of the law from the broader public consciousness.

Taken together, this evidence highlights the limitations of the existing law and the need for a more communicative response to work-related deaths. While regulatory law may be a useful tool for the attribution of responsibility in a factual sense, it appears to be less useful as a means of settling the more fundamental questions about the boundaries of acceptable conduct that underpin the distinction between legal and illegal behaviour. The desire for a manslaughter offence, or at least for a declaratory response to work-related deaths, is not driven simply by risk-intolerance or punitiveness but by the idea of punishment as what Duff calls 'purposive communication' (2001: 88); a means of reconciling the offender with the social values that provide the 'reasons against' the course of action embarked on, thereby securing commitment to the law. In this sense, the process is future-oriented, but these instrumental outcomes are grounded in the moral reasons for obeying the law, not in the content-independent and outcome-oriented rationale of regulation. Criminalisation is a means of defining certain forms of conduct as morally 'wrongful', not just as undesirable because harmful. As such, it goes beyond the capabilities of regulatory law in important ways, making a contribution to the process of enforcement as a communicative endeavour that is grounded in public deliberation.

The legitimatory functions of criminalisation

The argument made so far has suggested that the movement towards the criminal law in the context of work-related death has occurred because of the inability of systems of health and safety regulation to communicate the justificatory 'reasons to obey' that underpin them. This inability to ground instrumental legal controls in the normative sphere of the shared values of society has negative effects on the public status of health and safety law, and it distances it from both public understandings and from any content-dependent rationale that might imbue the law with moral authority. The consequences of this disjunction must be explored in order to understand why criminalisation, and the reconnection of instrumental regulatory law to its justificatory underpinnings, might be worthwhile. As discussed in Chapter 3, law is an integrative system of coercive controls which have a basis in democratic will-formation; legal controls must be able to trace back permission for the constraints imposed to a basis in communicative action. If the 'reasons for' the imposition of law are not clear, then the reasons for acceptance of that law are also eroded. The legitimacy of law relies upon this connection back to the normative structures which provide the motivation required to sustain it (Habermas 1973; 1992: 461).

Legitimacy refers to the foundation of authority, in the form of public validation, which underpins the actions of state institutions; it is contingent upon the belief in the value and correctness of a social order that is possessed by those subject to it. Weber describes legitimacy within the bureaucratic state as being based upon the 'belief in the legality of enacted rules and the right of those elevated to authority under such rules to issue commands' (1914: 215); Beetham clarifies three elements of this definition; legal validity, moral justifiability, and consent (1991: 15–25). Legal validity refers to procedural criteria, such as the requirements that due process be followed and that a public authority must have a legal basis for the decisions that it makes; this allows for the assertion that regulatory activities 'are the processes most meriting support according to recognized bench-marks' (Baldwin 1995: 57). Moral justifiability refers to moral content criteria, such as the requirement that the public authority's activities must accord with the values of society; this allows for the assertion that regulatory activities are 'right, proper, and appropriate... and can therefore make both an expressive claim founded in moral legitimacy and an instrumental claim derived from action in the public interest' (Hawkins 2002: 417). These two elements underpin the formation of the ultimate belief in the legitimacy of the public authority, the subjective evaluation of regulatory activity by audiences (the regulated population, general public, and political actors) which happens as a result of the process of making and enforcing laws (Almond 2007).

Habermas' thesis of 'legitimation crisis' (1973) identifies the social imperatives that lead to the legitimacy deficits experienced by governments and public institutions. Habermas argues that the process of juridification that has occurred in late-capitalist society, the expansion of instrumental law and the system imperatives of money and power that underpin it (1988), is driven by a need for increased state intervention to tackle emergent conflicts arising from structural risks within the capitalist market system, particularly those relating to the 'external costs of a private production that cannot adequately deal with the problem situations it itself creates' (1976: 194). The state responds to these risks by adopting a steering role, mitigating deficiencies and displacing conflict away from the economic system and onto more manageable issues in the social sphere (1976: 186). The expansion of social provision, such as health, education, and welfare programmes, occurs as a means of diverting economic crises via the construction of a socialised system of production, which involves a systematic overloading of the public budget; the state assumes the responsibility for offsetting the harmful side effects of the economic system, thereby representing the capitalist system as the best satisfaction of general social interests (1973: 36). But this budgetary overload amplifies the pressure on the state to legitimate the policies it enacts and to ensure that its primary function, the maintenance of economic stability, is not compromised (1973: 36). 'Legitimation crisis' occurs when the social system cannot succeed in providing both economic stability and social reform. When the state cannot do this, opposition to its steering role becomes prevalent and legitimacy is lost. This is a balancing act, in that two competing imperatives place different demands on the state; the imperatives of the economic system are intolerant of the fiscal burden that the socialising of production imposes, and citizens demand the continued enhancement of social welfare provision. The state must satisfy both of these interests in order to legitimate itself.

Legitimation and political risk

It is quite possible to conceive of health and safety regulation as a component of the state's steering function, mitigating the harmful side-effects of the economic system (Almond 2007; Haines and Gurney 2003; Haines and Sutton 2003). This builds on the observations of Carson (1979) and others that safety regulation emerged as a means of dispelling social conflict relating to the excesses of the emergent factory system, particularly the need to ensure that the physical harms inflicted did not compromise the system's long-term sustainability. Crucially however, the socialising role of health and safety regulation can be understood as one of legitimation, and this can be conceptualised in two main ways. The first is to view the issue in terms of political risk, as a project of securing support for 'the state' as a whole; on this view, health and safety regulation is part of the apparatus for the validation of the provider-state itself. Writers adopting this approach see health and safety regulation as serving the wider goal of state legitimation by alleviating structural tensions between workers and capital and so preventing fundamental conflicts from emerging that might threaten the stability of the system. The legitimation requirements here can be understood in terms of political risks; in Haines' terms (2011), the state must show that it can 'keep the economy going and make people feel safe', or perform its economic steering role while also mitigating the resultant risks of harm.

The role of regulation is to respond to challenges to the status of the government as protector of the security of the citizenry:

> even in the most complex societies, people have expectations that markets cannot satisfy. Politicians can never shift the legitimacy burden onto the economic system. Aware of this, politicians ... find themselves driven to develop mechanisms that will safeguard them in the event that markets 'let them down'.
>
> (Haines and Sutton 2003: 11)

Regulation is deployed in response to risks which challenge the legitimacy of government by prompting the withdrawal of consent, in the Weberian sense. Politicians must respond decisively to such risks, or else acknowledge their own bounded competence and thus provide grounds on which their performance may be challenged (Haines *et al.* 2007). The use of law as a tool of social control is one particularly effective means of responding to these risks because the act of legislating is highly visible and implies that the needs of the citizenry have been dealt with decisively (a 'legislative rationality': Simon 2007: 75); this helps explain the proliferation of law in the modern 'regulatory state'. Health and safety regulation is one example of a state-level response to a potential political risk, a dynamic that is particularly true in the aftermath of a major disaster or work-related death, when the desire for 'something to be done' is greatest (Haines 2011; Haines *et al.* 2007: 442).

Corporate manslaughter reforms can be understood as an example of this dynamic in action; a symbolically important means of responding to risk which cultivates the impression that the problem has been resolved via the creation of new legal powers. It also allows for the benefits of that symbolism to accrue to the political actor involved. Critical commentators have highlighted both the political self-interest that has underpinned the use of criminal law in this context, such as the British Labour government's need to preserve trade union support during a period when the influence of these actors was being fundamentally eroded (Gobert 2005; Hall and Johnstone 2005; Sarre and Richards 2005), and the potential of such an offence to be used as propaganda for lawmakers to claim a greater commitment to the values of health and safety regulation than they might actually possess (Haines and Hall 2004). Reform in this area has been driven by concerns that relate more to the political mileage to be gained from reform than by any commitment to the normative goals that underpin it. From this perspective, the communicative power of the new offence is utilised for essentially instrumental purposes, namely, the advancement of the interests of political actors. The primary legitimatory content of the new offence is the communication of a message about the government of the day, and where they wish to appear to stand in relation to the values associated with regulation; it is less concerned with whether those values are advanced.

Legitimation and institutional risk

The second way of understanding these issues of legitimacy within a regulatory context is as part of a process which addresses the legitimation needs of legal institutions themselves. For while law has a role in terms of the relationship between the political system and the social sphere, legal institutions and regulators must also legitimate their own existence 'by affirming the importance of the regulatory goal that [they are] directed at achieving and by demonstrating how effective [they are] in achieving that goal' (Haines and Gurney 2003: 372). By ensuring that they function in accordance with the shared values and understandings of the wider social community, legal institutions are able to make claims about their own value, and so strengthen their position relative to the challenges that they might face. In Hawkins' terms, this is about demonstrating a moral authority sufficient to motivate compliance and secure respect for the law: a 'lack of a moral mandate threatens [a] regulatory agency's legitimacy and enforcement authority' (2002: 13) to the extent that it may lose the support of regulated stakeholders and its political masters, fatally undermining its ability to fulfil its substantive goals.

Regulatory agencies are directly subjected to political risks, and must respond to these risks when discharging their functions. They have a direct link to the formal political sphere, being heavily influenced by the policies that emerge from the governmental surround within which they operate. A regulator may have to deal with a government that does not share its fundamental concerns, operating within a broader political context that is also hostile. But regulators are also political actors in their own right and must demonstrate their own legitimacy to stakeholders, politicians and the wider public in order to establish that they are deserving of support (Almond 2007: 299). The dynamics of political risk, expressed on the macro-level previously, also apply at the micro-level of legal institutions. If a safety regulator like HSE is cast in the role of the state apparatus in Habermas' model, it must regulate in such a way as to accord with the interests of business, which it does by fulfilling the advisory role dictated under the Robens approach. HSE must enforce the law in order to demonstrate its 'welfarist' credentials, justifying its existence by preventing harm to those it acts to protect (Haines and Gurney 2003: 372). The conflict between these two interest group constituencies (Almond 2007; Hawkins 1984: 9) creates considerable challenges, not least where governments demand that regulatory measures do not contradict their commitment to a broader economic liberalism.

In the case of work-related deaths, this means that a regulator must demonstrate its responsiveness in relation to a particular risk or event that constitutes a source of public concerns and align itself with the interests of its public constituency via that response. Work-related fatality cases have the potential to create crises for safety regulators because they provoke concern and public expectations that a declarative response, in the form of criminal sanctions, will follow (Almond 2007). For Habermas, crisis is a term that connotes a loss of social integration through a disintegration of the normative foundations of social institutions (1973: 3). When expectations of responsive action are not met, or the declaratory capacity of criminal enforcement is not used to restate the regulator's protective role, questions about the legitimacy of the regulator come into focus. Such a moment of crisis may occur in the aftermath of a work-related death, when the criminal law proves unable to bring a manslaughter prosecution against a culpable employer, or regulatory law imposes a fine which is not proportionate to the harm done. This inability to fulfil expectations can make it appear that the second component of the definition of legitimacy, moral justifiability, is missing, and so the normative foundations that the regulatory project relies upon, its connection to the 'reasons for regulating' that emerge from the public sphere, are eroded. In such situations, when 'the law is perceived as being discordant with popular, or individual, morality, it is morality rather than the law which takes priority' (Hutter 1988: 202). The reforms of the law so as to facilitate criminalisation can thus be read as a means of reasserting this connection between law and morality; it realigns the regulatory project with public expectations, allowing it to achieve outcomes commensurate with the values of the regulator's public constituencies.

In addition to the protection of their own legitimacy, regulators must enforce the law in order to fulfil their welfarist credentials, justifying their existence by preventing harm to those they act to protect (Haines and Gurney 2003: 372). This is actually a more complex process than the dynamics of political risk suggest because here, the regulator is concerned not only with the communication of its normative credentials but also with the advancement of the values that underpin the regulatory project. Similarly, the legitimation of regulation operates on this deeper level as well as on the institutional level; corporate manslaughter offences and the like have a role, not just in advertising where the regulator stands, but in promoting the claims that regulatory enforcement makes about the rightness of action in the public interest. Even the relative successes encountered by health and safety law in reducing instances of injury and death at work do not themselves advance the normative goals of the regulatory system; in Haines' terms, 'good outcomes from regulation cannot inspire the broader public as to their worth... defining the exact nature of the regulatory problem and the most effective method of amelioration cannot, in itself, bring about the necessary social and political commitment' (2011: 9). The commitment that is sought is an end in itself; the endorsement of a particular conception of the value of human life and the wrongfulness of endangering it via the pursuit of economic self-interest. Criminal law sanctions provide a means of restating these reasons for acting, meaning that the symbolic value and instrumental capacity of the law are advanced. But it is important to recognise that the pursuit of those values is not necessarily the motivating factor behind the introduction of law reforms. Politicians have introduced these offences in response to political risks that they face, and are thus motivated by self-interest and strategic considerations, rather than any concern over the alienation of regulation from its normative basis.

What 'values' does a corporate manslaughter offence pursue?

Viewing the new manslaughter offence as having the potential to advance a particular set of values begs a further question; what might these values be? On one level, it is possible to interrogate the form of the offence to identify the nature of the wrongdoing it seeks to criminalise. The rationale for the offence is contained in the terms on which liability is imposed. Criminal liability is normally understood as predicated upon two main component elements; an act which can be characterised as 'harmful' must be done by the defendant, and the doing of that act to produce that result must be 'wrongful' (Ashworth 2000: 240; Duff 2001: 127–128; Feinberg 1984; Husak 2008: 65–66; Warr 1989). Corporate manslaughter (under the Corporate Manslaughter and Corporate Homicide Act 2007) is an offence that is primarily defined according to two limiting criteria; the identity of the defendant (a corporate body) and the harm inflicted (death). This has been a source of criticism as it narrows the scope of the offence so as to exclude both the liability of individual directors and managers, and liability in relation to non-fatal harms, such as serious injury (Clarkson 2008; Gobert 2008; Tombs and Whyte 2007). It does at least signify that some form of 'non-trivial' harm (Husak 2008: 67) has been inflicted, in the sense of a physical 'thwarting, setting back, or defeating of an interest' (Feinberg 1984: 33), and this provides one justification for the offence; it aims at preventing serious harm. But consequences are not the only justification for criminalising conduct and are often taken as insufficient by themselves. Indeed, the harm-focused (in terms of risks of injury and death) Health and Safety at Work Act 1974 provides a good example of how the absence of any associated wrongfulness requirement can undermine the normative foundations of a criminal offence (Carson 1979; Norrie 2001; Warr 1989). The infliction of harm must be 'wrongful' in order to be culpable.

Why is it wrongful?

The concept of 'wrongfulness' is more complicated. There must be something about the way in which the harm is inflicted that makes it wrongful and thus an incident with which the criminal law should properly be concerned (Husak 2008: 73–76). Duff describes this as relating to the 'intentions and attitudes' that underpin a harmful action; it must be an 'attack on the... legitimate interests' of the victim which is 'malicious, contemptuous, or disrespectful' in nature (2001: 128). The criminal law utilises *mens rea* concepts such as intention and recklessness to express this wrongfulness in a form that can be evidentially proved. The corporate manslaughter offence (as defined in s. 1(1) of the Corporate Manslaughter and Corporate Homicide Act 2007) does not feature a traditional advertent fault element, instead imposing liability where 'the way in which [a corporate body's] activities are managed or organised (a) causes a person's death, and (b) amounts to a gross breach of a relevant duty of care' owed to the victim. The fault element here is a gross breach of a duty of care relating to the management of the company's activities such as those imposed under the Health and Safety at Work Act 1974 ss. 2–3 to 'ensure, so far as is reasonably practicable, the health, safety and welfare' of employees and the public. The wrongfulness of the offence is related to gross negligence, in that the breach of duty must fall far below the standards expected of the company in the circumstances (as defined by s. 1(3) of the CMCHA). Some theorists have criticised the notion of negligence as a basis for criminal liability on the basis that it does not involve advertence; a negligent offender will have acted carelessly or thoughtlessly, but will not have *chosen* the harmful outcome (Finkelstein 2005; Hall 1963; Williams 1961). Such offences are often seen as exceptions to the general rule that criminal liability requires advertent fault (although this rule is often observed only in the breach; Ashworth 2000; Husak 2008).

That said, it is generally recognised that negligence does involve wrongfulness on the part of the defendant because he fails to act as he should for the right reasons; he has inexcusably fallen short in the exercise of his rational capacities (Simester 2000). The defendant has good reasons to act but does not act, demonstrating a degree of culpability. The reasons to act here relate to the duty breached because undertaking such a duty involves the acceptance of conditions placed upon future conduct; a driver knows, when given their license to drive, that conditions about the nature and quality of their driving are placed upon them. Fletcher frames this in terms of conditions that 'put the actor on notice' or 'give him reasons to think' about the risks associated with his conduct (1971: 423); when these 'circumstances give the actor reason to think that his conduct risks harm to another, his failure to apprise himself of the risks latent in his conduct is culpable. There is thus reason to believe that culpable inadvertence is a form of mens rea' (1971: 426). Similarly, Hart argues that negligence is a normative term, implying that a degree of reproach should attach to an actor who 'failed to comply with a standard of conduct with which any ordinary man could and would have complied' (1968: 148); a negligent actor *could* have done different, and *should* have done so. Negligence is culpable because it involves 'a failure to exercise the capacity to advert to, and to think about and control, conduct and its risks' (1968: 157). An actor who chooses to undertake a risk (by driving a car or by employing another person) also undertakes associated obligations relating to the control of that risk, expressed in the form of a duty to those affected. Failure to heed these conditions makes the subsequent infliction of harm culpable.

It is suggested that the values addressed in the form of this offence relate to the nature of the attack on the interests of the victim; that a fundamental duty owed to the victim has not been fulfilled. What we assert, in imposing gross negligence liability, is that the defendant has not fulfilled the fundamental obligations to exercise his capacity and respond to risk incumbent upon him in his role as an employer. This is wrongful because it implies the kind of 'contempt or disrespect', in Duff's terms, that renders that failure an attack on the interests of those who are placed in danger. On one level, this idea of 'giving notice' as the basis of culpability is relatively proceduralistic, in that the wrongdoing seems to derive from ignoring the notice given, rather than any content-dependent feature or quality inherent in the substance of that notice. On Fletcher's reading, we might conclude that *all* breaches of duties are equally culpable because they involve the same mechanism of ignoring the notice given. On the other hand, it is the terms of specific duties that define why one breach is more wrongful than another; failing to stop at a pedestrian crossing is a more wrongful breach of a driver's duty than failing to switch off the ignition when stationary on the road,[3] but both constitute examples of failing to respond to notice given. Some duties matter more than others because of the nature of the interests and rights that they protect.

Why is a duty of care imposed?

As such, to understand what values the manslaughter offence seeks to reflect, we must look at the reasons why the duty to ensure the health and safety of employees and the public is imposed in the first place. Health and safety regulation constitutes a statement of a particular public good; the guarantee of non-exploitative citizenship rights and freedom from domination within the workplace. From an economic perspective, regulation has always involved the maintenance of the conditions governing access to markets (Braithwaite 2008; Carson 1979; Polanyi 1944). Regulation establishes rules that mean individuals can contract with one another as free and equal agents; market failure arises when these conditions are not present. So Baldwin and Cave see the rationale for health and safety regulation as the correction of unequal bargaining power between employer and employee, which limits the capacities of workers to make free choices about the risks they face (1999: 14); regulation involves protecting the autonomy of workers as contracting agents. The principles that civic republican scholars view regulation as pursuing, such as equality of citizenship, the strengthening of procedural law, and freedom as non-domination (Braithwaite 2008;

Feintuck 2004; Sunstein 1990) relate to the idea of market equality, in that they are concerned with preventing the exploitation of the powerless by the powerful (Prosser 2006: 382).

But these ideas transcend concerns over the rules of the market; Prosser argues that health and safety regulation is not simply about market failure, but is also about the quality of citizenship in a civilised society (2006: 370; 2011: 109), as reflected in the aspirational goals of civic republicanism (social solidarity and equality of welfare: Black 2000; Braithwaite 2008; Feintuck 2004; Sunstein 1990). Regulation prevents social fragmentation as a result of market forces, and so is not simply a market corrective; it aims to secure equal treatment and respect for citizens via the imposition of obligations that transcend individual interests. In the case of safety regulation, the core value being upheld is that of respect for the dignity of individuals as citizens, by securing basic levels of physical welfare for all in the interests of human rights and social solidarity (Prosser 2006: 383; 2011: 103). While the mitigation of unequal bargaining power is a component of 'civil' citizenship, relating to the rights required for individual freedom, the protection of welfare is an element of 'social' citizenship, relating to the rights to security, identity, and 'to live the life of a civilised being according to the standards prevailing in the society' (Marshall 1992: 8; also Ramsay 2006: 40–41). Regulatory criminal law exists to enrich the substance of civilised life, to reduce insecurity, and to ensure that these risks are not borne disproportionately by a particular group or class (Marshall 1992: 33; Prosser 2011: 103; Ramsay 2006: 49). Health and safety law establishes some of the basic conditions of social citizenship in modern society and requires others to uphold, or at least not compromise, those conditions in relation to others. It assists in realising a vision of the 'good society' (Haines and Gurney 2003).

Accordingly, regulatory law requires those who benefit from existing market relations (employers and businesses) to ensure that they do so without compromising these basic conditions (Prosser 2011: 103; Ramsay 2006: 49). The state has an interest in upholding the conditions of citizenship and so has the right to impose punishment where they are breached. For the corporate manslaughter offence, the underlying duty element is central here; it spells out the ways in which an employer must conceive of his employees, not as means to an end, but as ends in their own right, in a Kantian sense. Employees are ends because they hold rights relating to the nature and quality of their citizenship; it is culpable to breach those rights by failing to fulfil the obligations that they place onto one's own conduct. Health and safety law matters because it upholds the status of workers and the public as social citizens. The exploited workers of Morecambe Bay, along with the other insecure and marginalised workers in modern society, are just as deserving of the basic protections attached to social citizenship as the best-paid executives of the best-run corporations, and health and safety law exists to ensure this parity (Prosser 2011: 104). When this is breached, particularly with the kind of 'contempt or disrespect' that Duff (2001) argues constitutes an attack on the legitimate interests of the victim, then enforcement action takes place 'because it must'; not in pursuit of any instrumental advantage, but in order to uphold the bases of social citizenship. This is not a utilitarian basis for criminalisation (which may be insufficient itself to justify punishment: Husak 2008: 100–101), but rather justifies criminalisation on the basis of the wrong that is done to the citizen who is dominated, to society, and to the 'concept of' citizenship when these values are not observed.

Criminalisation as a deliberative forum

The final point to make in relation to the values that the corporate manslaughter reforms act in pursuit of is that it is just as important to safeguard the basis on which determinations about the nature of citizenship rights are made, as it is to protect those rights *per se*. To promote social citizenship is not to determine where the parameters of that concept might be drawn; if exposing another to a risk that compromises their social citizenship is wrongful, then where should the boundary between acceptable and unacceptable levels of risk to be drawn? It has been argued that the corporate manslaughter laws can be understood in relation to Habermas' account of communicative action as a means of normatively validating instrumental systems of law via the public sphere. This account is essentially value-neutral, providing a procedural basis for the validation of social action via communicative action. This was intended to avoid the difficulties associated with claiming any higher authority (whether derived from God or from natural law) for fundamental values; at the same time, however, a procedural emphasis would avoid the dead-end of moral relativism (Simon 1994). It is the outcomes of deliberative action, decisions reached through public discourse, that determine the values regulation should protect; this is neutral, meaning that expansive or minimal conceptions of regulation may predominate depending on the values that emerge (Habermas 1992). That said, Habermas himself implies certain solidaristic values through the qualifying conditions he places onto communicative action (it must be rational, ongoing, and inclusive: 1984; 1987), and the role he gives to law as a medium for the generalisation of norms (1992). The former conditions imply a basic degree of non-coerced freedom and equality of citizenship, and the latter prioritises an integrative, solidarity-building conception of the legal sphere.

But the point remains; substantive determinations about values are not necessarily dictated by the idea of law as a communicative medium. There are no 'concrete' preferences that we can ascribe to underlying 'shared values', apart from those that emerge via deliberative communicative action. The legitimation of the regulatory system is tied not to a predetermined model of enforcement. Instead, it is tied to the desire, expressed in public attitudes, for some kind of 'process' or 'forum' to be put in place for deliberation about the extent of social citizenship rights and their relationship to other considerations, such as the interests of the economic system. This is the kind of desire for deliberation that underpins regulatory approaches that prioritise participatory systems of regulation in order to make corporations 'permeable' to the normative influence of the lifeworld (Parker 2002: 40; also Aalders and Wilthagen 1997; Black 2001). This process of deliberation is central to the perceived need for criminalisation; it provides a forum for 'political judgement about the nature of fault in a social world dominated by economic calculation' in a way that the old law could not (Norrie 2001: 99). The demand for criminalisation has arisen pursuant to a particular set of solidarity-oriented values, but it is fundamentally about the provision of a public forum within which arguments about the nature of those values can be made out. A prosecution following a work-related death brings into focus arguments about the normative settlement of interests within society; the 'Herald of Free Enterprise' and 'Southall' prosecutions provide an example of this because they brought a wider project of neo-liberal economic reform into question by connecting processes such as privatisation to particularly harmful and damaging public outcomes. The new offence has the potential to offer a forum for more effective deliberation of this sort, with greater prospect of practical effect. There are reasons, however, to doubt whether the new offence will actually provide this forum for deliberation and to suspect that it represents a deeply imperfect solution to these problems. These reasons for caution will be discussed in the final chapter (Chapter 7).

7
The Limits of Corporate Manslaughter Reforms

This book has attempted to establish that the movement towards the criminalisation of work-related death cases, via the liberalisation of criminal law attribution rules and the introduction of corporate manslaughter offences, is reflective of a communicative deficit within systems of health and safety regulation. These systems tend to be instrumental in nature and technical in form, both factors that contribute to a distancing of the law from its legitimating foundations in deliberative public discourse. Criminal law, it is argued, has the potential to provide a more compelling public account of the 'reasons for' regulating, highlighting its connection to deeper social values. It can do this because it is an explicitly normative system of law that involves the censure of 'wrongdoing in which the public is properly interested' (Duff 2001: 61), and it involves making judgements about the accountability of the defendant for that wrong. It should make a statement about why compliance with the law is 'right' and so persuade the defendant and others of that rightness (Duff 2001: 80; Dzur and Mirchandani 2007: 156). In this way, the legitimacy of the regulatory system and the values it pursues are enhanced. Criminalisation is thus part of a constructive movement towards a more democratically constituted regulatory system.

But there are many reasons to doubt the criminal law's capacity to act in this way and these will be examined, along with reasons why criminalisation might be a less-than-ideal means of providing the kind of legitimatory input outlined above, and what the alternatives to this might be. In Chapter 2 it was noted that the shift towards criminalisation has been most pronounced in jurisdictions that are characterised by a political climate of neo-liberalism, and a commitment to free-market economics and a minimal welfare state. In societies where this model does not predominate, criminalisation is not pursued as a means of providing this legitimatory link, suggesting that alternative approaches exist focusing on regulation as expressive of shared social values, relating to welfarism, social solidarity, and participatory decision-making. The movement towards criminalisation represents a legitimatory 'crutch', a means of attaining the support for regulation which is provided organically in welfarist societies, but which does not emerge in market-oriented societies. A truly deliberative regulatory system would be a better guarantor of the benefits sketched out in Chapter 6 than criminalisation, which is itself an outcome of the social and political contexts in which it emerges.

The instrumental limits of corporate manslaughter

The first reason to exercise caution when assessing the transformative potential of criminalisation in the context of health and safety regulation is the seemingly modest instrumental impact that developments of this sort are able to produce. It is impossible to claim, and it is certainly not the intention to claim, that the symbolic effects of such reforms will extend to a significant practical impact; reform will not mean that the vast majority of cases are handled any differently than they were previously. The idea of symbolic enforcement is that the reach of the message that enforcement action promotes will exceed the extent of the immediate impact that it produces; in this way, a small number of instances can have significant effects (Almond 2007; Hawkins 2002). But there must be *some* instrumental effect, otherwise the law in question is recognised to be a dead letter, and any putative benefit is lost. Examples of underused criminal legislation abound (Law Commission 2010: 1.25), and if corporate manslaughter laws are to make a positive contribution to the health and safety agenda, they must put the values they espouse into effect. This issue was identified as soon as the Corporate Manslaughter and Corporate Homicide Act 2007 was passed: 'Cynical commentators might regard the Act as succeeding primarily in making a symbolic statement about corporate responsibility, which it will struggle to fulfil in practice' (Ormerod and Taylor 2008: 590). Of course, this symbolic statement may be the *raison d'être* of the new offence, but the underlying point remains; any attempt to symbolically declare some activity wrongful must be backed by a commitment to act on that declaration when it is appropriate to do so. And it appears that the UK's corporate manslaughter offence might be significantly constrained in its ability to give effect to the values that underpin it.

Firstly, there are 'internal' constraints on the implementation of this offence, which have been identified by commentators who have generally given it a rather lukewarm reception (Clarkson 2008; Gobert 2008; Ormerod and Taylor 2008). These relate to technical limitations such as the nature of the duty that must underpin the offence, the rather restrictive category of bodies covered by the Act, and uncertainties about whether the management failure test can overcome the evidential problems associated with the identification doctrine. Although broader in scope than the concept of 'directing mind and will', which set the parameters of responsibility under the identification doctrine, section 1(4) of the Act implies that the term 'management failure' requires that a connection be shown between the decisions of senior management and the actions of specific persons involved in forming organisational policy (Gobert 2008: 428). As such, the Act retains a role for individual fault, paving the way for argument about whether a specified individual was involved in forming policy, how broadly the parameters of 'senior management' should be drawn, and whether the contribution of any individual is substantial or not, all of which have the potential to undermine the new offence's ability to secure successful convictions. Similarly, the requirement that the management of corporate activities should amount to a gross breach of a duty of care allows for uncertainty to exist over exactly how bad a breach must be to be gross, and what kind and categories of duty will provide a basis for liability. Section 8(2) makes clear that health and safety duties will be particularly relevant, and section 8(3) permits reference to safety guidance, but also potentially to best practice across an industrial sector, when determining how bad a breach was. This has the potential to lead to lengthy arguments about what is relevant and what those comparative standards are (Ormerod and Taylor 2008: 603), and to make it difficult to obtain convictions under the new offence.

Secondly, there are 'external' constraints on the effectiveness of the new offence, relating to the prospects of it being used at all. Chief among these are the extra time and money required to bring a homicide prosecution rather than one under health and safety law. Although responsibility for bringing prosecutions under the new Act lies with the Police and Crown Prosecution Service (CPS), the HSE sets the context for this through its own use of prosecution as a 'last resort' in only the most serious cases and only where there is a significant prospect of securing a conviction (Hawkins 2002). Health and safety prosecutions themselves are rare enough; only around 1000 prosecutions are brought each year (following over 120,000 reported work-related injuries *per annum*), approximately 120 of which might relate to work-related deaths (Almond 2006; HSE 2010a; Tombs and Whyte 2010). Regulators are under-resourced and prosecution in this context is likely to be a much lower priority for the CPS than other areas of criminal offending. These concerns have been borne out by the lack of prosecutions since the offence came into law; only one has been brought, that relating to Cotswold Geotechnical,[1] and one other proceeding initiated,[2] in four years. This is significantly below the modest rate of 10–13 prosecutions per year envisaged by the Home Office when conducting its Regulatory Impact Assessment of the new offence (Home Office 2006: para. 25), which reflected an assumption that the Act must fit into existing prosecution practices, and thus be held back for use only in the very worst cases. From the Act's inception it was envisaged that prosecution would be an exceptional event.

So the instrumental impact of the offence has been very limited and it appears that it will not produce a significantly greater number of manslaughter convictions than the previous law (which managed seven convictions between 1994 and 2007). Many scholars have identified a role for criminal offences at the top of the 'enforcement pyramid', allowing the enforcer to utilise coercive sanctioning to reinforce a consensual system by illustrating the consequences of non-compliance (Ayres and Braithwaite 1992: Ch. 2; Gunningham and Johnstone 1999: Ch. 6). A corporate manslaughter conviction brings the possibility of a criminal penalty being levied, but this takes the form of a notionally unlimited fine, which the Sentencing Guidelines Council (SGC) specifies 'will seldom be less than £500,000 and may be measured in millions of pounds' (2010: para. 24). At the same time, however, a defendant is also liable to an unlimited fine following a conviction for a breach of sections 2 or 3 of the HSWA 1974 (albeit with actual fines normally set at a lower level: SGC 2010: para. 25). What this means is that there is little clear difference between the outcome of a manslaughter prosecution and one under health and safety law, apart from the symbolic benefit of a criminal conviction. This is an important caveat; when we talk about the new offence making a difference, we can only anticipate a 'symbolic' difference, not a concrete change in practice.

The manslaughter reforms as 'pure symbolism'?

A related objection is the notion that the corporate manslaughter offence might actually be counterproductive to the aims of the health and safety regulatory system because it provides a degree of false promise, giving the impression of decisive action while producing no instrumental change. The new law has been seen as a concession to trade union interests that had been sidelined within the Labour Party which introduced the offence (Gobert 2005). It has also been characterised as a component of the self-legitimating mechanisms of the capitalist system, ensuring that system's survival via a class-dialectical process of granting non-fundamental concessions to those whose long-term exploitation is secured as a result (Hall and Johnstone 2005: 75; Snider 1991: 211). Haines and Hall argue that manslaughter prosecutions 'may have significant negative effects – such as inducing a sense of complacency that something has actually been done to improve safety levels when no improvement has actually occurred' (2004: 269). In essence, the new law is a confidence trick; it buys loyalty and legitimacy but not at the cost of changing the balance of power in the workplace. Any future efforts to introduce new regulatory offences and penalties, or introduce a criminal offence of 'Corporate Grievous Bodily Harm' (Gobert 2008: 420) or 'corporate violence' (Tombs and Whyte 2007: 135), or to implement wholesale reform of corporate criminal law, as suggested by the Law Commission (2010), are likely to be unsuccessful given the concessions already made. In this sense, a symbolic offence is worse than nothing because it suppresses the interests it should serve.

There is also a concern that 'focusing on a few particularly serious cases and singling them out for "special treatment" [under the law of manslaughter] risks undermining the criminality of regulatory OHS [occupational health and safety] offences under OHS legislation' (Hall and Johnstone 2005: 73). On this objection, the symbolism of the new offence distracts from the pursuit of instrumental achievement, degrading the effectiveness of the laws that are relied on to achieve strategic safety goals. The distinction that the Home Office envisaged, between criminal offences and those that are 'merely regulatory' (2005: 58), is entrenched by a system that creates an artificial dichotomy of criminal (the minority) and non-criminal (the vast majority) work-related deaths. By saying that the minority are 'real crimes' that are deserving of being taken seriously, an implied message is also given out that the rest are not (Carson and Johnstone 1990). As a result, unless the criminal offence is 'symbolically rich' enough to reinforce health and safety law (Haines and Hall 2004: 269), it will have the effect of downgrading the status of regulation. The new offence addresses 'symptom and not cause' (Hall and Johnstone 2005: 76), reframing a small number of deaths as extraordinary and different to other, more regularly occurring deaths, which may therefore be classed as routine. Tombs and

Whyte add another dimension to this criticism when they state that a symbolic understanding of the corporate manslaughter offence tries to justify keeping criminalisation anomalous by limiting it to a small number of cases (2007: 48–9). On this reading, appeals to symbolism take place simply in order to obscure the deregulatory direction of neo-liberal regulatory policy. Further, this approach reflects a preoccupation with risks to legitimate middle-class victims, such as public transport users, and suppresses the seriousness of the deaths of workers who are killed while 'exchanging their labour power' (Tombs and Whyte 2010: 49). The manslaughter offence, as an initiative intended to address the concerns of public opinion, is actually about offering reassurance to a suburban elite of opinion-formers.

While there is some evidence from research into public attitudes to suggest that fatalities which 'cross the "factory fence"' are regarded as more serious than those involving workers (Almond 2008), the reality is more nuanced; concerns about public fatalities are not confined to any social demographic, and many of the most egregious 'work'-related deaths provoke very high ratings of perceived seriousness among the public (Almond 2008; Almond and Colover 2010). The primary purpose of criminalisation, under a communicative approach put forward here, is to provide a forum for action taken in the public interest which reinforces the normative 'reasons for' regulating to protect health and safety, reasons which relate to the preservation of the conditions of social citizenship. On this approach, it is important that enforcement action should achieve the maximum impact possible, but there is no overriding reason why one work-related death should be privileged by being criminalised, while another should not. To observe that public fatalities *do* communicate with audiences is not to demand that they *should* be utilised as the sole means of doing so.

A more preferable approach would be for manslaughter prosecutions to take place in the cases that display the greatest degree of wrongfulness, regardless of context or victim. Utilising a manslaughter offence in relation to more traditional breaches of workplace safety would allow for clarification of the relationship between the criminal law and the health and safety regulations that define the 'reasons for' prosecution (Gunningham and Johnstone 1999: 215). In fact, the point made by Haines and Hall that a manslaughter offence must possess a degree of symbolic richness in order to positively enhance health and safety law (2004: 269) positively 'demands' that the offence be connected to the regulatory laws that define the wrongfulness it seeks to censure. Symbolic richness requires use where these values are most grievously breached. Like Gunningham and Johnstone, who advocate the close harnessing of criminal and occupational health and safety laws (1999: 215), the argument advanced here would see the greatest benefit emerging from a mutually reinforcing connection between criminal and regulatory law. This requires that the duties underpinning corporate manslaughter be clarified in order to explicate the basis of the charge and that prosecution policy should emphasise the importance of the underlying regulatory breach, both in bringing charges and in explaining them at trial.

Issues of moral culpability have been shown to be highly significant in informing the prosecutorial decision-making of regulators like the HSE (Hawkins 2002; also Almond 2006); since the same regulator now has a key role in referring cases to the Police and CPS and in providing technical support to those bodies when they prosecute, it is plausible to assume that these factors will also feed into decision-making in relation to the new offence. The work of Hawkins (2002) and others (Hutter 1997; Hutter and Lloyd-Bostock 1990) has consistently highlighted the instrumental use of prosecution by safety regulators as a means of serving institutional interests such as the promotion of an image of invincibility, the highlighting of priority issues or particularly current concerns, and as a means of showing that the regulator is responsive to public and media concerns. But the approach argued for here is one that places greater emphasis on the use of prosecution, under criminal law, because it is 'deserved' and because it *must* take place, rather than for instrumental gain. The communicative value of an offence of this sort stems from the law's capacity to deliver judgements reflecting the approbation deemed appropriate according to shared social values. It is driven by a different rationale than regulatory enforcement, where calculation of impact is central to the decision to prosecute. The legitimation of the law via criminalisation occurs because there is a demonstrable connection between the outcomes reached and the expectations and values that inform the law. As such, symbolic enforcement is more about showing what the law means than showing where institutions stand in relation to it; they serve the law rather than it serving them.

Secondly, it is important to remember that the relationship between instrumental and symbolic outcomes is complex; the instrumental value of an offence is an outcome of its use when the values that it protects are violated. By restating the importance of the regulatory project, the symbolic offence reinforces the mandate of regulators and the law, and this has an instrumental impact in that it deters the regulated population from disregarding the 'reasons for' obeying the law, thus motivating future compliance. It can also increase the level of public and political support that the regulator enjoys, although these outcomes can be hard to measure. Much of the focus in discussions about instrumental benefit is placed upon the issue of punishment, and it is hard to envisage how a system of monetary penalties could muster sufficient instrumental impact given the limited nature of the fines levied and the ability of corporations to absorb these costs (Wells 2001: 166). This misses the point as, unlike civil damages, criminal punishments are not primarily about utilitarian cost-adjustment, but rather they are about signalling socio-cultural disapproval. Like other strands of regulatory theory, this process is about tapping into the willingness of actors to comply with laws that they think they *should* comply with (Ayres and Braithwaite 1992; Braithwaite 2002; 2008; Haines 1997; Parker 2002; Tyler 1990), making that 'should' as explicit as possible, rather than just aiming at mechanical deterrence. Regulation is a process of making the private sphere of business power permeable by the values of the wider public sphere, and this requires that enforcement must contribute to the 'regulatory conversation' in a positive way (Parker 2002; also Aalders and Wilthagen 1997; Black 2001; 2002). Rather than alienating the regulated via a commitment to a punitive enforcement policy, a normative approach has the potential to restate the 'reasons for' compliance which underpin the belief that obeying the law is the right thing to do, and thus contribute to a virtuous circle of commitment and reinforcement.

The final point to make about the symbolic conception of corporate manslaughter laws adopted here is that no prescriptive presumption about the extent to which such an offence will be used is imposed. If it is to strengthen the normative legitimacy of the regulatory system as a whole, it should be used to an extent that is sufficient to allow this to happen. Symbolic enforcement goals have been linked to a 'last-resort' strategy, whereby the communicative power of punitive law enforcement is used sparingly in order to maximise the impact that each prosecution has (Hawkins 2002). Such an approach is taken to militate against the widespread use of measures at the top of the enforcement pyramid and has been criticised for legitimating existing patterns of non-enforcement (Pearce and Tombs 1990; 1991; Tombs and Whyte 2010). For these critics, criminalisation must be used more widely in order to produce the level of deterrent effect required to prevent workplace death. But by emphasising that enforcement should occur when it *must* because it is deserved on the basis of the wrong in the individual case, arguments about the 'correct' amount of enforcement action become less relevant. It undermines the normative standing of the law if institutional constraints mean it is not used when it is deserved; conversely, if it is used when merited, then instrumental effects will follow. That said, it is reasonable to observe that current manslaughter prosecution practices are entirely insufficient for the fulfilment of the communicative goals sought. There should be more manslaughter prosecutions, and criminalisation should play a greater role in reinforcing the normative message that underpins regulation.

It is possible to arrive at some important conclusions about the implementation of corporate manslaughter offences, based upon this symbolic understanding of criminal law. Firstly, such an offence should be utilised in the most wrongful cases, not just those that generate publicity or provoke public concern. Secondly, if the offence is to be symbolically effective, it must be closely related to the broader regulatory project, as this is the system that it is intended to legitimate and which also defines the interests that it seeks to protect. Thirdly, it should be used as often as it is merited, rather than being driven by notional targets for enforcement rates. The internal, content-dependent reasons for prosecuting generate the legitimatory outcomes which the corporate manslaughter offence should be concerned with producing, not the external, content-independent, instrumental reasons that underpin regulatory policy. Only if these criteria are met will the symbolic potential of a corporate manslaughter offence be realised. The evidence available to date relating to the UK's experience in this regard (outlined above) suggests that they will not; the limited implementation of the new offence undermines any claims about transformative effect that the reforms might make.

The manslaughter reforms as 'penal populism'?

One important objection to the introduction of corporate manslaughter offences and a symbolic approach to enforcement is that such an approach constitutes a form of 'penal populism'. Many criminologists have attributed the emergence of punitive state-level criminal justice practices within the western world in the last 30 years to the increasing influence of public opinion within policy-making circles (Bottoms 1995; Garland 2001; Lacey 2008; Pratt 2000; Roberts *et al.* 2003; Simon 2007; Tonry 2004). Penal populism connotes the tendency of political decision-makers to be led by populist sentiment in shaping policy; the result is that 'punishment policy [is] developed primarily for its anticipated popularity' (Roberts *et al.* 2003: 65) rather than because it is likely to bring about any positive instrumental effect. And since public feelings of insecurity give rise to social preferences for emotive and retributive sanctioning, this dynamic of 'populist punitiveness' (Almond 2008; Bottoms 1995; Hutton 2005) leads to the pursuit of retributive, exclusionary sanctioning policies, an expanded penal infrastructure, and the marginalisation of offending populations (Garland 2001; Pratt 2000; Simon 2007; Tonry 2004; Young 1999).

The willingness of political leaders to respond to these pressures reflects the media's role as the primary forum for the transmission of public opinions (Ericson 1991; Roberts *et al.* 2003: 77), and the influence of 'late-modern' anxieties about social change (Garland 2001; King and Maruna 2009; Young 1999). This punitiveness also reflects the openness of political decision-making to external pressures; where executive power is not constrained by the need for negotiated decision-making (Lacey 2008; Simon 2007), and where checks on policy-making are eroded, punitive tendencies are more pronounced. In particular, the marginalisation of 'expertise' from governmental policy-making (Garland 2001: 150; Lacey 2008: 72; Loader 2006; Roberts *et al.* 2003: 70) has exposed political actors directly to the currents of public opinion. While not all elements of criminal justice policy-making conform to the punitive model outlined here, and there are empirical and conceptual reasons to doubt whether public attitudes are truly punitive (Almond 2011; Green 2006; Hutton 2005; Matthews 2005; Roberts and Hough 2005), the concern remains potent. Put simply, much criminal justice policy and law reform has tended to be ill-considered and unprincipled, and this trend reflects a common desire on the part of politicians to demonstrate their responsiveness to public demands.

It may be argued that the UK's Corporate Manslaughter and Corporate Homicide Act 2007 is an example of a penal populist response to public insecurity. This is part of Baldwin's (2004) critique of a 'new regulatory punitiveness', which he argues has led to a shift in legislative and regulatory approach so that the use of criminal sanctions plays a greater role and adversarial methods are increasingly widely used (2004: 352). There is evidence that elements of this regulatory punitiveness are present in other jurisdictions (2004: 354; Gray 2009), but Baldwin's main emphasis is on the regulatory legacy of the UK's New Labour governments. He attributes this shift to a media-driven 'blame culture' and a politically expedient desire to 'get' company directors (2004: 360), but does not fully explain the origins of this wider movement towards punitiveness. Baldwin also cites the corporate manslaughter offence and the HSE as examples of legislative and agency shifts towards a more punitive culture of resort to the 'big stick' in response to health and safety offences (also Lacey 2004: 162). The problems with Baldwin's account are twofold; firstly, there is little evidence of any groundswell of popular opinion putting pressure on politicians to get tough in this area (apart from the critical discourses outlined in Chapter 6), and secondly, there is little evidence that practices *have* actually got tough in this area, given the countervailing trends towards deregulation, reduced inspection and enforcement, and limited sanctions (Tombs and Whyte 2010).

Nevertheless, work-related deaths are capable of prompting public demands for a political response (Almond 2008; Almond and Colover 2010), and the corporate manslaughter offence does constitute a conceptual toughening of the law in this area. There was evidence of a penal populist dynamic at play in the reform process and of a willingness on the part of government to pursue symbolic gains ahead of meaningful outcomes (Baldwin 2004: 354; Gobert 2005; Ormerod and Taylor 2008). Gobert highlights the political manoeuvring and appeals to public concerns that characterised the Government's approach to the reform process and which are reflected in the Home Office's framing of reform in terms of the need to maintain 'public confidence' in the law (2000; 2005). Neither the Home Office nor the Law Commission (1996: 7.9) provided any evidence as to the extent of these concerns, seemingly assuming that critical media attitudes were representative of a wider public disquiet. The role of public disasters in driving the reforms illustrates that the process was akin to a kind of moral panic (Gobert 2005; Wells 2001), and the narrow focusing of the offence on only the most high-profile work-related deaths also suggests an overarching concern with media communication rather than coherent law reform. Haines and Hall summarise this by arguing that in the absence of a meaningful instrumental purpose, the new offence symbolises only the human appetite for blame and the willingness of political actors to capitalise on this for their own ends (2004: 271).

Three points can be made in response to these charges. Firstly, it is important to acknowledge that the law reform process has indeed been coloured by this kind of populist dynamic; it would be hard to argue that the new offence reflected a nuanced understanding of the legitimatory requirements of the regulatory system and that political expediency had played no role whatsoever in its introduction. The political calculation that led to the passing of the 2007 Act in the UK is typical of a populist approach to policy, in that the form of the offence and the focus on a specific element of a broader issue suggest a simplification of the policy-making process and a determination to be *seen to* have solved a problem. But the rather unpromising origins of the offence do not preclude it from having a real effect and do not mean that it cannot address the symbolic deficits of regulatory law. The contextual reasons why notions of corporate manslaughter gain traction, and the motivating reasons that explain why politicians reform the law, need not be the same, and the latter need not obscure the former. Penal populism involves the creation of criminal offences that are intended to communicate with a public audience, and so it seems reasonable to question whether such an offence may subsequently be used to communicate a more constructive message than the one its political progenitors envisaged. Additionally, the two limitations on Baldwin's 'regulatory punitiveness' thesis, the lack of popular public outrage and the lack of punitive regulatory practices, apply here also, suggesting that both the degree of 'populism' and the degree of 'penalism' embodied in the manslaughter reforms are less than might be suggested by Baldwin.

Secondly, it is important to be aware of the disjunction between public opinion as a perceived phenomenon that drives political decision-making, and true public 'attitudes', which are more nuanced than those perceptions allow (Green 2006; Hutton 2005; Roberts *et al.* 2003). To say that there is a public demand for punishment in relation to work-related deaths may be true, but such a characterisation obscures both the reasons for that demand and the nature of those preferences. In actuality, public attitudes are complex, not especially punitive, and focused on issues of accountability and prevention rather than retribution and exclusion (Almond 2008; Almond and Colover 2010, 2012). There is no simple or overwhelming reactionary clamour for punishment or blame and significant evidence to suggest that support for criminalisation here might be more akin to a genuine democratic preference than a search for vengeance; on this reading, there is a need to place a greater emphasis on the democratic components of Roberts *et al.*'s model of penal populism, rather than just those relating to political self-interest (2003: 62–64; 72). Punishment is a calculated preference, not a knee-jerk reaction.

Thirdly, there is a difference between responsiveness to mere opinion as a basis for criminal justice policy and the creation of policy with a genuinely deliberative component. Seeking public input does not automatically result in the sort of shallow populism displayed by, for instance, three-strike sentencing policies (Dzur and Mirchandani 2007: 161–164). A communicative approach to criminal law would argue that genuinely deliberative public engagement can assist in identifying problems and informing the decisions reached by formal institutions in resolving them. Rather than resulting in ill-considered policy choices, which are more likely to be the outcome of minimally deliberative policy formulation, a communicative approach to penal policy allows for a rational-critical debate over the settlement of interests and values to occur. This permits the creation of policy which gives effect to these values and which is more authentically representative of community norms. Even ostensibly punitive policies are compatible with a communicative approach to the law so long as they give effect to some degree of deliberative public will-formation. A genuinely communicative approach to the criminalisation of work-related deaths is a long way from being a license for reactionary punitiveness to take hold.

The manslaughter reforms as 'governing through crime'?

A final accusation that can be levelled at the corporate manslaughter reform process is that it constitutes an extension of the tendency for contemporary governments to use the criminal law as a tool of self-justification. Jonathan Simon, in his account of the process of 'Governing Through Crime' (2007), suggests that the exporting of dynamics and processes associated with the governance of crime into other spheres of social conduct is a key feature of contemporary politics, driven by a desire to secure political support via the control of social risks and to extend the power of the sovereign state. For Simon, social problems are redefined in terms of the analogy of crime and victimhood in a wide range of different contexts, including schools, the home, the welfare state, and the workplace, with the result that criminalisation becomes the default means of responding to these problems. On one level, this is because criminalisation is a much easier solution to implement than alternatives that actually seek to address the causes of the problem in question; on the other, it allows for the extension of executive government power into new spheres of social life via new agencies, laws, and capacity to systematically control swathes of the population. Finally, the emotive nature of crime, and the definition of the ordinary citizen as a victim, means that this extension of state power can be achieved with the consent of the population rather than via a contested political process.

Those writing from this perspective would view the new corporate manslaughter-type offences as examples of the extension of criminal law dynamics into new areas of civil life. For Simon, it is necessary to think long and hard before expanding the dynamic of criminalisation into areas like the workplace, even in the interests of protecting employees (for instance, via employment discrimination laws), because to do so inculcates an adversarial legalism which redefines 'the workplace as a field of battle' (2007: 256). On this front, Simon echoes the concerns raised by regulatory scholars about the potential that enforcement action possesses to increase levels of hostility to regulation among regulated stakeholders (Ayres and Braithwaite 1992; Bardach and Kagan 1982; Gunningham and Johnstone 1999; Hawkins 2002; Hutter 1997; May and Burby 1998; Robens 1972). And even though he sympathises with efforts to redress the 'increasingly stark asymmetry of power between management and workers' via law (2007: 236), Simon identifies many problems associated with the extension of criminal law in this way, including the tendency for areas of policy and practice to become fixated with actuarial processes of oversight and goal-setting via performance indicators, and with the aggregation of offenders into categories for the purposes of targeted intervention (Bottoms 1995; Feeley and Simon 1992; 1994). The result is an ends-focused legal infrastructure which dehumanises the individuals subject to it and facilitates the extension of power structures into ever more areas of social life.

There is a parallel between the concept of actuarialism and the notion of juridification, or the expansion of system imperatives of money and power into the sphere of the lifeworld, as identified by Habermas (1984; 1988). Both view the extension of the law as a process of colonisation, with political and economic interests driving an encroachment of rules into areas that traditionally had been thought to be outside the scope of government. Both are sceptical about the capacity of law to produce a positive change. And both see the State as having essentially self-interested motivations for encroaching in this way, either to expand its own power or to fulfil its steering role. The main difference is that Habermas explicitly recognises law's potential to have emancipatory effects if it is underpinned by meaningful deliberative public will-formation (1988; 1992). For Simon, however, the extension of criminalisation is almost never a good thing, and he is right to be sceptical; the spread of the dynamics of crime in the area of workplace safety has been associated with processes of responsibilisation and worker-blaming (2007: 237; also Gray 2006; 2009; Silbey 2009). After all, the criminal law is a system of State power which has been indicted as repressive and marginalising of the disadvantaged, as a hopelessly inadequate means of guaranteeing social justice and as effective only in obscuring the real bases of social conflicts (Cohen 1988; cited in Haines and Hall 2004: 269–270; Hall and Johnstone 2005). For these critics, criminalisation hides the power structures that underpin social relations and provides a forum for moral denunciation which does not indict the fundamental bases of the social and economic system.

But Habermas, while recognising the tendency for the law to become a tool of repression that serves powerful interests, also recognises the possibility that it may fulfil a positive solidarity-building social function, in the Durkheimian sense (1987; Prosser 2006). Once again, it comes down to the law's role as reflective of the shared mutual understandings of the lifeworld. Criminal enforcement has the capacity, when underpinned by a deliberative foundation in public opinion, to communicate effectively about the reasons to obey the law and to bring about more considered outcomes. It can work as a system of moral accountability and a mechanism for securing behavioural change, but only when it has this deeper legitimacy. Punishment must be done in the name of the community, must reflect the values of the community, and must reconcile the offender with those values and the community (Dzur and Mirchandani 2007; Weaver 2009). But a significant component of this is the affirmation of those values and the reinforcement of a social commitment to them via their enforcement. So although criminalisation is often negative, at least in the form that it often takes, it is also a necessary element of a broader approach which is not punitive in aspiration. As such, the use of an offence like corporate manslaughter should be closely associated with systems of regulatory oversight that are open and deliberative, and that allow for deliberative input from the public and stakeholders (Aalders and Wilthagen 1997; Black 2000; 2001; Parker 2002). The key is to facilitate 'governing through public democratic deliberation'; crime is just one tool that can be used in achieving this outcome.

Criminal law as an 'imperfect solution'?

Having explored the difficulties associated with the use of criminalisation in the regulatory sphere, it is necessary to return to the conclusions that emerged in Chapter 2, relating to the criminalisation of work-related deaths in different jurisdictions. In particular, one question arises: why, given the deficits of regulation identified throughout this book, and given the potential of criminalisation to address these deficits, do some countries continue to get by without corporate criminal law to back up their regulatory regimes? How is it that the shift towards manslaughter seen in so many national legal systems has not also occurred in countries which remain committed to the principle of *societas delinquere non potest*? Criminalisation is the product of particular socio-political contexts, and it is nations that have conformed most closely to the neo-liberal paradigm during the last 30 years which have moved furthest towards criminalisation during this period, suggesting that it is here that the communicative deficits of regulation are most acutely felt. Other jurisdictions which have to some extent retained a different socio-political context have not demonstrated the same need to use the criminal law to buttress regulation. The conclusion that can be drawn is that criminalisation, while a potentially productive step when it is needed, is not the only means through which the shortcomings of regulation can be offset; given the limitations of this communicative 'crutch' outlined above, it may be preferable to pursue a different approach, centred on a social recognition of the value of regulation.

Chapter 6 illustrated the problematic social and political context within which health and safety regulation operates. A poor-quality public dialogue about health and safety, founded on a crippled epistemology of myth, misinformation, and political opposition has meant that the communicative capacity of regulation has been eroded. In particular, the neo-liberal political climate that has become entrenched since the late 1970s has been instrumental in creating this hostile context. The neo-liberal state is defined as prioritising 'strong individual private property rights, the rule of law, and the institutions of freely functioning markets and free trade' as a means of guaranteeing individual freedoms (Harvey 2005: 64) and is thus hostile to the imposition of regulatory controls which curtail these interests. Individual responsibility for welfare, a small state infrastructure, and a resistance to government interference in the economic sphere are all features of the neo-liberal paradigm that help create a political climate in which safety regulators are regarded as inimical to the interests of the government of the day, and in which their funding, status, resources, and legitimacy are reduced accordingly (Gray 2009; Hawkins 2002; Tombs and Whyte 2007; 2010). Regulation is cast as a form of interference with individual freedoms which runs counter to the interests of society, which are best served via the maintenance of open markets in which individual economic choices can be pursued unencumbered. The emphasis on self-regulation, the shifting of regulatory burdens onto workers, the declining influence of worker representation, as well as changes in resourcing and enforcement philosophy have all been cited as consequences of the neo-liberal approach to safety regulation (Bittle and Snider 2006; Gray 2006; 2009; Tombs and Whyte 2007; 2010; Walters 2006).

But it appears that a countervailing tendency towards criminalisation is also associated with neo-liberalism; in Chapter 2, it was shown that the UK remains the only national jurisdiction to have a specific corporate manslaughter offence, and that the USA, Canada, and Australia have been among the most proactive proponents of criminalisation in this area. These nation states have also been among the most enthusiastic adherents to a neo-liberal political paradigm during the last 30 years (Harvey 2005; also Hall and Soskice 2001: 20; Lacey 2008). In the civil law jurisdictions which have reformed to allow for corporate criminality and manslaughter prosecutions (France, Belgium, the Netherlands, Denmark, and others), the overcoming of entrenched resistance to corporate crime has coincided with the emergence of neo-liberalism. Although the 'European model' is often presented as a social-democratic counterpoint to neo-liberalism, the European nations which have reformed to allow for corporate criminalisation are positioned more towards the liberal-market economy end of the political continuum than many of their neighbours. They display higher levels of stock market capitalisation, income inequality, and institutional and financial flexibility, and lower levels of employment protection, investment stability, and state intervention, than other, more coordinated, European economies (Hall and Soskice 2001: 19–33; Lacey 2008: 58–60; 111). It might also be suggested that they subscribe (at least in the case of France and the Netherlands) to a version of political progressivism which emphasises individual liberty and freedom, rather than social justice, as the goal of social democracy (Gibson and Caldeira 1996: 65–70; Harvey 2005: 41).

And it is in the nations of Europe where a social justice-oriented version of social democracy holds sway, and where there is a greater commitment to the maintenance of a coordinated economy (Sweden, Germany) that a strict divide between the regulatory and criminal spheres has been retained. These nations are most likely to retain a clearer commitment to welfare-oriented, representative, and protectionist cultures of labour and workplace politics (Thelen 2001) and to rely on systems of participatory regulation to govern these areas rather than adversarial approaches like the criminal law. This sketched thesis does oversimplify many issues, such as the criminalisation of corporate activity in apparently social-democratic jurisdictions like Denmark and Norway, and the resistance to criminalisation in nations like Greece, the Czech Republic, and Mexico, which derive their criminal law norms from the German system but not necessarily their political or economic culture (Gibson and Caldeira 1996; Hall and Soskice 2001). Nevertheless, it is clear that neo-liberalism may logically result in a diminution of state-led welfarist intervention in the corporate sphere. But why does a climate of neo-liberalism also lead to the introduction of corporate manslaughter offences?

Nicola Lacey's analysis (2008) of the punitiveness of Anglo-American criminal justice systems provides insights into the nature of debates about crime policy in different political contexts. She views the relative penal intolerance of the UK and the USA as an outcome, in part, of their political and economic systems, and particularly the influence of a neo-liberal dynamic of individualism and free marketism. Across multiple measures, including rates of imprisonment and criminal records, and the criminalisation of foreign nationals and ethnic minorities, societies that evidence the greatest conformity to neo-liberalism come out on top (2008: Ch. 3; also Cavadino and Dignan 2006; Wilkinson and Pickett 2009: Ch. 10). A greater penal tolerance is found in nations that conform to a social-democratic, corporatist political model (Cavadino and Dignan 2006; Kury 2008; Lacey 2008), although there is also evidence of a 'punitive turn' in recent years in many of these jurisdictions. The result is a significant differentiation of criminal justice policy, with the most extensive use of coercive state power occurring in jurisdictions that most clearly embody the neo-liberal values of the 'free economy and the strong state' (Gamble 1994), via a limited social justice infrastructure and an expanded security system (Harvey 2005).

According to Lacey, these differences reflect institutional and political decision-making processes. Coordinated economy jurisdictions tend to feature proportional representation, consensus-based political systems, and strong welfare states, all of which facilitate deliberative engagement and preclude aggressively adversarial policy-making. But free-market jurisdictions tend to feature minimal welfare states and majoritarian, adversarial political systems which privilege exclusionary policies and do not facilitate deliberative engagement (Lacey 2008: 62; also Hall and Soskice 2001); policy-making is unreflective and creates the kind of crippled epistemology outlined previously. Opportunities to participate in the democratic process occur rarely, and political actors are sensitive to fluctuations in public opinion as a result of their unmediated accountability at the polls, resulting in penal populist policy-making (Roberts *et al.* 2003). At the same time, however, these differences are not just institutional; neo-liberal states also promote political values of individualism, the exclusion of those who are not economically self-sufficient (Young 1999), and a retrenchment of the entitlements of citizens *vis-à-vis* the State. All of these tendencies help to explain the punitive tendencies of the neo-liberal world; punitiveness simply reflects the exclusionary and individualistic focus of the societies in which it occurs (Cavadino and Dignan 2006; Lacey 2008: Ch. 2).

This model also helps us to understand why health and safety regulation is increasingly vulnerable in these neo-liberal societies. As Braithwaite points out, areas of regulation such as health and safety do not tap into the same dynamic of social exclusion as mainstream criminal justice practices (2003). The features that incubate penal populism (free-marketism, majoritarian politics, minimal welfare state) also militate *against* welfarist policy interventions like health and safety law; regulation faces opposition from market-oriented interest groups (Almond 2009a; Gobert 2005; Hawkins 2002: 117), as well as deregulatory pressures from within the political system (Bain 1997; Beck and Woolfson 2000; Dodds 2006; Tombs and Whyte 2007; 2010). This is not offset by strong pro-regulatory interests; countries like the UK have lower levels of worker representation and trade union involvement in health and safety regulation than other European jurisdictions (Frick and Walters 1998; James and Walters 2002; Walters 1995). While other areas of provision have seen convergence across Europe, the historical gap between the social-democratic nations and the adversarial legalism of the common-law jurisdictions remains significant (Rehder 2009; Thelen 2001; Walters 1996: 307). In the European jurisdictions where any shift towards more extensive corporate criminalisation has been most fully resisted, most notably Germany and Sweden, the aims and purposes of the regulatory project are regarded as in the public interest, and health, safety, and environmental risks caused by business are more likely to be viewed as unacceptable (Vogel 2011: 18). Rates of worker participation are higher (Frick and Walters 1998), levels of employment protection are more developed, average working hours are lower (Hall and Soskice 2001: 22; Thelen 2001), there is a greater rights-culture of worker entitlement to welfare protection, and a greater level of public support for health and safety as a cooperative process (Koch and Salter 1999: 70). This culture of workplace welfarism serves to insulate these jurisdictions to some degree from the deregulatory pressures that exist elsewhere, limiting the extent to which safety regulation is undermined by broader political and economic trends.

Sweden and Germany in particular have also shown themselves to be more closely wedded to the 'precautionary principle' as a risk management philosophy, prioritising the protection of welfarist public interests by requiring that hazardous activities and materials be proved to be safe before they are permitted by regulators (Löfstedt 2004; 2011b). Britain and the USA, on the other hand, prefer a risk-based approach, which allows for judgements to be made about the economic costs and benefits of regulation, the probability and relative weighting of any harm being risked, and the desirability of the activity being regulated (Helm

2006; Löfstedt 2004; 2011b). While there are problems associated with a hazard-based approach, not least a tendency to produce outcomes that lack a robust evidence base and so appear disproportionately and irrationally restrictive (Löfstedt 2004; 2011b; Slovic 1986; Sunstein 2005; Viscusi 2000), this stance does signal an entrenched commitment to the protection of a particular set of values and socio-cultural considerations. The risk-based approach preferred in the neo-liberal world, on the other hand, is based on the scientific judgements of risk experts and an analysis of a much wider set of concerns, including the political and economic merits of the risk taken. This is a pragmatic, instrumental approach and, as such, there is more opportunity for Habermas' system imperatives (1988) to influence decision-making about the parameters of tolerability. Risk-based regulation allows for better-evidenced decisions to be made which increase the instrumental effectiveness of regulatory regimes, but it also contributes to a decline in the perceived trustworthiness of expert opinion, which is seen as unrepresentative of public concerns (Löfstedt 2011b: 161).

The disengagement of the regulatory process from the public sphere insulates processes of evidence-led decision-making from distortion by 'mere opinion', but it also distances it from the legitimating input of deliberative public engagement needed to justify its existence. This disengagement accounts for the normative deficits in regulation identified in previous chapters, and this in turn explains the shift towards criminalisation as a means of bringing these socio-political considerations back into the regulatory process. The neo-liberal perspective tends to conceive of occupational health and safety as a discrete system of rules that has its own internal logic and which functions on a value-neutral basis as an adjunct of the contractual relationship between employers and employees. It is a forum for the management of market practices and the facilitation of self-governance by autonomous legal actors, rather than for moral judgements about issues of justice. It is a steering mechanism; it displaces the structural conflicts inherent in the political and economic systems into a more manageable form (Almond 2007: Habermas 1973; 1988; Haines 2011; Haines and Sutton 2003). The construction of this model of health and safety regulation as a steering mechanism was set out in Chapter 4.

But why has corporate manslaughter emerged as an issue in more neo-liberal societies but not in jurisdictions where there might be a greater commitment to welfarism and social solidarity, ostensibly the values that such an offence seeks to promote? The answer is that it is not needed in these other jurisdictions precisely *because* they already have a commitment to welfarism and social solidarity. Systems of social regulation have a higher social profile in countries like Germany (Gräbe 1991); during the 1970s, there was a concerted interest in the development of safety protection and there remains a commitment to regulation as a means of securing particular welfare goals. Gräbe asserts, however, that there was (during the early 1990s) a greater 'consciousness' of safety issues in the UK than in Germany, where safety breaches were more easily accepted as a price to be paid for social progress (1991: 68). Two things can be said about this. Firstly, a relative lack of public engagement may reflect a more effective mechanism of worker engagement which allows for deliberative input without spilling over into the public sphere. If there is an effective forum for the settlement of these issues, then external pressure towards reform is less likely. Secondly, public 'consciousness' of health and safety does not necessarily guarantee public 'support' for that law, as evidenced in the UK, where much media discourse is devoted to the belittling of 'meddling' health and safety laws (Almond 2009b). And the public profile of health and safety at the start of the 1990s was driven by public disquiet about the profound failures of the existing system of regulation (see Chapter 5; also Wells 2001); so in this sense, the awareness evidenced was primarily an awareness of what was wrong with, rather than right with, regulation. As mentioned previously, the widespread culture of workplace welfarism in Germany and elsewhere serves to buttress safety regulation as one component of a broader social-democratic project, even though it may not stand out as a contested component in its own right.

In Sweden, levels of worker participation in safety regulation are significantly higher than elsewhere in Europe, as are rates of regulator engagement in pursuit of compliance (Frick and Walters 1998; Walters 1995), although this has declined in recent years (Walters *et al.* 2011). If German and Swedish health and safety regulation already has a more substantial emphasis on participation and deliberative decision-making than elsewhere, and thus renders the corporate sphere more open to input from a wider range of voices and social interests, then there is a viable alternative source of the legitimating social input that is missing in other countries. In Sweden, health and safety representatives are actively engaged in a participatory 'democratic dialogue' about safety provision via trade union committees and joint health and safety committees (Frick and Walters 1998; Gustavsen 1985). At the same time, rates of formal enforcement action taken by safety inspectors are low, and the powers of those inspectors to prosecute are heavily curtailed (Walters *et al.* 2011: 135). Similarly, the external political context is also less prone to the adversarialism associated with neo-liberal regimes. Not only is welfarism an accepted goal of political decision-making but also there is a greater capacity for the pursuit of mutually agreed outcomes via dialogic means; Sweden's traditions of high union membership rates and consensus politics mean that it is a society with a relatively high degree of acceptance of occupational health and safety provision as a legitimate goal of social policy (Frick and Walters 1998: 382). This means that the instrumental systems of occupational health and safety are already embedded within the broader democratic contexts from which they derive their meaning. There is a basis for debate about how to balance the interests of the economic and welfarist constituencies and for expression of the normative value attached to notions of welfare rights-protection and social citizenship. The regulatory system is connected to the 'reasons for' regulating that underpin it and is, as a result, accepted as a means of addressing these reasons and fulfilling the social interests that inform them.

Criminalisation can thus be understood as a product of the status of systems of health and safety regulation within contemporary neo-liberal societies, but also as reflective of the long history of adversarial, impartial government, and values of liberal self-determination that predominate in those societies, while a history of hierarchical but also accommodative politics in countries like Sweden might mitigate against such an outcome. As such, 'it is not surprising . . . that American policymakers chose an occupational safety and health compliance system based on punishment meted out through the legal system . . . [N]or is it surprising that Swedish policymakers chose to use normative inducements, with legal punishments only as a backup' (Kelman 1984: 115). In the latter case, there is no need to pursue symbolic criminal law enforcement as a means of justifying the interference with individual interests that regulation involves. Regulatory law is capable of speaking for itself. And while the outcomes achieved may not attain the same level of public censure as criminal law is capable of doing, it 'does not need to do so' in order to communicate the requisite message about the legitimacy of the regulatory system. Put simply, if regulatory law 'matters', then it will be more able to secure the legitimacy that it requires. There may be shortcomings in these regulatory systems' capacity to achieve justice in serious cases, or in the rates of workplace death and injury achieved, or in terms of how effective processes of deliberative engagement are, but there are still reasons to believe that regulatory systems with these characteristics have a significant legitimatory advantage over those in other national jurisdictions. They may not speak as loudly as adversarial neo-liberal legal systems that carry 'big sticks' (Ayres and Braithwaite 1992), but they perhaps speak 'more clearly', especially with regard to their own legitimacy as protectors of established social values.

Conclusions

This book has outlined the development of criminal laws in many national jurisdictions in the last 20 years that allow for the pursuit of manslaughter prosecutions against corporate bodies that cause deaths. This trend has involved the development of both specific corporate manslaughter offences (such as the one passed into UK law in 2007) and more general methods for the attribution of criminal fault to corporate bodies, allowing them to be liable for the same manslaughter offences as human defendants. This trend has been most pronounced in the common-law world, with the UK, the USA, Canada, and Australia leading the way, but there has increasingly been a similar movement in European civil law jurisdictions as well. This development must be understood as a result of the communicative status of regulatory systems of health and safety law within contemporary societies. Systems of regulatory control over workplace safety developed over time in order to grant and protect the social citizenship rights of individual workers and citizens, but this process has increasingly involved the construction of a system of regulation which is instrumental in nature. This instrumentalism makes health and safety regulation more ends-focused and concerned about the relative costs and benefits of regulation, and increases the capacity of that system to maximise positive outcomes. It emphasises notions of targeted intervention, compliance-seeking, and the fulfilment of strategic goals as the primary aims of the regulatory system.

At the same time, however, it also renders the regulatory system more technical and bureaucratic, more distant from the lives and understandings of citizens, and more focused on internal rationality than on external moral values. Because it is an effective tool for the fulfilment of specific goals, it is also open to domination by the interests of systems of money and power that predominate in a capitalist society. The goals which the regulatory system seeks to fulfil become differentiated from the social priorities that it is supposed to pursue, even as its instrumental ability to fulfil those goals is increased. As a result, systems of health and safety regulation lose their grounding in the normative values of the life-world, which provides the 'reasons for' regulating. The development of criminal laws (such as the manslaughter offence) constitutes a response to the inability of instrumental systems of regulation to communicate about the normative bases on which they operate, and so establish the source of their legitimacy. Criminal enforcement is not instrumental in nature, for the most part, and involves the declaration of the unacceptability of particular forms of offending behaviour. This is done via explicit reference to normative values, and so the use of criminal law in the regulatory sphere offers the possibility of constructing a forum for the consideration of those issues in explicitly moralised terms.

But this is an imperfect solution. Criminalisation is an ambivalent measure and does not always achieve the kind of communicative outcomes that might be hoped for. It is a blunt tool which has detrimental side effects and cannot normally be characterised as progressive in nature. And there are significant concerns about how far the new laws that have been introduced are capable of having any meaningful practical effect or are backed up by a political commitment sufficient to ensure that they are used proactively enough to have any symbolic effect. There is a risk that these offences are 'Potemkin villages' (Gray 2006), symbolic gestures rather than genuinely communicative tools that can legitimate systems of regulation. In some other jurisdictions, there has not been a move towards criminalisation, and this reflects the possibility that the necessary legitimatory outcomes can be achieved via a more deliberative approach to regulation. As such, these criminal laws can be seen as 'legitimatory crutches', tools to assist in propping up systems of regulation that are too normatively weak to stand on their own. Criminalisation is a non-optimal means of making regulated business interests permeable to outside influence from the socio-cultural sphere and of ensuring that some form of deliberation takes place over the proper balance to be drawn between welfarist and economic interests.

But in reaching this conclusion, it is important to reflect on the contextual conditions that give rise to this weakness of the regulatory system. It is the adversarial style of government, resistance to welfarist state intervention to secure socially just outcomes, and commitment to principles of individualism and economic freedom found in contemporary neo-liberal political systems that have incubated this collapse of regulatory capacity. If regulation is seen as the enemy of government, and thus of the people, it should come as no surprise that a poor-quality and hostile public dialogue about health and safety emerges as a result. Add this to a structural political choice to downgrade the capacity of regulatory systems by, for instance, withdrawing funding, and you have a combination which erases the popular support that the regulatory project needs to sustain itself. There are good reasons for regulating, which are embedded within public attitudes but marginalised within media and public debate, and which do not permeate through to policy formation or regulatory practice. While criminalisation might help re-establish the standing of health and safety regulation by reinforcing these 'reasons for' regulating, the greater challenge is to address the political and cultural assumptions that created this low standing in the first place. This is a bigger task, one which criminalisation is unlikely to be able to achieve alone. A truly deliberative, democratic basis for regulation, which gives effect to fundamental social values relating to social citizenship, is required in order to establish health and safety regulation as a key component in the realisation of a vision of the good society, but this appears unlikely. Corporate manslaughter offences may make a difference to how health and safety law is perceived, but they cannot bring about change of this sort by themselves.

Notes

Introduction

1. The case of *R v OLL Ltd.* (1994) Unreported, *The Independent*, 9 December 1994.

1 The Shift from 'Regulation' to 'Crime'

1. *R v Cotswold Geotechnical (Holdings) Ltd.* [2011] EWCA Crim 1337; [2011] All ER (D) 100 (May).
2. www.oed.com defines a fatality as 'a disastrous event; a calamity, misfortune; a disaster resulting in death; a fatal accident or occurrence', thereby implying both inadvertence and accidentalness.
3. These 'core' industries are agriculture, hunting, and forestry; Manufacturing; Electricity, gas and water supply; Construction; Wholesale and retail trade; repair of motor vehicles, motorcycles, and personal and household goods; Hotels and restaurants; Transport, storage and communication; Financial intermediation; and Real estate, renting and business activities (EUROSTAT 2010b).
4. The Reporting of Injuries, Diseases and Dangerous Occurrences Regulations (1995) S.I. No. 3163. London: HMSO, available online at: http://www.opsi.gov.uk/si/si1995/Uksi_19953163_en_1.htm#end [last accessed 20 July 2010].
5. These figures are based on rates of fatal injury (180) reported to HSE in 2008/9 (HSE 2009a): http://www.hse.gov.uk/statistics/causinj/index-ld.htm#kind1
6. Another example of the hazards of people-trafficking is provided by the deaths of 58 Chinese migrants from asphyxiation while being transported through the port of Dover in a lorry in 2000 (*R v Wacker* [2003] 4 All ER 295). In this case, it was held that even illegitimate enterprises can bear criminal responsibility because there is a public interest in controlling the risks involved.
7. *R v P&O European Ferries (Dover) Ltd.* [1991] 93 Cr. App. R 72.
8. At the time of the trial, the offence of manslaughter utilised an objective recklessness standard, as established in *R v Lawrence* [1982] AC 510 and *R v Seymour* [1983] 2 AC 493, rather than the gross negligence standard utilised following the subsequent decision in *R v Adomako* [1995] 1 AC 171.
9. (1994) Unreported, *The Independent*, 9 December 1994.
10. *R v Jackson Transport (Ossett) Ltd.* (1996) Unreported, *Health and Safety at Work*, 11/1996 p. 4.
11. *Attorney-General's Reference (No. 2 of 1999)* [2000] 3 All ER 183, relating to the prosecution case of *R v Great Western Trains Co. Ltd.* (1999), Unreported, Central Criminal Court, 13 August 1999.

12. *H. L. Bolton (Engineering) Co. Ltd. v. T.J. Graham & Sons Ltd.* [1957] 1 QB 159 at p. 172.
13. *R v Adomako* [1995] 1 AC 171; *Attorney-General's Reference (No. 2 of 1999)* [2000] 3 All ER 182; *R v Misra and Srivastava* [2005] 1 Cr. App. R. 328; also Virgo (1995); Quick (2010).

2 The International 'Corporate Manslaughter' Phenomenon

1. (1994) 6 VIR 157. The case involved the death of a commercial driver when the brakes of the company vehicle he was driving failed; the defendant company was fined $120,000 (Sarre and Richards 2005: 95).
2. *Meridian Global Funds Management Asia Ltd. v Securities Commission* [1995] 2 AC 500.
3. R v *Birmingham and Gloucester Railway Co* (1842) 3 Q.B. 223; R v *Great North of England Railway Co* (1846) 9 Q.B. 315.
4. 212 U.S. 481 (1909).
5. 134 F. 592 (1904).
6. *State v Lehig Valley Railroad* 103 A. 685 (1917).
7. 195 NY 102, 107 (1909).
8. *United States v Basic Construction Co.* 711 F.2d. 570 at p. 573 (4th Cir. 1983).
9. *United States v Bank of New England* 484 U.S. 943 (1987).
10. [1985] 1 SCR 662.
11. *Hospital Case,* Rechtbank Leeuwarden, 23 December 1987 (N.J. 1988, 981); Field and Jörg (1991: 158).
12. Hoge Raad, 23 February 1954 (N.J. 1954, 378).
13. Hoge Raad, 1 July 1981 (N.J. 1982, 80). This case involved breaches of fishing regulations committed by the skipper of a vessel.
14. As an example, in April 2011 the senior national managers of Thyssenkrupp (a German steel company) in Italy were convicted of voluntary homicide following the deaths of seven workers in a factory fire in Turin (see http://www.dw-world.de/dw/article/0,,14993772,00.html; last accessed 25 July 2012).
15. *Meridian Global Funds Management Asia Ltd. v Securities Commission* [1995] 2 AC 500.
16. This according to the policies of the Swedish Work Environment Authority (at http://www.av.se/inenglish/inspections/thedifference.aspx; last accessed 25 July 2012).

3 Work-Related Deaths as Symbolic Events

1. Habermas identifies these structural risks as including 'interruptions of the accumulation process conditioned by the business cycle, the external costs of a private production that cannot adequately deal with the problem situations it itself creates, and a pattern of privilege whose core is a structurally conditioned unequal distribution of wealth and income' (1976: 194).

4 Regulating Work-Related Death – A History

1. 'Exhausted children were beaten to work, and sickness, mutilation by machinery and even deaths from malnutrition and long confinement were regular occurrences... little children suffered horrible existences in many lonely mills' (Ward 1962: 16).
2. *Priestley v Fowler* [1837] 150 Eng. Rep. 1030; Stein (2008: 944).
3. For example, Sir Francis Burdett asserted in Parliament that 'We hear of slavery abroad, but, good God, have we ever heard of any such instance of overworking as has been published with respect to the labour of children in the cotton manufactories?' (Hansard 1825, XIII: 643–649; cited by Thomas 1948: 28).
4. Parliamentary Papers (1835) XL, p. 698 (cited in Thomas 1948: 76).
5. *per* Lord Oaksey in *Marshall v Gotham* [1954] AC 360 at p. 370; see also *Austin Rover v H.M. Inspector of Factories* [1989] 3 WLR 520.
6. The Code for Crown Prosecutors sets out a two-stage test for determining whether prosecution is appropriate. These are: that there be a realistic prospect of conviction; and that there be a public interest in the bringing of the case (DPP 1985).

5 Criminalising Work-Related Death

1. The European Court of Human Rights determines whether a legal proceeding is a matter of 'criminal' law by reference to the outcome involved; if a charge may result in a *penalty* being imposed, it will be deemed criminal: *Benham v United Kingdom* (1996) 22 EHRR 293.
2. (1688) 80 ER 1085 (2 Bulstrode 233); Clarkson (1996).
3. (1842) 3 QB 223.
4. (1846) 9 Q.B. 315.
5. [1917] 2 KB 836.
6. [1927] 1 KB 810.
7. [1944] KB 146; [1944] KB 551; [1944] 2 All ER 515.
8. *H. L. Bolton (Engineering) Co. Ltd. v T.J. Graham & Sons Ltd.* [1957] 1 QB 159 at p. 172.
9. [1972] AC 153.
10. *Attorney-General's Reference (No. 2 of 1999)* [2000] 3 All ER 182, per Rose LJ at p. 191.
11. *Tesco v Brent London Borough Council* [1993] 2 All ER 718.
12. *Meridian Global Funds Management Asia Ltd. v Securities Commission* [1995] 2 AC 500 (PC).
13. *R v P&O European Ferries (Dover) Ltd.* [1991] 93 Cr. App. R 72.
14. *R v Great Western Trains* (1999) Central Criminal Court 30 June 1999, case ref. C7800570.
15. *Attorney-General's Reference (No. 2 of 1999)* [2000] 3 All ER 182.
16. *R v OLL Ltd.* (1994) Unreported, *The Independent*, 9 December 1994.
17. *R v Jackson Transport (Ossett) Ltd.* (1996) Unreported, *Health and Safety at Work*, v18(11) p. 4; *R v English Brothers Ltd.* (2001) Unreported, Northampton Crown Court 30 July 2001; *R v Dennis Clothier and Sons Ltd.* (2002)

Unreported, Bristol Crown Court 23 March 2002; *R v Teglgaard Hardwood (UK) Ltd.* (2003) Unreported, Hull Crown Court 24 February 2004.

18. Following the decisions in *R v British Steel* [1995] 1 WLR 1356, *R v F. Howe and Son (Engineers) Ltd.* [1999] 2 Cr.App.R. 37, and other cases, which were critical of sentencing trends.
19. David Cameron, speech to Policy Exchange think-tank, 1 December 2009.
20. *The Guardian*, 15 August 2011 (available online at http://www.guardian.co.uk/uk/2011/aug/15/david-cameron-riots-broken-society).

6 The Purpose of Corporate Homicide Liability

1. See the HSE website at http://www.hse.gov.uk/risk/principles.htm.
2. 'This attitude, this whole health and safety, human rights act culture, has infected every part of our life. If you're a police officer you now cannot pursue an armed criminal without first filling out a risk assessment form...' Speech to Conservative Party conference, *The Guardian*, 01/10/2008; and 'Something has gone seriously wrong with the spirit of health and safety in the past decade. When children are made to wear goggles by their headteacher to play conkers... what began as a noble intention to protect people from harm has mutated into a stultifying blanket of bureaucracy...' Speech to Policy Exchange, 1 December 2009.
3. As defined in the UK Highway Code s. 109 (Road Traffic Act 1988 s. 36), and UK Highway Code s. 123 (Road Vehicles (Construction & Use) Regulations 1986 ss. 98, 107).

7 The Limits of Corporate Manslaughter Reforms

1. *R v Cotswold Geotechnical (Holdings) Ltd.* [2011] EWCA Crim 1337; [2011] All ER (D) 100 (May).
2. *R v Lion Steel Equipment Ltd.* (2012) Unreported, Manchester Crown Court, 20 July 2012 (online at http://www.judiciary.gov.uk/Resources/JCO/Documents/Judgments/hhj-gilbart-qc-sentence-remarksr-v-lion-steel.pdf; last accessed 25 July 2012).

Bibliography

M. Aalders and T. Wilthagen (1997) 'Moving Beyond Command-and-Control: Reflexivity in the Regulation of Occupational Health and Safety and the Environment', *Law and Policy*, 19/4: 415–443.

G. W. Alger (1900) 'The Courts and Factory Legislation', *The American Journal of Sociology*, 6/3: 396–406.

P. Almond (2006) 'An Inspector's-Eye View: The Prospective Enforcement of Work-Related Fatality Cases', *British Journal of Criminology*, 46/5: 893–916.

P. Almond (2007) 'Regulation Crisis: Evaluating the Potential Legitimizing Effects of "Corporate Manslaughter" Cases', *Law and Policy*, 29/3: 285–310.

P. Almond (2008) 'Public Perceptions of Work-Related Fatality Cases: Reaching the Outer Limits of "Populist Punitiveness" ', *British Journal of Criminology*, 48/4: 448–467.

P. Almond (2009a) 'Understanding the Seriousness of Corporate Crime: Some Lessons for the "Corporate Manslaughter" Reform Project', *Criminology and Criminal Justice*, 9/2: 145–164.

P. Almond (2009b) 'The Dangers of Hanging Baskets: Regulatory Myths' and Media Representations of Health and Safety Regulation', *Journal of Law and Society*, 36/3: 352–375.

P. Almond (2011) 'Corporate Crime and the "Crippled Epistemology" of Punitiveness' in H. Kury and E. Shea (eds.) *Punitivity – International Developments vol. 1: Punitiveness – An International Phenomenon?* (Bochum: Univ. Brockmeyer), pp. 53–72.

P. Almond and S. Colover (2010) 'Mediating Punitiveness: Understanding Public Attitudes Towards Work-Related Fatality Cases', *European Journal of Criminology*, 7/5: 1–16.

P. Almond and S. Colover (2012) 'Communication and Social Regulation: The Criminalization of Work-Related Death', *British Journal of Criminology*, 52/5 (in press).

American Law Institute (1962) *Model Penal Code* (Philadelphia, PA: ALI).

H. W. Arthurs (1985) *Without the Law: Administrative Justice and Legal Pluralism in 19th Century England* (Toronto, ON: University of Toronto Press).

A. Ashworth (2000) 'Is the Criminal Law a Lost Cause?' *Law Quarterly Review*, 116/2: 225–256.

A. B. Atkinson (1998) 'Social Exclusion, Poverty and Unemployment' in A. B. Atkinson and J. Hills (eds.) *Exclusion, Employment and Opportunity: CASE Paper 4* (London: London School of Economics), pp. 1–20.

J. Atkinson (1985) 'The Changing Corporation' in D. Clutterbuck (ed.) *New Patterns of Work* (Aldershot: Gower), pp. 13–34.

I. Ayres and J. Braithwaite (1992) *Responsive Regulation: Transcending the Deregulation Debate* (Oxford: Oxford University Press).

S. Bacigalupo (1999) ' "Accessory Consequences" Applicable to Legal Entities Under the Spanish Criminal Code of 1995' in A. Eser, G. Heine, and B. Huber (eds.) *Criminal Responsibility of Legal and Collective Entities* (Berlin: Edition Iuscrim), pp. 255–266.

P. Bain (1997) 'Human Resource Malpractice: The Deregulation of Health and Safety at Work in the USA and Britain', *Industrial Relations Journal,* 28/3: 176–191.

P. Bal (1996) 'Discourse Ethics and Human Rights in Criminal Procedure' in M. Deflem (ed.) *Habermas, Modernity, and Law* (London: Sage), pp. 71–99.

R. Baldwin (1987) 'Health and Safety at Work: Consensus and Self-Regulation' in R. Baldwin and C. McCrudden (eds.) *Regulation and Public Law* (London: Weidenfeld and Nicholson), pp. 132–158.

R. Baldwin (1995) *Rules and Governmen*t (Oxford: Clarendon Press).

R. Baldwin (2004) 'The New Punitive Regulation', *Modern Law Review,* 67/3: 351–383.

R. Baldwin and J. Black (2008) 'Really Responsive Regulation', *Modern Law Review,* 71/1: 59–94.

R. Baldwin and M. Cave (1999) *Understanding Regulation: Theory, Strategy, and Practice* (Oxford: Oxford University Press).

R. Baldwin, C. Scott, and C. Hood (1998) *A Reader on Regulation* (Oxford: Oxford University Press).

S. Banks (2009) 'Woodley v Metropolitan District Railway Company (1877)' in C. Mitchell and P. Mitchell (eds.) *Landmark Cases in the Law of Tort* (Oxford: Hart), pp. 127–152.

E. Bardach and R. A. Kagan (1982) *Going by the Book: The Problem of Regulatory Unreasonableness* (New Brunswick, NJ: Transaction Press).

E. Bardasi and M. Francesconi (2004) 'The Impact of Atypical Employment on Individual Wellbeing: Evidence from a Panel of British Workers', *Social Science & Medicine,* 58/9: 1671–1688.

J. A. Bargh (1997) 'The Automaticity of Everyday Life' in R. S. Wyer Jr. (ed.) *The Automaticity of Everyday Life* (Hillsdale, NJ: Lawrence Erlbaum Associates), pp. 1–62.

I. Bartle and P. Vass (2007) 'Self-Regulation Within the Regulatory State: Towards a New Regulatory Paradigm?' *Public Administration,* 85/4: 885–905.

P. Bartrip (2002) *The Home Office and the Dangerous Trades: Regulating Occupational Disease in Victorian and Edwardian Britain* (Amsterdam: Editions Rodopi B.V.).

P. Bartrip and P. T. Fenn (1983) 'The Evolution of Regulatory Style in the Nineteenth Century British Factory Inspectorate', *Journal of Law and Society,* 10/2: 201–222.

P. Bartrip and P. T. Fenn (1988) 'Factory Fatalities and Regulation in Britain, 1878–1913', *Explorations in Economic History,* 25/1: 60–74.

P. Bartrip and R. Hartwell (1997) 'Profit and Virtue: Economic Theory and the Regulation of Occupational Health in Nineteenth and Early Twentieth Century Britain' in K. Hawkins (ed.) *The Human Face of Law: Essays in Honour of Donald Harris* (Oxford: Oxford University Press), pp. 45–64.

Z. Bauman (2000) *Liquid Modernity* (Cambridge: Polity Press).

S. S. Beale and A. G. Safwat (2004) 'What Developments in Western Europe Tell Us about American Critiques of Corporate Criminal Liability', *Buffalo Criminal Law Review,* 8: 89–163.

M. Beck and M. O'Brien (2000) 'Corporate Criminal Liability', *American Criminal Law Review,* 37/2: 261–289.

M. Beck and C. Woolfson (2000) 'The Regulation of Health and Safety in Britain: From Old Labour to New Labour', *Industrial Relations Journal,* 31/1: 35–49.

U. Beck (1992) *Risk Society: Towards a New Modernity* Trans. M. Ritter (London: Sage).

P. J. Becker, A. J. Jipson, and A. S. Bruce (2002) '*State of Indiana v. Ford Motor Company* Revisited', *American Journal of Criminal Justice,* 26/2: 181–202.

D. Beetham (1991) *The Legitimation of Power* (London: Macmillan).

R. S. Belous (1995) 'The Rise of the Contingent Workforce: The Key Challenges and Opportunities', *Washington and Lee Law Review,* 52/3: 863–878.

T. J. Bernard (1984) 'The Historical Development of Corporate Criminal Liability', *Criminology,* 22/1: 3–17.

Better Regulation Executive (2009) *Better Regulation, Better Benefits: Getting the Balance Right: Main Report* (London: Department for Business, Innovation & Skills).

S. Bittle and L. Snider (2006) 'From Manslaughter to Preventable Accident: Shaping Corporate Criminal Liability', *Law and Policy,* 28/4: 470–496.

J. Black (1998) 'Talking About Regulation', *Public Law,* 77–105.

J. Black (2000) 'Proceduralizing Regulation: Part I', *Oxford Journal of Legal Studies,* 20/4: 597–614.

J. Black (2001) 'Proceduralizing Regulation: Part II', *Oxford Journal of Legal Studies,* 21/1: 33–58.

J. Black (2002) 'Regulatory Conversations', *Journal of Law and Society,* 29/2: 163–196.

J. Black (2005) 'The Emergence of Risk-based Regulation and the new Public Risk Management in the United Kingdom', *Public Law,* 512–549.

J. Black (2007) 'Tensions in the Regulatory State', *Public Law,* 58–73.

J. Black and R. Baldwin (2010) 'Really Responsive Risk-Based Regulation', *Law and Policy,* 32/2: 181–213.

W. Blackstone (1809) *Commentaries on the Laws of England (15th ed.)* (London: Cadell and Davies).

BMJ (1879) 'Factory Inspection', *British Medical Journal,* 1/961: 824.

M. Böse (2011) 'Corporate Criminal Liability in Germany' in M. Pieth and R. Ivory (eds.) *Corporate Criminal Liability: Emergence, Convergence, and Risk* (New York: Springer), pp. 227–254.

A. Bottoms (1995) 'The Philosophy and Politics of Punishment and Sentencing' in C. Clarkson and R. Morgan (eds.) *The Politics of Sentencing Reform* (Oxford: Clarendon Press), pp. 17–49.

J. Braithwaite (1985) *To Punish or Persuade: The Enforcement of Coal Mine Safety* (Albany, NY: State University of New York Press).

J. Braithwaite (2002) *Restorative Justice and Responsive Regulation* (Oxford: Oxford University Press).

J. Braithwaite (2003) 'What's Wrong with the Sociology of Punishment?' *Theoretical Criminology,* 7/1: 5–28.

J. Braithwaite (2008) *Regulatory Capitalism: How It Works, Ideas for Making It Work Better* (Cheltenham: Edward Elgar).

J. Braithwaite and P. Pettit (1990) *Not Just Desserts: A Republican Theory of Criminal Justice* (Oxford: Oxford University Press).

G. Breakwell (2007) *The Psychology of Risk* (Cambridge: Cambridge University Press).

S. Breyer (1982) *Regulation and Its Reform* (Cambridge, MA: Harvard University Press).

K. Brickey (1981), 'Corporate Criminal Accountability: A Brief History and an Observation', *Washington University Law Quarterly,* 60: 393–424.

A. Briggs (1959) *The Age of Improvement 1783–1867* (London: Longman).

G. D. Brown and D. O'Rourke (2003) 'The Race to China and Implications for Global Labor Standards', *International Journal of Occupational and Environmental Health,* 9/4: 299–301.

A. Brudner (1993) 'Agency and Welfare in the Penal Law' in S. Shute, J. Gardner, and J. Horder (eds.) *Action and Value in Criminal Law* (Oxford: Clarendon Press), pp. 22–54.

J. H. Brunvand (1981) *The Vanishing Hitchhiker: American Urban Legends and Their Meaning* (New York: W.W. Norton).

P. Cappelli (1999) *The New Deal at Work: Managing the Market-Driven Workforce* (Boston, MA: Harvard Business School Press).

B. Carlsson (2002) 'Jurgen Habermas and the Sociology of Law' in R. Banakar and M. Travers (eds.) *An Introduction to Law and Social Theory* (Oxford: Hart), pp. 77–96.

W. G. Carson (1970) 'White-Collar Crime and the Enforcement of Factory Legislation', *British Journal of Criminology,* 10/4: 383–398.

W. G. Carson (1979) 'The Conventionalization of Early Factory Crime', *International Journal of the Sociology of Law,* 7: 37–60.

W. G. Carson and R. Johnstone (1990) 'The Dupes of Hazard: Occupational Health and Safety and the Victorian Sanctions Debate', *Australian and New Zealand Journal of Sociology,* 26/1: 126–141.

M. Cavadino and J. Dignan (2006) *Penal Systems: A Comparative Approach* (London: Sage).

C. M. V. Clarkson (1996) 'Kicking Corporate Bodies and Damning their Souls', *Modern Law Review,* 59: 557–572.

C. M. V. Clarkson (2005) 'Corporate Manslaughter: Yet more Government Proposals', *Criminal Law Review,* 677–689.

C. M. V. Clarkson (2008) 'Corporate Manslaughter: Need for a Special Offence?' in C. Clarkson and S. Cunningham (eds.) *Criminal Liability for Non-Aggressive Death* (Aldershot: Ashgate), pp. 79–96.

J. Clough (2008) 'Punishing the Parent: Corporate Criminal Liability in Human Rights Abuses', *Brooklyn Journal of International Law,* 33/3: 899–931.

J. C. Coffee (1983) 'Corporate Criminal Responsibility' in S. Kadish (ed.) *Encyclopedia of Crime and Justice* (New York: Free Press), pp. 253–264.

J. C. Coffee (1999) 'Corporate Criminal Liability: An Introduction and Comparative Survey' in A. Eser, G. Heine, and B. Huber (eds.) *Criminal Responsibility of Legal and Collective Entities* (Berlin: Edition Iuscrim), pp. 9–38.

S. Cohen (1988) *Against Criminology* (New Brunswick, NJ: Transaction Press).

S. Cohn (2007) 'After the Black Death: Labour Legislation and Attitudes towards Labour in Late-medieval Western Europe', *Economic History Review,* 60/3: 457–485.

A. Crawford (2009) 'Governing Through Anti-Social Behaviour: Regulatory Challenges to Criminal Justice', *British Journal of Criminology*, 49/5: 810–831.

F. T. Cullen, B. G. Link, and C. W. Polanzi (1982) 'The Seriousness of Crime Revisited: Have Attitudes Toward White-Collar Crime Changed?' *Criminology*, 20/1: 83–102.

Lord Cullen (1990) *The Public Inquiry into the Piper Alpha Disaster* Cm 1310 (London: HMSO).

N. Davies (2010) 'Sentencing Guidance: Corporate Manslaughter and Health and Safety Offences Causing Death – Maintaining the Status Quo?' *Criminal Law Review*, 402–406.

S. Dawson, P. Willman, A. Clinton, and M. Bamford (1988) *Safety at Work: The Limits of Self-Regulation* (Cambridge: Cambridge University Press).

K. Deckert (2011) 'Corporate Criminal Liability in France' in M. Pieth and R. Ivory (eds.) *Corporate Criminal Liability: Emergence, Convergence, and Risk* (New York: Springer), pp. 147–176.

M. Deflem (1994) 'Social Control and the Theory of Communicative Action', *International Journal of the Sociology of Law*, 22: 355–373.

C. de Maglie (2011) '*Societas Delinquere Potest*? The Italian Solution' in M. Pieth and R. Ivory (eds.) *Corporate Criminal Liability: Emergence, Convergence, and Risk* (New York: Springer), pp. 255–270.

Department of Transport (1987) *MV Herald of Free Enterprise: Report of the Court No. 8047 (The Sheen Report)* (London: HMSO).

DETR [Department of Environment, Transport and the Regions] (2000) *Revitalising Health and Safety: Strategy Statement* (London: Crown).

'Developments' (1979) 'Developments in the Law: Corporate Crime: Regulating Corporate Behaviour Through Criminal Sanctions', *Harvard Law Review*, 92/2: 1227–1375.

DPP [Director of Public Prosecutions] (1985) The Code for Crown Prosecutors (available online at http://www.cps.gov.uk/publications/docs/code2010english.pdf; last accessed 25 July 2012).

A. V. Dicey (1914) *Lectures on the Relation between Law and Public Opinion in England During the Nineteenth Century* (London: Macmillan).

E. B. Diskant (2008) 'Comparative Corporate Criminal Liability: Exploring the Uniquely American Doctrine through Comparative Criminal Procedure', *Yale Law Journal*, 118: 126–176.

A. Dodds (2006) 'The Core Executive's Approach to Regulation: From "Better Regulation" to "Risk-Tolerant Deregulation"', *Social Policy & Administration*, 40/5: 526–542.

M. Douglas (1992) *Risk and Blame: Essays in Cultural Theory* (London: Routledge).

M. Douglas and A. B. Wildavsky (1982) *Risk and Culture: An Essay on the Selection of Technical and Environmental Dangers* (Berkeley, CA: University of California Press).

M. Dowie (1977) 'Pinto Madness', *Mother Jones*, 2: 18–32.

C. D. Drake and F. B. Wright (1983) *Law of Health and Safety at Work: The New Approach* (London: Sweet and Maxwell).

R. A. Duff (2001) *Punishment, Communication, and Community* (Oxford: Oxford University Press).

C. Dyer (2003) 'Revitalising Blank Forces HSE to Change Its "Mindset"', *Health and Safety Bulletin*, 315: 2–4.

A. W. Dzur and R. Mirchandani (2007) 'Punishment and Democracy: The Role of Public Deliberation', *Punishment and Society,* 9/2: 151–175.

H. Eckert (2004) 'Inspections, Warnings, and Compliance: The Case of Petroleum Storage Regulation', *Journal of Environmental Economics and Management,* 47/2: 232–259.

V. Eichener (1997) 'Effective European Problem-Solving: Lessons from the Regulation of Occupational Safety and Environmental Protection', *Journal of European Public Policy*, 4/4: 591–608.

J. R. Elkins (1976) 'Corporations and the Criminal Law: An Uneasy Alliance', *Kentucky Law Journal,* 65/1: 73–129.

C. Emsley (1987) *Crime and Society in England 1750–1900* (London: Longman).

R. Ericson (1991) 'Mass Media, Crime, Law and Justice: An Institutional Approach', *British Journal of Criminology,* 31/3: 219–249.

R. V. Ericson and K. D. Haggerty (1997) *Policing the Risk Society* (Oxford: Clarendon Press).

A. Eser, G. Heine, and B. Huber (1999) *Collective Responsibility of Legal and Collective Entities* (Berlin: Editions Iuscrim).

C. Estlund (2003) *Working Together: How Workplace Bonds Strengthen a Diverse Democracy* (Oxford: Oxford University Press).

EUROSTAT (2001) *European Statistics on Accidents at Work (ESAW): Methodology* (Luxembourg: European Commission).

EUROSTAT (2009) *Statistics in Focus: 63/2009: 8.6% of Workers in the EU Experienced Work-Related Health Problems* (Luxembourg: European Commission).

EUROSTAT (2010a) *The Social Situation in the European Union 2009* (Luxembourg: Publications Office of the European Union).

EUROSTAT (2010b) *Accidents at Work: Reference Metadata in Euro SDMX Metadata Structure* (available online at http://epp.eurostat.ec.europa.eu/cache/ITY_SDDS/en/hsw_acc_work_esms.htm; last accessed 25 July 2012).

F. Ewald (2002) 'The Return of Descartes' Malicious Demon: An Outline of a Philosophy of Precaution' in T. Baker and J. Simon (eds.) *Embracing Risk: The Changing Culture of Insurance and Responsibility* (Chicago: University Of Chicago Press), pp. 273–301.

M. Faure (1999) 'Criminal Responsibilities of Legal and Collective Entities: Developments in Belgium' in A. Eser, G. Heine, and B. Huber (eds.) *Criminal Responsibility of Legal and Collective Entities* (Berlin: Edition Iuscrim), pp. 105–112.

M. Feeley and J. Simon (1992) 'The New Penology: Notes on the Emerging Strategy of Corrections and its Implications', *Criminology,* 30/4: 449–474.

M. Feeley and J. Simon (1994) 'Actuarial Justice: The Emerging New Criminal Law' in D. Nelken (ed.) *The Futures of Criminology* (London: Sage), pp. 173–201.

J. Feinberg (1984) *Harm to Others* (New York: Oxford University Press).

M. Feintuck (2004) *The Public Interest in Regulation* (Oxford: Oxford University Press).

G. Ferguson (1999) 'The Basis for Criminal Responsibility of Collective Entities in Canada' in A. Eser, G. Heine, and B. Huber (eds.) *Criminal Responsibility of Legal and Collective Entities* (Berlin: Edition Iuscrim), pp. 153–180.

S. Field (1990) 'Without the Law? Professor Arthurs and the Early Factory Inspectorate', *Journal of Law and Society,* 17/4: 445–468.

S. Field and N. Jorg (1991) 'Corporate Liability and Manslaughter: Should We Be Going Dutch?' *Criminal Law Review*, 156–171.

C. Finkelstein (2005) 'Responsibility for Unintended Consequences', *Ohio State Journal of Criminal Law*, 2: 579.

G. P. Fletcher (1971) 'The Theory of Criminal Negligence: A Comparative Analysis', *University of Pennsylvania Law Review*, 119/3: 401–438.

G. P. Fletcher (1978) *Rethinking Criminal Law* (Boston, MA: Little, Brown).

J. Francis (1993) *The Politics of Regulation: A Comparative Perspective* (Oxford: Blackwell).

A. Fraser (2001) 'A Marx for the Managerial Revolution: Habermas on Law and Democracy', *Journal of Law and Society*, 28/3: 361–383.

P. French (1984) *Collective and Corporate Responsibility* (New York: Columbia University Press).

K. Frick and D. R. Walters (1998) 'Worker Representation on Health and Safety in Small Enterprises: Lessons from a Swedish Approach', *International Labour Review*, 137/3: 367–389.

A. Gamble (1994) *The Free Economy and the Strong State: The Politics of Thatcherism (2nd ed.)* (London: Macmillan).

D. Garland (1985) *Punishment and Welfare: A History of Penal Strategies* (Aldershot: Gower Press).

D. Garland (2001) *The Culture of Control: Crime and Social Order in Contemporary Society* (Oxford: Oxford University Press).

P. Gaskell (1936) *Artisans and Machinery: The Moral and Physical Condition of the Manufacturing Population* (London: Frank Cass & Co.).

H. Genn (1993) 'Business Responses to the Regulation of Health and Safety in England', *Law and Policy*, 15/3: 219–233.

J. L. Gibson and G. A. Caldeira (1996) 'The Legal Cultures of Europe', *Law & Society Review*, 30/1: 55–86.

A. Giddens (1991) *Modernity and Self Identity: Self and Society in the Late Modern Age* (Cambridge: Polity Press).

S. Gilad (2011) 'It Runs in the Family: Meta-Regulation and its Siblings', *Regulation & Governance*, 4/3: 485–506.

J. Gilboy (1995) 'Regulatory and Administrative Agency Behaviour: Accommodation, Amplification and Assimilation', *Law and Policy*, 17/1: 3–22.

P. Gill (2002) 'Policing and Regulation: What is the Difference?' *Social and Legal Studies* 11/4: 523–546.

D. Glassner (1999) *The Culture of Fear: Why Americans are Afraid of the Wrong Things* (New York: Basic Books).

P. Glazebrook (2002) 'A Better Way of Convicting Businesses of Avoidable Deaths and Injuries?' *Cambridge Law Journal*, 61/2: 405–422.

J. Gobert (2005) 'The Politics of Corporate Manslaughter – The British Experience', *Flinders Journal of Law Reform*, 8/1: 1–38.

J. Gobert (2008) 'The Corporate Manslaughter and Corporate Homicide Act 2007 – Thirteen Years in the Making But Was It Worth the Wait?' *Modern Law Review*, 71/3: 413–433.

J. Gobert and E. Mugnai (2002) 'Coping with Corporate Crime – Some Lessons from Italy', *Criminal Law Review*, 619–629.

E. Goffman (1969) *The Presentation of Self in Everyday Life* (London: Allen Lane).

S. Gräbe (1991) 'Regulatory Agencies and Interest Groups in Occupational Health and Safety in Great Britain and West Germany: A Perspective from West Germany', *Law and Policy*, 13/1: 55–72.

G. Gray (2002) 'A Socio-Legal Ethnography of the Right to Refuse Dangerous Work', *Studies in Law, Politics, and Society*, 24: 133–169.

G. Gray (2006) 'The Regulation of Corporate Violations: Punishment, Compliance, and the Blurring of Responsibility', *British Journal of Criminology*, 46/5: 875–892.

G. Gray (2009) 'The Responsibilization Strategy of Health and Safety: Neo-liberalism and the Reconfiguration of Individual Responsibility for Risk', *British Journal of Criminology*, 49/3: 326–342.

R. L. Gray (1995) 'Eliminating the (Absurd) Distinction between *Malum in Se* and *Malum Prohibitum* Crimes', *Washington University Law Quarterly*, 73: 1369–1398.

W. B. Gray and J. T. Scholz (1991) 'Analyzing the Equity and Efficiency of OSHA Enforcement', *Law and Policy*, 13/3: 185–214.

W. B. Gray and J. T. Scholz (1993) 'Does Regulatory Enforcement Work? A Panel Analysis of OSHA Enforcement', *Law & Society Review*, 27/1: 177–213.

D. A. Green (2006) 'Public Opinion Versus Public Judgment About Crime: Correcting the "Comedy of Errors" ', *British Journal of Criminology*, 46/4: 131–154.

D. Green (2009) 'Feeding Wolves: Punitiveness and Culture', *European Journal of Criminology*, 6/6: 517–536.

C. O. Gregory (1951) 'Trespass to Negligence to Absolute Liability', *Virginia Law Review*, 37/3: 359–398.

F. W. Guldenmund (2000) 'The Nature of Safety Culture: A Review of Theory and Research', *Safety Science*, 34/3: 215–257.

N. Gunningham and J. Rees (1997) 'Industry Self-Regulation: An Institutional Perspective', *Law and Policy*, 19/4: 363–414.

N. Gunningham and P. Grabosky (1998) *Smart Regulation: Designing Environmental Policy* (Oxford: Oxford University Press).

N. Gunningham and R. Johnstone (1999) *Regulating Workplace Safety: Systems and Sanctions* (Oxford: Oxford University Press).

J. R. Gusfield (1981) *The Culture of Public Problems: Drinking-Driving and the Symbolic Order* (Chicago: University of Chicago Press).

B. Gustavsen (1985) Workplace Reform and Democratic Dialogue', *Economic and Industrial Democracy*, 6/4: 461–479.

J. Habermas (1973) *Legitimation Crisis [Legitimationsprobleme im Spatkapitalismus]* Trans. T. McCarthy (London: Heinemann).

J. Habermas (1976) *Communication and the Evolution of Society [Zur Rekonstruktion des Historichen Materialismus]* Trans. F. Lawrence (Boston, MA: Beacon Press).

J. Habermas (1984) *The Theory of Communicative Action Vol. I: Reason and the Rationalization of Society [Theorie des Kommunikativen Handelns, Band I: Handlungsrationalitat und gesellschaftliche Rationalisierung]* Trans. T. McCarthy (Cambridge: Polity Press).

J. Habermas (1987) *The Theory of Communicative Action Vol. II: The Critique of Functionalist Reason [Theorie des Kommunikativen Handelns, Band II: Zur Kritik der funktionalistischen Vernunft]* Trans. T. McCarthy (Cambridge: Polity Press).

J. Habermas (1988) 'Law as Medium and Law as Institution' in G. Teubner (ed.) *Dilemmas of Law in the Welfare State* (Berlin: Walter de Gruyter), pp. 203–220.

J. Habermas (1992) *Between Facts and Norms [Faktizitat und Geltung]* Trans. W. Rehg (Cambridge: Polity Press).

F. Haines (1997) *Corporate Regulation: Beyond 'Punish or Persuade'* (Oxford: Clarendon Press).

F. Haines (2003) 'Regulatory Reform in Light of Regulatory Character: Assessing Industrial Safety Change in the Aftermath of the Kader Toy Factory Fire in Bangkok, Thailand', *Social & Legal Studies,* 12/4: 461–487.

F. Haines (2011) *The Paradox of Regulation: What Regulation Can Achieve and What It Cannot* (Cheltenham: Edward Elgar).

F. Haines and D. Gurney (2003) 'The Shadows of the Law: Approaches to Regulation and the Problem of Regulatory Conflict', *Law and Policy,* 25/4: 353–380.

F. Haines and A. Hall (2004) 'The Law and order Debate in Occupational Health and Safety', *Journal of Occupational Health and Safety: Australia and New Zealand,* 20/3: 263–273.

F. Haines and A. Sutton (2003) 'The Engineer's Dilemma: A Sociological Perspective on Juridification and Regulation', *Crime, Law & Social Change,* 39/1: 1–22.

F. Haines and A. Sutton (2007) 'The Importance of Being Ambiguous: Theorising White-Collar Crime' in A. Brannigan and G. Pavlich (eds.) *Governance and Regulation in Social Life: Essays in Honour of W. G. Carson* (Abingdon: Routledge Cavendish), pp. 21–32.

F. Haines, A. Sutton, and C. Patania-Phung (2007) 'It's All About Risk Isn't It? Science, Politics, Public Opinion and Regulatory Reform', *Flinders Journal of Law Reform,* 10: 435–453.

A. Hall and R. Johnstone (2005) 'Exploring the Re-criminalising of OHS Breaches in the Context of Industrial Death', *Flinders Journal of Law Reform,* 8: 57–92.

J. Hall (1963) 'Negligent Behaviour Should Be Excluded from Penal Liability', *Columbia Law Review,* 63: 632.

P. A. Hall and D. Soskice (2001) 'An Introduction to Varieties of Capitalism' in P. A. Hall and D. Soskice (eds.) *Varieties of Capitalism: The Institutional Foundations of Comparative Advantage* (Oxford: Oxford University Press), pp. 1–70.

W. Haltom and M. McCann (2004) *Distorting the Law: Politics, Media, and the Litigation Crisis* (Chicago: University of Chicago Press).

P. Hämäläinen, K. L. Saarela, and J. Takala (2009) 'Global Trends According to Estimated Number of Occupational Accidents and Fatal Work-related Diseases at Region and Country Level', *Journal of Safety Research,* 40: 125–139.

P. Hampton (2005) *Reducing Administrative Burdens: Effective Inspection and Enforcement (The Hampton Review)* (London: HM Treasury).

J. F. Handler (1992) 'Discretion: Power, Quiescence, and Trust' in K. Hawkins (ed.) *The Uses of Discretion* (Oxford: Clarendon Press), pp. 331–360.

M. Hansel (1987) 'Citizen Crime Stereotypes – Normative Consensus Revisited', *Criminology,* 25/3: 455–485.

B. Harcourt (2010) 'Neoliberal Penality: A Brief Genealogy', *Theoretical Criminology,* 14/1: 74–92.

R. Hardin (2002) 'The Crippled Epistemology of Extremism' in A. Breton, G. Galeotti, P. Salmon, and R. Wintrobe (eds.) *Political Extremism and Rationality* (Cambridge: Cambridge University Press), pp. 3–22.

J. W. Harlow (2011) 'Corporate Criminal Liability for Homicide: A Statutory Framework', *Duke Law Journal*, 61/1: 123–166.

H. L. A. Hart (1968) *Punishment and Responsibility: Essays in the Philosophy of Law* (Oxford: Clarendon Press).

D. Harvey (2005) *A Brief History of Neoliberalism* (Oxford: Oxford University Press).

K. Hawkins (1983) 'Bargain and Bluff: Compliance Strategy and Deterrence in the Enforcement of Regulation', *Law and Policy*, 5/1: 35–73.

K. Hawkins (1984) *Environment and Enforcement: Regulation and the Social Definition of Pollution* (Oxford: Clarendon Press).

K. Hawkins (1990) 'Compliance Strategy, Prosecution Policy, and Aunt Sally: A Comment on Pearce and Tombs', *British Journal of Criminology*, 30/4: 444–466.

K. Hawkins (1991) 'Enforcing Regulation: More of the Same from Pearce and Tombs', *British Journal of Criminology*, 31/4: 427–430.

K. Hawkins (2002) *Law as Last Resort: Prosecution Decision-Making in a Regulatory Agency* (Oxford: Oxford University Press).

K. Hawkins and J. M. Thomas (1984) 'The Enforcement Process in Regulatory Bureaucracies' in K. Hawkins and J. M. Thomas (eds.) *Enforcing Regulation* (Dordrecht: Kluwer-Nijhoff), pp. 3–22.

D. Hay (1975) 'Property, Authority and the Criminal Law' in D. Hay, P. Linebaugh, J. G. Rule, E. P. Thompson, and C. Winslow (eds.) *Albion's Fatal Tree: Crime and Society in Eighteenth-Century England* (London: Pantheon), pp. 17–63.

R. Hefendehl (2000) 'Corporate Criminal Liability: Model Penal Code Section 2.07 and Development in Western Legal Systems', *Buffalo Criminal Law Review*, 4: 283–300.

D. Helm (2006) 'Regulatory Reform, Capture, and the Regulatory Burden', *Oxford Review of Economic Policy*, 22/2: 169–185.

E. Hobsbawm (1964) *The Age of Revolution: Europe 1789–1848* (London: Weidenfeld & Nicholson).

E. Hobsbawm (1975) *The Age of Capital: 1848–1875* (London: Weidenfeld & Nicholson).

E. Hobsbawm (1987) *The Age of Empire: 1875–1914* (London: Abacus).

E. Hobsbawm (1994) *The Age of Extremes: The Short Twentieth Century 1914–1848* (London: Abacus).

A. R. Hochschild (1997) *The Time Bind: When Work Becomes Home and Home Becomes Work* (New York: Basic Books).

W. Holdsworth (1938) *A History of English Law* (Boston, MA: Little, Brown).

Home Office (2000) *Reforming the Law of Involuntary Manslaughter: The Government's Proposals* (London: Home Office).

Home Office (2005) *Corporate Manslaughter: The Government's Draft Bill for Reform* (London: The Stationery Office).

Home Office (2006) *Corporate Manslaughter and Corporate Homicide: A Regulatory Impact Assessment of the Government's Bill* (available online at http://webarchive.nationalarchives.gov.uk/+/http://www.homeoffice.gov.uk/documents/ria-corporate-manslaughter.pdf?view= Binary; last accessed 14 June 2011).

T. Honoré (1999) *Responsibility and Fault* (Oxford: Hart).

C. Hood, H. Rothstein, and R. Baldwin (2001) *The Government of Risk: Understanding Risk Regulation Regimes* (Oxford: Oxford University Press).

A. Hopkins (1994) 'Compliance with What?: The Fundamental Regulatory Question', *British Journal of Criminology,* 34/4: 431–443.

A. Hopkins (2009) *Failure to Learn: The BP Texas City Refinery Disaster* (Sydney, NSW: CCH Australia).

HSE (1988) *Blackspot Construction* (London: HSE).

HSE (2009a) *Health and Safety Statistics 2008/9* (London: HSE).

HSE (2009b) *HSE Enforcement Policy Statement* (London: HSE) (available online at http://www.hse.gov.uk/pubns/hse41.pdf; last accessed 25 July 2012).

HSE (2010a) *Statistics on Fatal Injuries in the Workplace 2009/10* (London: HSE).

HSE (2010b) *The Health and Safety Executive Annual Report and Accounts 2009/10* (London: HSE).

B. Hudson (2003) *Justice in the Risk Society* (London: Sage).

D. Husak (2008) *Overcriminalization: The Limits of the Criminal Law* (New York: Oxford University Press).

B. L. Hutchins and A. Harrison (1911) *A History of Factory Legislation (2nd ed.)* (London: P. S. King & Son).

B. Hutter (1986) 'An Inspector Calls: The Importance of Proactive Enforcement in the Regulatory Context', *British Journal of Criminology,* 26/2: 114–128.

B. Hutter (1988) *The Reasonable Arm of the Law? The Law Enforcement Procedures of Environmental Health Officers* (Oxford: Clarendon Press).

B. Hutter (1989) 'Variations in Regulatory Enforcement Styles', *Law and Policy,* 11/2: 153–174.

B. Hutter (1997) *Compliance: Regulation and Environment* (Oxford: Clarendon Press).

B. Hutter and S. Lloyd-Bostock (1990) 'The Power of Accidents: The Social and Psychological Impact of Accidents and the Enforcement of Safety Regulations', *British Journal of Criminology,* 30/4: 409–422.

B. Hutter and P. Manning (1990) 'The Contexts of Regulation: The Impacts Upon Health and Safety Inspectorates in Britain', *Law and Policy,* 12/2: 103–136.

N. Hutton (2005) 'Beyond Populist Punitiveness?' *Punishment & Society,* 7/3: 243–258.

W. Hutton (1995) *The State We're In* (London: Vintage Press).

M. Innes (2004) 'Signal Crimes and Signal Disorders: Notes on Deviance as Communicative Action', *British Journal of Sociology,* 55/3: 335–355.

P. James (1992) 'Reforming British Health and Safety Laws', *Industrial Law Review,* 21/1: 83–105.

P. James and D. R. Walters (2002) 'Worker Representation in Health and Safety: Options for Regulatory Reform', *Industrial Relations Journal,* 33/2: 141–156.

L. Jiachen (1999) 'The Legislation and Judicial Practice on Punishment of Unit Crime in China' in A. Eser, G. Heine, and B. Huber (eds.) *Criminal Responsibility of Legal and Collective Entities* (Berlin: Edition Iuscrim), pp. 71–80.

JISHA (2010) *Industrial Accidents Statistics in Japan* (available online at http://www.jisha.or.jp/english/statistics/index.html; last accessed 25 July 2012).

C. Johnson (2008) 'Ten Contentions of Corporate Manslaughter Legislation: Public Policy and the Legal Response to Workplace Accidents', *Safety Science,* 46: 349–370.

R. Johnstone (2004) *Occupational Health and Safety Law and Policy (2nd ed.)* (Sydney, NSW: Thomson).

S. Douglas Jones (1991) 'State prosecutions for Safety-Related Crimes in the Workplace: Can D.A.'s Succeed Where OSHA Failed?' *Kentucky Law Journal,* 79/1: 139–158.

R. A. Kagan (1984) 'On Regulatory Inspectorates and Police' in K. Hawkins and J. M. Thomas (eds.) *Enforcing Regulation* (Boston, MA: Kluwer-Nijhof), pp. 37–64.

R. A. Kagan and J. T. Scholz (1984) 'The "Criminology" of the Corporation and Regulatory Enforcement Strategies' in K. Hawkins and J. M. Thomas (eds.) *Enforcing Regulation* (Boston, MA: Kluwer-Nijhoff), pp. 67–95.

S. Kelman (1984) 'Enforcement of Occupational Safety and Health Regulations: A Comparison of Swedish and American Practices' in K. Hawkins and J. M. Thomas (eds.) *Enforcing Regulation* (Boston, MA: Kluwer-Nijhoff), pp. 97–120.

R. Kerr, E. Kintisch, and E. Stokstad (2010) 'Will *Deepwater Horizon* Set a New Standard for Catastrophe?' *Science,* 328/5979: 674–675.

B. F. Keulen and E. Gritter (2011) 'Corporate Criminal Liability in the Netherlands' in M. Pieth and R. Ivory (eds.) *Corporate Criminal Liability: Emergence, Convergence, and Risk* (New York: Springer), pp. 177–192.

V. S. Khanna (1996) 'Corporate Criminal Liability: What Purpose Does it Serve?' *Harvard Law Review,* 109/7: 1477–1532.

A. King and S. Maruna (2009) 'Is a Conservative Just a Liberal Who Has Been Mugged?: Exploring the Origins of Punitive Views', *Punishment & Society,* 11/2: 147–169.

J. Kitsuse and A. Cicourel (1963) 'A Note on the Uses of Official Statistics', *Social Problems,* 11/2: 131–139.

J. Klayman and Y.-W. Ha (1987) 'Confirmation, Disconfirmation and Information in Hypothesis Testing', *Psychological Review,* 94/2: 211–228.

K. Koch and N. Salter (1999) 'The Health and Safety System in the Federal Republic of Germany', *Industrial Relations Journal,* 30/1: 61–71.

H. Kury (2008) *Fear of Crime – Punitivity: New Developments in Theory and Research* (Bochum: Brockmeyer).

S. Kydd ('Alfred') (1857) *The History of the Factory Movement: From the Year 1802, to the Enactment of the Ten Hours' Bill in 1847* (Two Volumes) (London: Simpkin, Marshall & Co.).

J. Kyriakakis (2009) 'Corporate Criminal Liability and the ICC Statute: The Comparative Law Challenge', *Netherlands International Law Review,* 56: 333–366.

N. Lacey (2001) 'In Search of the Responsible Subject: History, Philosophy and Social Sciences in Criminal Law Theory', *Modern Law Review,* 64: 350–371.

N. Lacey (2004) 'Criminalization as Regulation: The Role of Criminal Law' in C. Parker, C. Scott, N. Lacey, and J. Braithwaite (eds.) *Regulating Law* (Oxford: Oxford University Press), pp. 144–167.

N. Lacey (2008) *The Prisoners' Dilemma: Political Economy and Punishment in Contemporary Democracies* (Cambridge: Cambridge University Press).

Law Commission (1994) *Consultation Paper 135: Involuntary Manslaughter* (London: HMSO).

Law Commission (1996) *Report 237: Legislating the Criminal Code: Involuntary Manslaughter* (London: HMSO).

Law Commission (2010) *Consultation Paper 195: Criminal Liability in Regulatory Contexts* (London: HMSO).

D. Levi-Faur (2005) 'The Global Diffusion of Regulatory Capitalism', *Annals of the American Academy of Political and Social Science,* 598: 12–32.

R. Lewis (1976) 'The Historical Development of Labour Law', *British Journal of Industrial Relations,* 14/1: 1–17.

S. Livingstone and P. Lunt (2007) 'The Politics of Consumption/The Consumption of Politics: Representing Citizens and Consumers in Media and Communications Regulation', *The Annals of The American Academy of Political and Social Science,* 611: 51–65.

S. Lloyd-Bostock (1992) 'The Psychology of Routine Discretion: Accident Screening by British Factory Inspectors', *Law and Policy,* 14/1: 45–60.

I. Loader (1996) *Youth, Policing and Democracy* (London: Palgrave Macmillan).

I. Loader (2006) 'Fall of the "Platonic Guardians": Liberalism, Criminology and Political Responses to Crime in England and Wales', *British Journal of Criminology,* 46/4: 561–586.

M. Lodge (2002) 'The Wrong Type of Regulation? Regulatory Failure and the Railways in Britain and Germany', *Journal of Public Policy,* 22/3: 271–297.

R. Löfstedt (2004) 'The Swing of the Regulatory Pendulum in Europe: From Precautionary Principle to (Regulatory) Impact Analysis', *The Journal of Risk and Uncertainty,* 28/3: 237–260.

R. Löfstedt (2011a) *Reclaiming Health and Safety for All: An Independent Review of Health and Safety Legislation [The Löfstedt Review]* (London: Crown).

R. Löfstedt (2011b) 'Risk versus Hazard – How to Regulate in the 21st Century', *European Journal of Risk Regulation,* 2/2: 149–168.

D. MacPherson (2005) 'Reforming the Doctrine of Attribution: A Canadian Solution to British Concerns?' in S. Tully (ed.) *Research Handbook of Corporate Legal Responsibility* (Cheltenham: Edward Elgar), pp. 194–214.

R. Macrory (2006) *Regulatory Justice: Sanctioning in a Post-Hampton World (The Macrory Review)* (London: Better Regulation Executive).

G. Majone (1997) 'From the Positive to the Regulatory State: Causes and Consequences of Changes in the Mode of Governance', *Journal of Public Policy,* 17/2: 139–167.

T. H. Marshall (1992) *Citizenship and Social Class* (London: Pluto).

K. Marx (1887) [1990] *Capital* (London: Penguin).

P. Mascini and D. Houtman (2011) 'Resisting Administrative Tolerance in the Netherlands: A Rightist Backlash?' *British Journal of Criminology,* 51/4: 690–706.

R. Matthews (2005) 'The Myth of Punitiveness', *Theoretical Criminology,* 9/2: 175–201.

P. May and R. Burby (1998) 'Making Sense out of Regulatory Enforcement', *Law and Policy,* 20/2: 157–182.

C. Mayhew and M. Quinlan (1999) 'The Effects of Outsourcing on Occupational Health and Safety: A Comparative Study of Factory-Based Workers and Outworkers in the Australian Clothing Industry', *International Journal of Health Services,* 29/1: 83–107.

J. Mendeloff and W. B. Gray (2005) 'Inside the Black Box: How do OSHA Inspections Lead to Reductions in Workplace Injuries?' *Law and Policy,* 27/2: 219–237.

H. A. Mess (1926) *Factory Legislation and Its Administration 1891–1924* (London: P. S. King & Son).

J. Meyer (1999) 'Criminal Responsibilities of Legal and Collective Entities: Comments on Developments in Germany' in A. Eser, G. Heine, and B. Huber (eds.) *Criminal Responsibility of Legal and Collective Entities* (Berlin: Edition Iuscrim), pp. 129–134.

V. Militello (1999) 'The Basis for Criminal Responsibility of Collective Entities in Italy' in A. Eser, G. Heine, and B. Huber (eds.) *Criminal Responsibility of Legal and Collective Entities* (Berlin: Edition Iuscrim), pp. 181–188.

B. Morgan (2003) 'The Economization of Politics: Meta-Regulation as a Form of Nonjudicial Legality', *Social & Legal Studies,* 12/4: 489–523.

G. T. Nielsen (1999) 'Criminal Liability of Collective Entities: The Danish Model' in A. Eser, G. Heine, and B. Huber (eds.) *Criminal Responsibility of Legal and Collective Entities* (Berlin: Edition Iuscrim), pp. 189–194.

P. Nonet and P. Selznick (1978) *Law and Society in Transition: Toward Responsive Law* (New York: Harper Colophon Books).

A. Norrie (2001) *Crime, Reason, and History (2nd ed.)* (Cambridge: Cambridge University Press).

C. Norris and M. McCahill (2006) 'CCTV: Beyond Penal Modernism?' *British Journal of Criminology,* 46/1: 97–118.

NWISP (2009) *National Work Injury Statistics Program Summary Table of Accepted Time-Loss Injuries/Diseases and Fatalities by Jurisdiction* (available online at http://www.awcbc.org/en/nationalworkinjuriesstatisticsprogramnwisp.asp; last accessed 20 July 2010).

M. O'Connell and A. Whelan (1996) 'Taking Wrongs Seriously: Public Perceptions of Crime Seriousness', *British Journal of Criminology,* 36/2: 299–318.

P. O'Malley (1999) 'Volatile and Contradictory Punishment', *Theoretical Criminology,* 3/2: 175–196.

R. O'Neill (2010) 'Once in a Lifetime?' *Hazards,* 110 (available online at http://www.hazards.org/deadlybusiness/onceinalifetime.htm; last accessed 14 October 2010).

A. Ogus (1992) 'Regulatory Law: Some Lessons from the Past', *Legal Studies,* 12/1: 1–19.

A. Ogus (1994) *Regulation: Legal Forms and Economic Theory* (Oxford: Clarendon Press).

A. Ogus (1995) 'Rethinking Self-Regulation', *Oxford Journal of Legal Studies,* 15/1: 97–108.

L. Orland and C. Cachera (1995) 'Corporate Crime and Punishment in France: Criminal Responsibility of Legal Entities (Personnes Morales) Under the New French Criminal Code (Nouveau Code Penal)', *Connecticut Journal of International Law,* 11: 111–168.

D. Ormerod and R. Taylor (2008) 'The Corporate Manslaughter and Corporate Homicide Act 2007', *Criminal Law Review,* 589–611.

OSHA (2010) *2008 Census of Fatal Occupational Injuries (revised data)* (Washington, DC: U.S. Department of Labor, Bureau of Labor Statistics).

W. Outhwaite (1996) *The Habermas Reader* (Cambridge: Polity Press).

E. Palti (1998) 'Patroklos's Funeral and Habermas's Sentence', *Law and Social Inquiry,* 23/4: 1017–1044.

C. Parker (2002) *The Open Corporation: Effective Self-Regulation and Democracy* (Cambridge: Cambridge University Press).

C. Parker (2006) 'The "Compliance" Trap: The Moral Message in Responsive Regulatory Enforcement', *Law & Society Review,* 40/3: 591–622.

A. E. Peacock (1984) 'The Successful Prosecution of the Factory Acts 1833–55', *The Economic History Review,* 37/2: 197–210.

F. Pearce and S. Tombs (1990) 'Ideology, Hegemony, and Empiricism', *British Journal of Criminology,* 30/4: 423–443.

F. Pearce and S. Tombs (1991) 'Policing Corporate "Skid Rows": A Reply to Keith Hawkins', *British Journal of Criminology,* 31/4: 415–426.

S. Pemberton (2005) 'Moral Indifference and Corporate Manslaughter: Compromising Safety in the Name of Profit?' in S. Tully (ed.) *Research Handbook on Corporate Legal Responsibility* (Cheltenham: Edward Elgar), pp. 177–193.

C. Perrow (1984) *Normal Accidents: Living with High-Risk Technologies* (London: HarperCollins).

N. Pidgeon, I. Lorenzoni, and W. Poortinga (2008) 'Climate Change or Nuclear Power – No Thanks! A Quantitative Study of Public Perceptions and Risk Framing in Britain', *Global Environmental Change,* 18/1: 69–85.

M. Pieth and R. Ivory (eds.) (2011) *Corporate Criminal Liability: Emergence, Convergence, and Risk* (New York: Springer).

K. Polanyi (1944) *The Great Transformation: The Political and Economic Origins of Our Time* (Boston, MA: Beacon Hill).

J. Pratt (2000) 'Emotive and Ostentatious Punishment: Its Decline and Resurgence in Modern Society', *Punishment and Society,* 2/4: 417–440.

T. E. Pringle and S. D. Frost (2003) '"The Absence of Rigor and the Failure of Implementation": Occupational Health and Safety in China', *International Journal of Occupational and Environmental Health,* 9/4: 309–316.

T. Prosser (2006) 'Regulation and Social Solidarity', *Journal of Law and Society,* 33/3: 364–387.

T. Prosser (2011) *The Regulatory Enterprise: Government, Regulation, and Legitimacy* (Oxford: Oxford University Press).

O. Quick (2010) 'Medical Mistakes and Manslaughter: A Criminal Combination?' *Cambridge Law Journal,* 69/1: 186–203.

M. Quinlan (1999) 'The Implications of Labour Market Restructuring in Industrialized Societies for Occupational Health and Safety', *Economic and Industrial Democracy,* 20/3: 427–460.

P. Ramsay (2006) 'The Responsible Subject as Citizen: Criminal Law, Democracy and the Welfare State', *Modern Law Review,* 69/1: 29–58.

B. Rehder (2009) '"Adversarial Legalism" in the German System of Industrial Relations?' *Regulation & Governance,* 3/3: 217–234.

I. Reiner and J. Chatten-Brown (1989) 'When It Is Not an Accident, But a Crime: Prosecutors Get Tough with OSHA Violations', *Northern Kentucky Law Review,* 17/1: 83–103.

A. J. Reiss Jr. (1984) 'Selecting Strategies of Control Over Organizational Life' in K. Hawkins and J. M. Thomas (eds.) *Enforcing Regulation* (Boston, MA: Kluwer-Nijhoff), pp. 23–35.

L. Rhinehart (2008) 'Workers at Risk: The Unfulfilled Promise of the Occupational Safety and Health Act', *West Virginia Law Review,* 111: 117–134.

K. P. Richard (1997) *The Westray Story: A Predictable Path to Disaster (Report of the Westray Mine Public Inquiry)* (Halifax: Westray Mine Public Inquiry).

G. Richardson (1987) 'Strict Liability for Regulatory Crime: The Empirical Research', *Criminal Law Review,* 295–306.

A. Ridley and L. Dunford (1997) 'Corporate Killing – Legislating for Unlawful Death', *Industrial Law Journal,* 26: 99–113.

Lord Robens (1972) *Safety and Health at Work: Report of the Committee 1970–72 (The Robens Report)* (London: HMSO).

J. V. Roberts and M. Hough (2005) *Understanding Public Attitudes to Criminal Justice* (Maidenhead: Open University Press).

J. V. Roberts, L. J. Stalans, D. Indermaur, and M. Hough (2003) *Penal Populism and Public Opinion: Lessons from Five Countries* (Oxford: Oxford University Press).

E. Rodriguez (2002) 'Marginal Employment and Health in Britain and Germany: Does Unstable Employment Predict Health?' *Social Science & Medicine,* 55/6: 963–979.

S. P. Rosenmerkel (2001) 'Wrongfulness and Harmfulness as Components of Seriousness of White-Collar Offenses', *Journal of Contemporary Criminal Justice,* 17/4: 308–327.

H. Rothstein, P. Irving, T. Walden, and R. Yearsley (2006) 'The Risks of Risk-Based Regulation: Insights from the Environmental Policy Domain', *Environment International,* 32: 1056–1065.

Safe Work Australia (2011) *Work-Related Traumatic Injury Fatalities, Australia 2008–09* (Canberra, ACT: Safe Work Australia).

N. Sargent (1989) 'Law, Ideology and Corporate Crime: A Critique of Instrumentalism', *Canadian Journal of Law and Society,* 4/1: 39–75.

R. Sarre (2007) 'White Collar Crime and Prosecution for "Industrial Manslaughter" as a Means to Reduce Workplace Deaths' in H. Pontell and G. Geis (eds.) *International Handbook on White Collar Crime* (New York: Springer), pp. 648–662.

R. Sarre and J. Richards (2005) 'Responding to Culpable Corporate Behaviour: Current Developments in the Industrial Manslaughter Debate', *Flinders Journal of Law Reform,* 8/1: 93–111.

A. Schneider (2009) 'Corporate Liability for Manslaughter: A Comparison between English and German Law', *Zeitschrift für Internationale Strafrechtsdogmatik [Review of International Criminal Law Doctrine],* 1/2009: 22–43.

J. T. Scholz (1984) 'Cooperation, Deterrence, and the Ecology of Regulatory Enforcement', *Law & Society Review,* 18/2: 179–224.

J. T. Scholz (1997) 'Enforcement Policy and Corporate Misconduct: The Changing Perspective of Deterrence Theory', *Law and Contemporary Problems,* 60/3: 253–268.

P. Selznick (1985) 'Focusing Organisational Research on Regulation' in R. Noll (ed.) *Regulatory Policy and the Social Sciences* (Berkeley, CA: University of California Press), pp. 363–367.

R. Sennett (1998) *The Corrosion of Character: The Personal Consequences of Work in the New Capitalism* (New York and London: W. W. Norton).

Sentencing Guidelines Council (2010) *Corporate Manslaughter & Health and Safety Offences Causing Death: Definitive Guideline* (London: Crown).

T. Serra (1999) 'Establishing a Basis for Criminal Responsibility of Collective Entities' in A. Eser, G. Heine, and B. Huber (eds.) *Criminal Responsibility of Legal and Collective Entities* (Berlin: Edition Iuscrim), pp. 203–216.

D. Sharma (2005) 'Bhopal: 20 Years On', *The Lancet*, 365/9454: 111–112.

P. Shrivastava (1987) *Bhopal: Anatomy of a Crisis* (Cambridge: Ballinger).

S. Silbey (2009) 'Taming Prometheus: Talk About Safety Culture', *Annual Review of Sociology*, 35: 341–369.

M. Silverstein (2008) 'Getting Home Safe and Sound: Occupational Safety and Health Administration at 38', *Health Policy and Ethics*, 98/3: 416–423.

A. P. Simester (2000) 'Can Negligence Be Culpable?' in J. Horder (ed.) *Oxford Essays in Jurisprudence (4th Series)* (Oxford: Oxford University Press), pp. 85–106.

J. Simon (1994) 'Between Power and Knowledge: Habermas, Foucault, and the Future of Legal Studies', *Law & Society Review*, 28/4: 947–961.

J. Simon (2007) *Governing Through Crime: How the War on Crime Transformed American Democracy and Created a Culture of Fear* (Oxford: Oxford University Press).

J. Simon (2010) 'Consuming Obsessions: Housing, Homicide, and Mass Incarceration since 1950', *University of Chicago Legal Forum*, 165–204.

S. S. Simpson (2002) *Corporate Crime, Law and Social Control* (Cambridge: Cambridge University Press).

D. Sinclair (1997) 'Self-Regulation Versus Command-and-Control? Beyond False Dichotomies', *Law and Policy*, 19/4: 529–559.

G. Slapper (1993) 'Corporate Manslaughter: An Examination of the Determinants of Prosecutorial Policy', *Social & Legal Studies*, 2/4: 423–443.

G. Slapper (1999) *Blood in the Bank: Legal and Societal Aspects of Workplace Deaths* (London: Ashworth).

P. Slovic (1986) 'Informing and Educating the Public about Risk', *Risk Analysis*, 6/4: 403–415.

P. Slovic (1987) 'Perception of Risk', *Science*, 236: 280–285.

P. Slovic, B. Fischhoff, and S. Lichtenstein (1979) 'Rating the Risks', *Environment*, 2/3: 14–39.

K. Snell and S. Tombs (2011), ' "How Do You Get Your Voice Heard When No-One Will Let You?" Victimization at Work', *Criminology & Criminal Justice*, 11/3: 207–223.

L. Snider (1991) 'The Regulatory Dance: Understanding Reform Processes in Corporate Crime', *International Journal of the Sociology of Law*, 19/2: 209–236.

J. R. Spencer and M. Brajeux (2010) 'Criminal Liability for Negligence – A Lesson From Across the Channel?' *International and Comparative Law Quarterly*, 59/1: 1–24.

M. A. Stein (2008) 'Victorian Tort Liability for Workplace Industry', *University of Illinois Law Review*, 2008/3: 933–984.

G. Stessens (1994) 'Corporate Criminal Liability: A Comparative Perspective', *International and Comparative Law Quarterly*, 43: 493–520.

J. Stiglitz (2009) 'Regulation and Failure' in D. Moss and J. Cisternino (eds.) *New Perspectives on Regulation* (Cambridge, MA: The Tobin Project), pp. 11–23.

B. Sullivan (2001) 'Corporate Killing – Some Government Proposals', *Criminal Law Review*, 31–39.

C. Sunstein (1990) *After the Rights Revolution: Reconceiving the Regulatory State* (Cambridge, MA: Harvard University Press).

C. Sunstein (2005) *Laws of Fear: Beyond the Precautionary Principle* (Oxford: Oxford University Press).

C. Sunstein and A. Vermeule (2009) 'Conspiracy Theories', *Journal of Political Philosophy,* 17/2: 202–227.

V. L. Swigert and R. A. Farrell (1981) 'Corporate Homicide: Definitional processes in the Creation of Deviance', *Law & Society Review,* 15/1: 161–182.

V. Tadros (2005) *Criminal Responsibility* (Oxford: Oxford University Press).

B. Tamanaha (1997) *Realistic Socio-Legal Theory: Pragmatism and a Social Theory of Law* (Oxford: Clarendon Press).

B. Tamanaha (2006) *Law as a Means to an End: Threat to the Rule of Law* (Cambridge: Cambridge University Press).

M. Tausig and R. Fenwick (2001) 'Unbinding Time: Alternate Work Schedules and Work-Life Balance', *Journal of Family and Economic Issues,* 22/2: 101–119.

G. Teubner (1987) 'Juridification: Concepts, Aspects, Limits, Solutions' in R. Baldwin, C. Scott, and C. Hood (eds.) *A Reader on Regulation* (Oxford: Oxford University Press), pp. 389–440.

K. Thelen (2001) 'Varieties of Labor Politics in the Developed Democracies' in P. A. Hall and D. Soskice (eds.) *Varieties of Capitalism: The Institutional Foundations of Comparative Advantage* (Oxford: Oxford University Press), pp. 71–103.

M. W. Thomas (1948) *The Early Factory Legislation: A Study in Legislative and Administrative Evolution* (Leigh-on-Sea: Thames Bank).

D. Thornton, N. A. Gunningham, and R. A. Kagan (2005) 'General Deterrence and Corporate Environmental Behavior', *Law and Policy,* 27/2: 262–288.

S. Tombs (2004) 'Workplace Injury and Death: Social Harms and the Illusion of Law' in P. Hillyard, C. Pantazis, S. Tombs, and D. Gordon (eds.) *Beyond Criminology: Taking Harms Seriously* (London: Pluto), pp. 156–177.

S. Tombs and D. Whyte (2007) *Safety Crimes* (Cullompton: Willan).

S. Tombs and D. Whyte (2010) 'A Deadly Consensus: Worker Safety and Regulatory Degradation under New Labour', *British Journal of Criminology,* 50/1: 46–65.

M. Tonry (2004) *Thinking About Crime: Sense and Sensibility in American Penal Culture* (Oxford: Oxford University Press).

E. Tucker (1995) 'And Defeat Goes On: An Assessment of Third-Wave Health and Safety Regulation' in F. Pearce and L. Snider (eds.) *Corporate Crime: Contemporary Debates* (Toronto, ON: University of Toronto Press), pp. 245–267.

T. Tyler (1990) *Why People Obey the Law* (Princeton, NJ: Princeton University Press).

T. Tyler and J. Darley (2000) 'Building a Law-abiding Society: Taking Public Views about Morality and the Legitimacy of Legal Authorities into Account When Formulating Substantive Law', *Hofstra Law Review,* 28/3: 707–739.

R. M. Unger (1975) *Knowledge and Politics* (New York: Free Press).

I. van Kamp, P. G. van der Velden, R. K. Stellato, J. Roorda, J. van Loon, R. J. Kleber, B. R. Gersons, and E. Lebret (2006) 'Physical and Mental Health Shortly after a Disaster: First Results From the Enschede Firework Disaster Study', *European Journal of Public Health,* 16/3: 252–258.

D. Vaughan (1999) 'The Dark Side of Organizations: Mistake, Misconduct, and Disaster', *Annual Review of Sociology,* 25: 271–305.

C. G. Veljanovski (1983) 'Regulatory Enforcement: An Economic Study of the British Factory Inspectorate', *Law & Policy Quarterly,* 5/1: 75–96.

G. Virgo (1995) 'Reconstructing Manslaughter on Defective Foundations', *Cambridge Law Journal,* 54/1: 14–16.

W. K. Viscusi (2000) 'Corporate Risk Analysis: A Reckless Act?' *Stanford Law Review*, 52: 547–597.

D. J. Vogel (2011) 'The Transatlantic Shift in Health, Safety & Environmental Risk Regulation, 1960 to 2010', *Jerusalem Papers in Regulation and Governance*, Working Paper No. 38.

J. Walls, N. Pidgeon, A. Weyman, and T. Horlick-Jones (2004) 'Critical Trust: Understanding Lay Perceptions of Health and Safety Risk Regulation', *Health, Risk, and Society*, 6/2: 133–150.

C. J. Walsh and A. Pyrich (1995) 'Corporate Compliance Programs as a Defense to Criminal Liability: Can a Corporation Save its Soul?' *Rutgers Law Review*, 47: 605–689.

D. R. Walters (1995) 'Employee Representation and Occupational Health and Safety: The Significance of Europe', *Journal of Loss Prevention in the Process Industries*, 8/6: 313–318.

D. R. Walters (1996) 'Health and Safety Strategies in Europe', *Journal of Loss Prevention in the Process Industries*, 9/5: 297–308.

D. R. Walters (2006) 'One Step Forward, Two Steps Back: Worker Representation and Health and Safety in the United Kingdom', *International Journal of Health Services*, 36/1: 87–111.

D. Walters, R. Johnstone, K. Frick, M. Quinlan, G. Baril-Gingras, and A. Thébaud-Mony (eds.) (2011) *Regulating Workplace Risks: A Comparative Study of Inspection Regimes in Times of Change* (Cheltenham: Edward Elgar).

J. T. Ward (1962) *The Factory Movement 1830–1855* (London: Macmillan).

M. Warr (1989) 'What Is the Perceived Seriousness of Crimes?' *Criminology*, 27/4: 795–820.

B. Weaver (2009) 'Communicative Punishment as a Penal Approach to Supporting Desistance', *Theoretical Criminology*, 13/1: 9–29.

M. Weber (1914) *Economy and Society* Trans. G. Roth and C. Wittich (Berkeley, CA: University of California Press).

T. Weigend (2008) 'Societas Delinquere Non Potest?: A German Perspective', *Journal of International Criminal Justice*, 6/5: 927–945.

C. Wells (1988) 'The Decline and Rise of English Murder: Corporate Crime and Individual Responsibility', *Criminal Law Review*, 788–801.

C. Wells (1996) 'The Corporate Manslaughter Proposals: Pragmatism, Paradox and Peninsularity', *Criminal Law Review*, 545–553.

C. Wells (2001) *Corporations, Crime and Accountability (2nd ed.)* (Oxford: Oxford University Press).

C. Wells (2005) 'Corporate Criminal Responsibility' in S. Tully (ed.) *Research Handbook on Corporate Legal Responsibility* (Cheltenham: Edward Elgar), pp. 147–158.

C. Wells (2010) 'Corporate Crime: Opening the Eyes of the Sentry', *Legal Studies*, 30/3: 370–390.

M. Wilkinson (2003) 'Corporate Criminal Liability: The Move Towards Recognising Genuine Corporate Fault', *Canterbury Law Review*, 9: 142.

R. Wilkinson and K. Pickett (2009) *The Spirit Level: Why Equality is Better for Everyone* (London: Penguin).

G. Williams (1955) 'The Definition of a Crime', *Current Legal Problems*, 8/1: 107.

G. Williams (1961) *Criminal Law, The General Part (2nd ed.)* (London: Stevens & Sons).

K. Williams (2006) 'Politics, the Media and Refining the Notion of Fault: Section 1 of the Compensation Act 2006', *Journal of Personal Injury Law,* 4: 347–353.

J. Witt (1998) 'The Transformation of Work and the Law of Workplace Accidents, 1842–1910', *Yale Law Journal,* 107: 1467.

C. Woolfson, J. Foster, and M. Beck (1996) *Paying for the Piper: Capital and Labour in Britain's Offshore Oil Industry* (London: Mansell).

F. Wright (1997) *Law of Health and Safety at Work* (London: Sweet and Maxwell).

F. Wright (2008) 'Effective Regulation and Sanctioning in Health and Safety Law in the European Union', *Web Journal of Current Legal Issues,* 2008/1.

J. Young (1999) *The Exclusive Society: Social Exclusion, Crime and Difference in Late Modernity* (London: Sage).

Lord Young (2010) *Common Sense, Common Safety [The Young Review]* (London: Crown).

L. Zedner (2006) 'Policing Before and After the Police: The Historical Antecedents of Contemporary Crime Control', *British Journal of Criminology,* 46/1: 78–96.

D. Zohar (1980) 'Safety Climate in Industrial Organizations: Theoretical and Applied Implications', *Journal of Applied Psychology,* 65/1: 96–102.

Index

Printed and bound in the United States of America